Mathematics for the IB Diploma
Higher Level Topic 10
Series and differential equations

Hugh Neill and Douglas Quadling

Series Editor Hugh Neill

CAMBRIDGE
UNIVERSITY PRESS

CAMBRIDGE UNIVERSITY PRESS
Cambridge, New York, Melbourne, Madrid, Cape Town, Singapore, São Paulo, Delhi

Cambridge University Press
The Edinburgh Building, Cambridge CB2 8RU, UK

www.cambridge.org
Information on this title: www.cambridge.org/9780521714648

First published 2008

A catalogue record for this publication is available from the British Library

ISBN   978-0-521-71464-8 paperback

The authors and the publishers are grateful to the following examination boards for permission to reproduce
questions from past examination papers, identified in the text as follows.
OCR   Oxford, Cambridge and RSA Examinations
IBO   International Baccalaureate Organization
The authors, and not the examination boards, are responsible for the method and accuracy of the answers
to examination questions given; these may not necessarily constitute the only possible solutions.

This material has been developed independently of the International Baccalaureate Organization (IBO).
This text is in no way connected with, nor endorsed by, the IBO.

Contents

Introduction

Series and differential equations has been written especially for the International Baccalaureate Mathematics HL and FM examinations. This book covers the syllabus for Topic 10.

There are 11 chapters on series followed by 3 chapters on differential equations, and these are completely independent of each other. Students could, if they wish, begin work on the differential equations chapters as soon as they have completed the associated chapters 23 and 27 in Higher Level Book 2. There is a small amount of material which extends a topic beyond the syllabus as printed, with the aim of enhancing students' appreciation of the subject. This is indicated by an asterisk (*) at the appropriate place in the text.

Occasionally within the text paragraphs appear in *this type style*. These paragraphs are usually outside the main stream of the mathematical argument, but may help to give insight, or suggest extra work or different approaches.

Students are expected to have access to graphic display calculators and the text places considerable emphasis on their potential for supporting the learning of mathematics.

There are plenty of exercises throughout. At the end of the book there is a Review exercise which includes some questions from past International Baccalaureate examinations, but on a different syllabus. At the time of writing, there are few current versions of the Higher Level examinations, so there is no backlog of examination questions on the newer parts of the syllabus.

The authors thank OCR and IBO for permission to use some examination questions and Cambridge University Press for their help in producing this book. Particular thanks are due to Brian Fugard, for his help and advice. However, the responsibility for the text, and for any errors, remains with the authors.

1 Summing finite series

When the terms of a series are given algebraically, it may be possible to find a formula for the sum of n terms. When you have completed this chapter, you should

- know how to use the method of differences to find the sums of series
- be able to express algebraic fractions as the sum of partial fractions, and use these in conjunction with the method of differences to sum series.

1.1 The method of differences

You already know a number of formulae for the sums of series of different kinds. Here are some examples.

Sums of powers of integers:

$$\sum_{i=1}^{n} i = 1 + 2 + 3 + \ldots + n = \tfrac{1}{2}n(n+1) \qquad \text{(HL Book 1 Section 2.3)}$$

$$\sum_{i=1}^{n} i^2 = 1^2 + 2^2 + 3^2 + \ldots + n^2 = \tfrac{1}{6}n(n+1)(2n+1) \qquad \text{(HL Book 2 Section 1.6)}$$

Geometric series:

$$\sum_{i=1}^{n} r^{i-1} = 1 + r + r^2 + \ldots + r^{n-1} = \frac{1 - r^n}{1 - r} \quad (r \neq 1) \qquad \text{(HL Book 1 Section 30.3)}$$

Various methods have been used to prove these: from a diagram, by mathematical induction, or by a special algebraic method which depends on a particular property of the sequence of terms.

Finding a formula for the sum of a series is called 'summing' the series.

This section describes a general method which can be used to sum a number of series. It depends on being able to find a function f so that a general term u_i of the series can be expressed in the form

$$u_i = f(i) - f(i-1).$$

Then the sum of the series is

$$\sum_{i=1}^{n} u_i = (f(1) - f(0)) + (f(2) - f(1)) + (f(3) - f(2)) + \ldots + (f(n) - f(n-1)).$$

Now in this sum you have $f(1)$ in the first bracket and $-f(1)$ in the second, $f(2)$ in the second bracket and $-f(2)$ in the third, and so on. All that is left is $-f(0)$ in the first bracket and $f(n)$ in the last. So

$$\sum_{i=1}^{n} u_i = f(n) - f(0).$$

This is called the **method of differences**, and the series is summed by **telescoping**.

> **Method of differences**   If, given a sequence u_i, you can find a function f such that $u_i = f(i) - f(i-1)$, then
>
> $$\sum_{i=1}^{n} u_i = f(n) - f(0).$$

The difficult part, of course, is finding a function f with the required property. This is a 'trial and error' process (or perhaps better, 'trial and modify'). The following examples suggest some methods which often work.

Example 1.1.1

Sum $\displaystyle\sum_{i=1}^{n} i(i+1)$.

The general term u_i is the product of two consecutive integers, so try taking for $g(i)$ the product of three consecutive integers $i(i+1)(i+2)$. (Think 'g stands for guess'!) Then

$$g(i-1) = (i-1)(i-1+1)(i-1+2)$$
$$= (i-1)i(i+1).$$

Notice that both $g(i)$ and $g(i-1)$ have $i(i+1)$ as a factor. So

$$g(i) - g(i-1) = i(i+1)(i+2) - (i-1)i(i+1)$$
$$= i(i+1)((i+2) - (i-1))$$
$$= i(i+1) \times 3.$$

The first guess is just 3 times u_i. So modify the guess by dividing the first guess by 3. If $f(i) = \frac{1}{3}g(i) = \frac{1}{3}i(i+1)(i+2)$, then

$$f(i) - f(i-1) = \frac{1}{3}(g(i) - g(i-1))$$
$$= \frac{1}{3} \times i(i+1) \times 3$$
$$= i(i+1).$$

You have now found a function with the desired property, so by the result in the shaded box

$$\sum_{i=1}^{n} i(i+1) = f(n) - f(0)$$
$$= \frac{1}{3}n(n+1)(n+2) - \frac{1}{3} \times 0 \times 1 \times 2$$
$$= \frac{1}{3}n(n+1)(n+2).$$

It is a good idea to check your answer numerically with a small value for n. For example, if $n = 2$, the left side is $1 \times 2 + 2 \times 3 = 2 + 6 = 8$, and the right side is $\frac{1}{3} \times 2 \times 3 \times 4 = 8$.

It is worth noticing that the result of Example 1.1.1 gives another method of summing $\sum_{i=1}^{n} i^2$. Since, by the addition rule (Higher Level Book 1 Section 2.6),

$$\sum_{i=1}^{n} i(i+1) = \sum_{i=1}^{n} (i^2 + i) = \sum_{i=1}^{n} i^2 + \sum_{i=1}^{n} i,$$

it follows that

$$\sum_{i=1}^{n} i^2 = \sum_{i=1}^{n} i(i+1) - \sum_{i=1}^{n} i$$
$$= \tfrac{1}{3} n(n+1)(n+2) - \tfrac{1}{2} n(n+1)$$
$$= \tfrac{1}{6} n(n+1)(2(n+2) - 3)$$
$$= \tfrac{1}{6} n(n+1)(2n+1).$$

Example 1.1.2

Write $\dfrac{1}{1 \times 2} + \dfrac{1}{2 \times 3} + \dfrac{1}{3 \times 4} + \ldots + \dfrac{1}{98 \times 99} + \dfrac{1}{99 \times 100}$ as a single fraction.

This sum could be written as $\sum_{i=1}^{99} \dfrac{1}{i(i+1)}$, so you want to find a function f such that

$$f(i) - f(i-1) = \frac{1}{i(i+1)}.$$

It is obviously no good starting as in Example 1.1.1 by guessing $g(i) = \dfrac{1}{i(i+1)(i+2)}$, since then $g(i-1)$ would be $\dfrac{1}{(i-1)i(i+1)}$ and $g(i) - g(i-1)$ would be a fraction with four factors in the denominator, $(i-1)i(i+1)(i+2)$.

But this gives a hint how you might find $f(i)$. To get a fraction so that $f(i) - f(i-1)$ has just two factors in the denominator, perhaps you should begin with fractions $f(i)$ and $f(i-1)$ each having one factor in the denominator.

The obvious guess is that $g(i)$ is $\dfrac{1}{i+1}$. Then $g(i-1) = \dfrac{1}{i-1+1} = \dfrac{1}{i}$. So

$$g(i) - g(i-1) = \frac{1}{i+1} - \frac{1}{i}$$
$$= \frac{i-(i+1)}{(i+1)i} = \frac{-1}{i(i+1)}.$$

This is almost what you want, except for the minus sign. So take $f(i) = -g(i) = \dfrac{-1}{i+1}$. Then

$$f(i) - f(i-1) = \frac{-1}{i+1} - \frac{-1}{i}$$
$$= \frac{-i+(i+1)}{(i+1)i} = \frac{1}{i(i+1)}.$$

Using $\frac{1}{i(i+1)} = \frac{-1}{i+1} - \frac{-1}{i}$ with $i = 1, 2, 3, \ldots, 99$ in turn,

$$\frac{1}{1 \times 2} + \frac{1}{2 \times 3} + \frac{1}{3 \times 4} + \cdots + \frac{1}{98 \times 99} + \frac{1}{99 \times 100}$$

$$= \left(\frac{-1}{2} - \frac{-1}{1}\right) + \left(\frac{-1}{3} - \frac{-1}{2}\right) + \left(\frac{-1}{4} - \frac{-1}{3}\right) + \cdots + \left(\frac{-1}{99} - \frac{-1}{98}\right) + \left(\frac{-1}{100} - \frac{-1}{99}\right)$$

$$= \left(1 - \tfrac{1}{2}\right) + \left(\tfrac{1}{2} - \tfrac{1}{3}\right) + \left(\tfrac{1}{3} - \tfrac{1}{4}\right) + \cdots + \left(\tfrac{1}{98} - \tfrac{1}{99}\right) + \left(\tfrac{1}{99} - \tfrac{1}{100}\right)$$

$$= 1 - \tfrac{1}{100} = \tfrac{99}{100}.$$

Example 1.1.3

Simplify $f(i) - f(i-1)$ when $f(i) = i^2(i+1)^2$. Use your answer to sum $\sum_{i=1}^{n} i^3$.

$$f(i) - f(i-1) = i^2(i+1)^2 - (i-1)^2 i^2$$

$$= i^2\left((i+1)^2 - (i-1)^2\right)$$

$$= i^2\left((i+1) - (i-1)\right)\left((i+1) + (i-1)\right) \qquad \text{(difference of two squares)}$$

$$= i^2 \times 2 \times 2i = 4i^3.$$

Then, using the method of differences,

$$f(n) - f(0) = \sum_{i=1}^{n} 4i^3 = 4\sum_{i=1}^{n} i^3,$$

so

$$\sum_{i=1}^{n} i^3 = \tfrac{1}{4}\left(n^2(n+1)^2 - 0^2 \times (0+1)^2\right)$$

$$= \tfrac{1}{4} n^2(n+1)^2.$$

You may have noticed that the process of finding a function f such that $u_i = f(i) - f(i-1)$ is rather like finding an indefinite integral. Compare $\sum_{i=1}^{n} u_i = f(n) - f(0)$ with $\int_a^b f(x)\,\mathrm{d}x = I(b) - I(a)$. Can you see any other similarities?

Exercise 1A

1   Use the method of Example 1.1.2 to prove that $\displaystyle\sum_{i=1}^{n} \frac{1}{i(i+1)} = \frac{n}{n+1}$.

2   (a) Find a function f such that $f(i) - f(i-1) = i(i+1)(i+2)$. Hence sum $\displaystyle\sum_{i=1}^{n} i(i+1)(i+2)$.

   (b) Find a function f such that $f(i) - f(i-1) = \dfrac{1}{i(i+1)(i+2)}$. Hence sum $\displaystyle\sum_{i=1}^{n} \frac{1}{i(i+1)(i+2)}$.

3   Simplify $i^3(i+1)^3 - (i-1)^3 i^3$. Hence, using the result of Example 1.1.3, sum $\displaystyle\sum_{i=1}^{n} i^5$.

Check your answer with a numerical value for n.

4   Sum the series

(a) $\displaystyle\sum_{i=1}^{n} \ln\left(1+\frac{1}{i}\right),$ (b) $\displaystyle\sum_{i=1}^{n} \frac{i-1}{i!}.$

5   If $f(i) = (i+1)!$, show that $f(i) - f(i-1) = i \times i!$. Hence sum $\displaystyle\sum_{i=1}^{n} i \times i!$.

6   Find the value of $\displaystyle\sum_{i=1}^{100} \frac{1}{(2i-1)(2i+1)}$.

7   Simplify $(2i+1)^5 - (2i-1)^5$. Hence sum $\displaystyle\sum_{i=1}^{20} i^4$.

Check your answer by using a calculator to sum the series.

8   (a) Show that $ir^i - (i-1)r^{i-1} = r^{i-1} - (1-r)ir^{i-1}$. Use this result to find $\displaystyle\sum_{i=1}^{n} ir^{i-1}$.

(b) Check your answer by differentiating the sum $\displaystyle\sum_{i=0}^{n} r^i$.

9   Prove that $\sin\left(i+\tfrac{1}{2}\right)\theta - \sin\left(i-\tfrac{1}{2}\right)\theta = 2\cos i\theta \sin\tfrac{1}{2}\theta$. Hence sum $\displaystyle\sum_{i=1}^{n} \cos i\theta$.

1.2 Partial fractions

In Example 1.1.2 the expression $\dfrac{1}{i(i+1)}$ was split into two simpler fractions as $\dfrac{-1}{i+1} - \dfrac{-1}{i}$, which is

$\dfrac{1}{i} - \dfrac{1}{i+1}$. This process is called **splitting into partial fractions**. It is a very useful technique, not only for summing series but also for differentiation, integration, curve sketching and many other applications.

When you add two fractions $\dfrac{a}{x-p} + \dfrac{b}{x-q}$ you get a single fraction

$$\frac{a(x-q) + b(x-p)}{(x-p)(x-q)}, \quad \text{which can be written as} \quad \frac{(a+b)x - (aq+bp)}{(x-p)(x-q)}.$$

The denominator is a quadratic polynomial in factor form. The numerator is usually a linear polynomial, but if $a+b=0$ it is simply a constant. In any case, the degree of the numerator is 1 or less.

If you increase the number of fractions to three, $\dfrac{a}{x-p} + \dfrac{b}{x-q} + \dfrac{c}{x-r}$, you get

$$\frac{a(x-q)(x-r) + b(x-p)(x-r) + c(x-p)(x-q)}{(x-p)(x-q)(x-r)}.$$

The denominator is now a cubic polynomial. The numerator is a polynomial of degree 2, or possibly less. The important point is that the degree of the numerator is less than the number of factors in the denominator.

If you have a fraction with two or more linear factors in the denominator and a polynomial of lower degree in the numerator, you can reverse the process and express it as the sum of partial fractions of the form $\dfrac{a}{x-p}$.

Example 1.2.1

Split $\dfrac{4}{(x-1)(3x+1)}$ into partial fractions.

The aim is to find numbers A and B such that

$$\frac{A}{x-1} + \frac{B}{3x+1} \equiv \frac{4}{(x-1)(3x+1)}.$$

Notice the use of $\equiv$ to denote an identity. The two sides have to be equal for all the values of x for which they have a meaning.

Begin by finding A. To do this, multiply both sides of the identity by $x-1$ to get another identity

$$A + \frac{B(x-1)}{3x+1} \equiv \frac{4}{3x+1}.$$

Notice that on the right the effect of multiplying by $x-1$ is simply to remove the factor $(x-1)$ from the denominator.

Now, to find A without involving B, you want to cut out the second term on the left side. You can do this by putting x equal to 1, which makes $x-1=0$. This gives

$$A + \frac{B \times 0}{3 \times 1 + 1} = \frac{4}{3 \times 1 + 1},$$

so $A + 0 = \dfrac{4}{4}$,   giving $A = 1$.

You can use a similar method to find B. This time multiply both sides of the original identity by $3x+1$ to get

$$\frac{A(3x+1)}{x-1} + B \equiv \frac{4}{x-1}.$$

The effect of this is to remove the factor $(3x+1)$ from the denominator on the right.

To find B without involving A, put $x = -\tfrac{1}{3}$, which makes $3x+1=0$. This gives

$$\frac{A \times 0}{-\frac{1}{3}-1} + B = \frac{4}{-\frac{1}{3}-1},$$

so $0 + B = \dfrac{4}{-\frac{4}{3}}$,   giving $B = -3$.

Putting all this together,

$$\frac{4}{(x-1)(3x+1)} \equiv \frac{1}{x-1} + \frac{-3}{3x+1}$$

$$\equiv \frac{1}{x-1} - \frac{3}{3x+1}.$$

Example 1.2.2

Split $\dfrac{4x+1}{(x-2)(2x-1)}$ into partial fractions.

You want to find A and B such that

$$\frac{A}{x-2} + \frac{B}{2x-1} \equiv \frac{4x+1}{(x-2)(2x-1)}.$$

To find A, multiply by $x-2$:

$$A + \frac{B(x-2)}{2x-1} \equiv \frac{4x+1}{2x-1}.$$

The factor $(x-2)$ has disappeared from the denominator on the right. Now put $x = 2$:

$$A + \frac{B \times 0}{2 \times 2 - 1} = \frac{4 \times 2 + 1}{2 \times 2 - 1}.$$

So $A + 0 = \dfrac{9}{3}$,   giving $A = 3$.

To find B, multiply by $2x-1$:

$$\frac{A(2x-1)}{x-2} + B \equiv \frac{4x+1}{x-2}.$$

The factor $(2x-1)$ has disappeared from the denominator on the right. Now put $x = \frac{1}{2}$:

$$\frac{A \times 0}{\frac{1}{2} - 2} + B = \frac{4 \times \frac{1}{2} + 1}{\frac{1}{2} - 2}.$$

So $0 + B = \dfrac{3}{-\frac{3}{2}}$,   giving $B = -2$.

Therefore, in partial fractions,

$$\frac{4x+1}{(x-2)(2x-1)} \equiv \frac{3}{x-2} - \frac{2}{2x-1}.$$

It is worth checking the answer, by combining the partial fractions to make sure that they give the correct numerator. In Example 1.2.2 the numerator is $3(2x-1) - 2(x-2)$, which can be simplified as $6x - 3 - 2x + 4 \equiv 4x + 1$, as required.

You will soon find that you can write down the partial fractions without setting out the intermediate steps in full. In Example 1.2.2, to find A you remove $(x-2)$ from the denominator and then put $x=2$. To find B you remove $(2x-1)$ from the denominator and put $x=\frac{1}{2}$.

Example 1.2.3

Split $\dfrac{x^2+2}{x(x+1)(x-2)}$ into partial fractions.

You want

$$\frac{A}{x}+\frac{B}{x+1}+\frac{C}{x-2} \equiv \frac{x^2+2}{x(x+1)(x-2)}.$$

To find A, remove x from the denominator on the right and put $x=0$:

$$A = \frac{0^2+2}{(0+1)(0-2)} = \frac{2}{-2} = -1.$$

To find B, remove $(x+1)$ from the denominator on the right and put $x=-1$:

$$B = \frac{(-1)^2+2}{(-1)(-1-2)} = \frac{3}{3} = 1.$$

To find C, remove $(x-2)$ from the denominator on the right and put $x=2$:

$$C = \frac{2^2+2}{2(2+1)} = \frac{6}{6} = 1.$$

So $\dfrac{x^2+2}{x(x+1)(x-2)} \equiv -\dfrac{1}{x}+\dfrac{1}{x+1}+\dfrac{1}{x-2}.$

Exercise 1B

1 Split the following into partial fractions.

(a) $\dfrac{2x+8}{(x+5)(x+3)}$ (b) $\dfrac{10x+8}{(x-1)(x+5)}$ (c) $\dfrac{x}{(x-4)(x-5)}$ (d) $\dfrac{28}{(2x-1)(x+3)}$

2 Split the following into partial fractions.

(a) $\dfrac{8x+1}{x^2+x-2}$ (b) $\dfrac{25}{x^2-3x-4}$ (c) $\dfrac{10x-6}{x^2-9}$ (d) $\dfrac{3}{2x^2+x}$

3 Split into partial fractions

(a) $\dfrac{35-5x}{(x+2)(x-1)(x-3)}$,   (b) $\dfrac{8x^2}{(x+1)(x-1)(x+3)}$,   (c) $\dfrac{15x^2-28x-72}{x^3-2x^2-24x}.$

1.3 Summation using partial fractions

You can often use partial fractions to express the terms of a series in the form $f(i) - f(i-1)$, and hence to sum the series.

Example 1.3.1

Find the sum of the first n terms of the series $\dfrac{1}{1\times 4} + \dfrac{1}{4\times 7} + \dfrac{1}{7\times 10} + \dots$.

The numbers $1, 4, 7, \dots$ form an arithmetic sequence, and the ith number in the sequence is $1 + 3(i-1) = 3i - 2$. So a general term of the series is $\dfrac{1}{(3i-2)(3i+1)}$, which can be expressed in partial fractions as

$$\frac{\frac{1}{3}}{3i-2} - \frac{\frac{1}{3}}{3i+1}.$$

You can write this as

$$\frac{\frac{1}{3}}{3(i-1)+1} - \frac{\frac{1}{3}}{3i+1},$$

which is $f(i) - f(i-1)$ with $f(i) = -\dfrac{\frac{1}{3}}{3i+1}$.

So, using the method of differences, the sum of the series is

$$f(n) - f(0) = -\frac{\frac{1}{3}}{3n+1} + \frac{\frac{1}{3}}{1} = \frac{1}{3} - \frac{1}{3(3n+1)}.$$

Example 1.3.2

Find the value of $\displaystyle\sum_{i=1}^{50} \frac{i}{(i+1)(i+2)(i+3)}$.

You can check for yourself that, in partial fractions,

$$\frac{i}{(i+1)(i+2)(i+3)} \equiv -\frac{\frac{1}{2}}{i+1} + \frac{2}{i+2} - \frac{\frac{3}{2}}{i+3}.$$

There are two possible ways to continue.

Method 1   You may not see how this expression can be put into the form $f(i) - f(i-1)$. But if you write out the first few and the last few terms using the partial fraction form you may spot a way of finding the sum.

$$\sum_{i=1}^{50} \frac{i}{(i+1)(i+2)(i+3)} = \frac{1}{2\times 3\times 4} + \frac{2}{3\times 4\times 5} + \frac{3}{4\times 5\times 6} + \dots$$

$$+ \frac{48}{49\times 50\times 51} + \frac{49}{50\times 51\times 52} + \frac{50}{51\times 52\times 53}.$$

Writing the terms on the right downwards, and using the identity above, you get

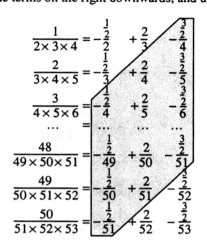

$$\frac{1}{2\times3\times4}=-\frac{\frac12}{2}+\frac{2}{3}-\frac{\frac32}{4}$$

$$\frac{2}{3\times4\times5}=-\frac{\frac12}{3}+\frac{2}{4}-\frac{\frac32}{5}$$

$$\frac{3}{4\times5\times6}=-\frac{\frac12}{4}+\frac{2}{5}-\frac{\frac32}{6}$$

$$\cdots=\cdots\quad\cdots\quad\cdots$$

$$\frac{48}{49\times50\times51}=-\frac{\frac12}{49}+\frac{2}{50}-\frac{\frac32}{51}$$

$$\frac{49}{50\times51\times52}=-\frac{\frac12}{50}+\frac{2}{51}-\frac{\frac32}{52}$$

$$\frac{50}{51\times52\times53}=-\frac{\frac12}{51}+\frac{2}{52}-\frac{\frac32}{53}$$

Look at the terms inside the shaded region. If you add these up along lines parallel to the sloping sides you get a lot of sums running from $-\frac{\frac12}{4}+\frac{2}{4}-\frac{\frac32}{4}$ to $-\frac{\frac12}{51}+\frac{2}{51}-\frac{\frac32}{51}$, all of which are 0. So the sum of all the numbers inside the shaded region is 0, and all that is left is

$$-\frac{\frac12}{2}-\frac{\frac12}{3}+\frac{2}{3}+\frac{2}{52}-\frac{\frac32}{52}-\frac{\frac32}{53}=-\frac{\frac12}{2}+\frac{\frac32}{3}+\frac{\frac12}{52}-\frac{\frac32}{53},$$

which is $\frac{1275}{5512}$.

Method 2   You might notice that, if you split 2 as $-\left(-\frac32\right)+\frac12$, the expression in partial fractions for the general term of the series could be written as $f(i)-f(i-1)$, with $f(i)=\frac{\frac12}{i+2}-\frac{\frac32}{i+3}$. So, by the method of differences,

$$\sum_{i=1}^{50}\frac{i}{(i+1)(i+2)(i+3)}=f(50)-f(0)$$

$$=\left(\frac{\frac12}{52}-\frac{\frac32}{53}\right)-\left(\frac{\frac12}{2}-\frac{\frac32}{3}\right)=\frac{1275}{5512}.$$

Example 1.3.3*

Sum $\displaystyle\sum_{i=1}^{n}\frac{2i+1}{(i+1)(i+2)}\,3^i$.

In partial fractions,

$$\frac{2i+1}{(i+1)(i+2)}\equiv-\frac{1}{i+1}+\frac{3}{i+2}.$$

So $\dfrac{2i+1}{(i+1)(i+2)}3^i = -\dfrac{3^i}{i+1} + \dfrac{3^{i+1}}{i+2}$.

This is $f(i) - f(i-1)$ with $f(i) = \dfrac{3^{i+1}}{i+2}$.

So, by the method of differences,

$$\sum_{i=1}^{n}\dfrac{2i+1}{(i+1)(i+2)}3^i = f(n) - f(0)$$

$$= \dfrac{3^{n+1}}{n+2} - \dfrac{3}{2}.$$

Exercise 1C

1 Find the sum of the first n terms of the following series.

(a) $\dfrac{1}{1\times 3} + \dfrac{1}{3\times 5} + \dfrac{1}{5\times 7} + \cdots$

(b) $\dfrac{1}{2\times 5} + \dfrac{1}{5\times 8} + \dfrac{1}{8\times 11} + \cdots$

(c) $\dfrac{1}{1\times 3\times 5} + \dfrac{1}{3\times 5\times 7} + \dfrac{1}{5\times 7\times 9} + \cdots$

(d) $\dfrac{1}{3\times 5\times 7} + \dfrac{3}{5\times 7\times 9} + \dfrac{5}{7\times 9\times 11} + \cdots$

2* Sum the following series.

(a) $\displaystyle\sum_{i=1}^{n}\dfrac{i}{(i+1)(i+2)}2^i$

(b) $\displaystyle\sum_{i=1}^{n}\dfrac{i+3}{(i+1)(i+2)}\left(\tfrac{1}{2}\right)^i$

(c) $\displaystyle\sum_{i=1}^{n}\dfrac{i+1}{(2i-1)(2i+1)}\left(\tfrac{1}{3}\right)^i$

2 Infinite series

This chapter introduces methods of determining whether infinite series are convergent or divergent. When you have completed it, you should

- be able to deduce the sums of convergent infinite series when the sum to n terms can be found
- be able to use comparison methods to decide whether a series of positive terms is convergent or divergent
- be able to use inequalities to find an upper bound for the sum to infinity of a series of positive terms.

2.1 From n to infinity

You will remember that the sum of the geometric series

$$1 + r + r^2 + r^3 + \dots$$

converges to a limit as the number of terms tends to infinity, provided that the common ratio r is between -1 and 1 (Higher Level Book 1 Section 30.4). The way you proved this was to begin with the formula for the sum of n terms,

$$S_n = \frac{1 - r^n}{1 - r}.$$

S_n is called a **partial sum** of the infinite geometric series, and its values for $n = 1, 2, 3, \dots$ form the **sum sequence**. You can split S_n into two terms, the first of which doesn't involve n, as

$$S_n = \frac{1}{1-r} - \frac{1}{1-r} \times r^n.$$

Then, if $-1 < r < 1$, the factor r^n in the second term tends to 0 as n tends to infinity, so that

$$\lim_{n \to \infty} S_n = \frac{1}{1-r}.$$

This is the **sum to infinity** of the series, and it is usually denoted by $S_\infty = \sum_{i=1}^{\infty} r^{i-1}$. You say that the infinite series $\sum r^{i-1}$ is **convergent** if $-1 < r < 1$.

You can use a similar argument with other series which you know how to sum.

In the rest of this chapter all the series have positive terms.

Example 2.1.1

Investigate whether the series $\dfrac{1}{1 \times 4} + \dfrac{1}{4 \times 7} + \dfrac{1}{7 \times 10} + \dots$ converges to a limit as $n \to \infty$.

It was shown in Example 1.3.1 that the sum of n terms of this series is $S_n = \frac{1}{3} - \dfrac{1}{3(3n+1)}$.

The second term of this expression can be made as small as you like by making n large enough, so that $\lim\limits_{n\to\infty} \dfrac{1}{3(3n+1)} = 0$. So the series is convergent and the sum to infinity is

$$S_\infty = \lim_{n\to\infty} S_n = \tfrac{1}{3} - 0 = \tfrac{1}{3}.$$

The series converges to a limit of $\tfrac{1}{3}$ as $n \to \infty$.

Example 2.1.2*

Investigate the convergence of $\displaystyle\sum \frac{2i+3}{(2i-1)(2i+1)}\left(\tfrac{1}{2}\right)^i$.

The symbol $\displaystyle\sum$ without stating the values of i is used because you don't yet know whether the series is convergent or not. Once it has been proved convergent, you can use $\displaystyle\sum_{i=1}^{\infty}$ to denote its sum to infinity.

It is often worth beginning by calculating a few terms.

$$S_1 = \frac{5}{1\times 3}\times\tfrac{1}{2} = 0.8333\ldots, \qquad S_2 = S_1 + \frac{7}{3\times 5}\times\tfrac{1}{4} = 0.95,$$

$$S_3 = S_2 + \frac{9}{5\times 7}\times\tfrac{1}{8} = 0.9821\ldots, \qquad S_4 = S_3 + \frac{11}{7\times 9}\times\tfrac{1}{16} = 0.9930\ldots\ .$$

It looks as if the sum sequence might tend to a limit, possibly 1. To test this, try to sum the series to find a formula for S_n.

In partial fractions, $\dfrac{2i+3}{(2i-1)(2i+1)} \equiv \dfrac{2}{2i-1} - \dfrac{1}{2i+1}$,

so $\qquad \dfrac{2i+3}{(2i-1)(2i+1)}\left(\tfrac{1}{2}\right)^i \equiv \dfrac{\left(\tfrac{1}{2}\right)^{i-1}}{2i-1} - \dfrac{\left(\tfrac{1}{2}\right)^i}{2i+1}.$

The expression on the right has the form $f(i) - f(i-1)$ where $f(i) = \dfrac{-\left(\tfrac{1}{2}\right)^i}{2i+1}$. It follows that

$$\begin{aligned}
S_n &= \sum_{i=1}^{n} \frac{2i+3}{(2i-1)(2i+1)}\left(\tfrac{1}{2}\right)^i \\
&= f(n) - f(0) \\
&= \frac{-\left(\tfrac{1}{2}\right)^n}{2n+1} - \frac{-1}{1}.
\end{aligned}$$

You can see at once that S_n is less than 1 for all values of n. In the first term, the numerator $-\left(\tfrac{1}{2}\right)^n$ tends to 0 as $n \to \infty$, and the denominator increases without limit, so this term certainly tends to 0. So $S_n \to 0 - (-1) = 1$, and the sum to infinity is

$$\sum_{i=1}^{\infty} \frac{2i+3}{(2i-1)(2i+1)}\left(\tfrac{1}{2}\right)^i = 1.$$

The series converges to a limit of 1.

Exercise 2A

1   Find the sums of the following infinite series.

(a) $\displaystyle\sum_{i=1}^{\infty}\frac{1}{i(i+1)}$

(b) $\displaystyle\sum_{i=1}^{\infty}\frac{1}{i(i+1)(i+2)}$

(c) $\displaystyle\sum_{i=1}^{\infty}\frac{1}{(2i-1)(2i+1)}$

(d) $\displaystyle\sum_{i=1}^{\infty}\frac{1}{(3i-1)(3i+2)}$

(e) $\displaystyle\sum_{i=1}^{\infty}\frac{1}{(4i-3)(4i+1)}$

(f) $\displaystyle\sum_{i=1}^{\infty}\frac{1}{(2i-1)(2i+1)(2i+3)}$

2*   Find the sums of the following infinite series.

(a) $\displaystyle\sum_{i=1}^{\infty}\frac{i-1}{(i+1)(i+2)(i+3)}$

(b) $\displaystyle\sum_{i=1}^{\infty}\frac{i+1}{(2i-1)(2i+1)}\left(\tfrac{1}{3}\right)^{i}$

(c) $\displaystyle\sum_{i=1}^{\infty}\frac{i+3}{i(i+1)}\left(\tfrac{2}{3}\right)^{i}$

3   (a) Prove that $\displaystyle\sum_{i=1}^{\infty}\frac{i-1}{i!}=1$.   (b) Find $\displaystyle\sum_{i=1}^{\infty}\frac{i^{2}-i-1}{i!}$.

2.2   Series which cannot be summed

The series in the last section were easy to deal with because it was possible to find a formula for S_n. But there are many series which can't be summed in this way, which may or may not converge to a limit. The examples in this section illustrate both possibilities.

Example 2.2.1

Investigate whether the series $\dfrac{1}{\sqrt{1}}+\dfrac{1}{\sqrt{2}}+\dfrac{1}{\sqrt{3}}+\ldots$ converges to a limit.

What do you think? In some respects this series resembles those in the last section; for example, the terms get steadily smaller, and tend to 0 as $n\to\infty$. Is this enough to ensure that the series converges?

It is worth beginning experimentally. Your calculator may have a program for finding the sum of a given number of terms of a series defined by a formula. Table 2.1 gives some values of $S_n=\displaystyle\sum_{i=1}^{n}\frac{1}{\sqrt{i}}$ found in this way.

n	50	100	200	500	999
S_n	12.752...	18.589...	26.859...	43.283...	61.769...

Table 2.1

The reason for stopping at 999 is that the 'sum sequence' program on the calculator used to make this table was limited to values of n less than 1000. If you want to go further you may have to split the sum into several parts, or write a program to do the calculations. If 'sum sequence' is not available you can use the $\sum$ program to find each value of S_n separately.

Another possibility is to use a calculator to produce a graph of the sum sequence, defined by

$$S_1 = 1, \quad S_n = S_{n-1} + \frac{1}{\sqrt{n}}.$$

This is shown, for $1 \le n \le 50$, in Fig. 2.2. Again, the calculator may restrict the values of n for which you can do this.

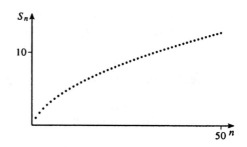

Fig. 2.2

You would probably suspect by now that the series doesn't converge to a limit, but the experimental evidence isn't conclusive. What is needed is an algebraic argument.

For this series it is quite easy to prove that the series doesn't converge. It has already been remarked that the terms get steadily smaller, and this means that all the terms $\frac{1}{\sqrt{1}}, \frac{1}{\sqrt{2}}, \frac{1}{\sqrt{3}}, \dots, \frac{1}{\sqrt{n-1}}$ are greater than $\frac{1}{\sqrt{n}}$. It follows that, if $n > 1$,

$$S_n = \frac{1}{\sqrt{1}} + \frac{1}{\sqrt{2}} + \frac{1}{\sqrt{3}} + \dots + \frac{1}{\sqrt{n-1}} + \frac{1}{\sqrt{n}}$$
$$> \frac{1}{\sqrt{n}} + \frac{1}{\sqrt{n}} + \frac{1}{\sqrt{n}} + \dots + \frac{1}{\sqrt{n}} + \frac{1}{\sqrt{n}}$$
$$= n \times \frac{1}{\sqrt{n}} = \sqrt{n}.$$

You can show this inequality numerically by adding a third row to Table 2.1, to give Table 2.3.

n	50	100	200	500	999
S_n	12.752...	18.589...	26.859...	43.283...	61.769...
$\sqrt{n}$	7.071...	10	14.142...	22.360...	31.606...

Table 2.3

Now $\sqrt{n}$ doesn't tend to a limit as $n \to \infty$. You can make it as large as you like by taking a large enough value for n. Since S_n is larger than $\sqrt{n}$, the same is true of the sum sequence S_n. This means that the series $\sum \frac{1}{\sqrt{i}}$ is not convergent.

A series which does not converge is said to be **divergent**. In Example 2.2.1 the sum sequence 'diverges to infinity'. You write $S_n \to \infty$ as $n \to \infty$.

Example 2.2.2
Investigate whether the series $\sum \frac{1}{i^2}$ is convergent.

As in the previous example, begin with some numerical calculations. Table 2.4 gives the values of $S_n = \sum_{i=1}^{n} \frac{1}{i^2}$ for a selection of values of n, and Fig. 2.5 shows the graph of S_n for $1 \le n \le 50$.

n	50	100	200	500	999
S_n	1.6251...	1.6349...	1.6399...	1.6429...	1.6439...

Table 2.4

This series behaves quite differently from $\sum \dfrac{1}{\sqrt{i}}$.

It is clearly convergent, though the value of the sum to infinity is not at all obvious.

You have in fact seen Fig. 2.5 before. It is Fig. 9.14 in Higher Level Book 1 Section 9.6, and it was stated there that the series converges to the limit $\frac{1}{6}\pi^2$.

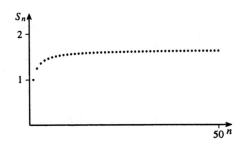

Fig. 2.5

In Example 2.2.1, where you wanted to prove that the series is divergent, you found an inequality which showed that the partial sums are greater than another function which tends to infinity. To prove that a series is convergent, you try to prove that the partial sums are less than another function which tends to a limit as $n \to \infty$. In this example you can do this by finding another series which is convergent and whose terms are greater than those of $\sum \dfrac{1}{i^2}$.

To get a fraction $\dfrac{1}{\cdots}$ greater than $\dfrac{1}{i^2}$, the denominator has to be *less* than i^2. A good choice is to take a denominator of $i^2 - \frac{1}{4}$. The reason for this is that you can then express the fraction in partial fractions as

$$\frac{1}{i^2 - \frac{1}{4}} \equiv \frac{1}{\left(i - \frac{1}{2}\right)\left(i + \frac{1}{2}\right)} \equiv \frac{1}{i - \frac{1}{2}} - \frac{1}{i + \frac{1}{2}};$$

and these partial fractions have the form $f(i) - f(i-1)$, with $f(i) = -\dfrac{1}{i + \frac{1}{2}}$. So

$$\sum_{i=1}^{n} \frac{1}{i^2 - \frac{1}{4}} = f(n) - f(0) = -\frac{1}{n + \frac{1}{2}} + \frac{1}{\frac{1}{2}} = 2 - \frac{1}{n + \frac{1}{2}}.$$

And since $\dfrac{1}{n + \frac{1}{2}} \to 0$ as $n \to \infty$, this series is convergent, and $\sum_{i=1}^{\infty} \dfrac{1}{i^2 - \frac{1}{4}} = 2$.

This completes the argument. You know that, for each positive integer i,

$$\frac{1}{i^2} < \frac{1}{i^2 - \frac{1}{4}}, \quad \text{so that} \quad S_n = \sum_{i=1}^{n} \frac{1}{i^2} < \sum_{i=1}^{n} \frac{1}{i^2 - \frac{1}{4}}.$$

Also the series on the right converges to the limit 2. So S_n converges to a limit which is less than or equal to 2.

2.3   Some general rules

The examples in the last two sections will have suggested to you some properties which are true of many infinite series. One almost obvious property is that, if a series is convergent, then the size of the individual terms u_i must tend to 0 as $n \to \infty$. This is easy to prove. If S_n and S_{n-1} are the partial sums of n and $n-1$ terms of the series $\sum u_i$, then

$$S_n = S_{n-1} + u_n, \quad \text{so that} \quad u_n = S_n - S_{n-1}.$$

But if the series is convergent, both S_n and S_{n-1} tend to the sum to infinity S_∞. So

$$\lim_{n\to\infty}(S_n - S_{n-1}) = \lim_{n\to\infty} S_n - \lim_{n\to\infty} S_{n-1} = S_\infty - S_\infty = 0.$$

It follows that $\lim_{n\to\infty} u_n = 0$.

What is less obvious is that the converse is not true. You can have series, such as the one in Example 2.2.1, for which $\lim_{n\to\infty} u_n = 0$ but which are not convergent. One way of expressing this in words is:

> For $\sum u_i$ to be convergent it is necessary, but not sufficient, that $\lim_{n\to\infty} u_n = 0$.

All the examples in this chapter are series of positive terms, but this rule is still true for series with some terms positive and some negative. The proof is exactly the same.

It follows from this that:

> If $\lim_{n\to\infty} u_n \neq 0$, or if the limit does not exist, the series is divergent.

Example 2.3.1
Prove that $\sum \cos^2 i$ is divergent.

The method is to show that there are numbers i as large as you like for which $\cos^2 i$ is greater than a positive constant, so that it cannot tend to 0 as $i \to \infty$.

Since $\pi > 3$, $\frac{1}{6}\pi > \frac{1}{2}$. So, for every positive integer m, there is at least one integer i between $m\pi - \frac{1}{6}\pi$ and $m\pi + \frac{1}{6}\pi$. For these values of i,

$$\cos^2 i > \cos^2\left(m\pi \pm \frac{1}{6}\pi\right) = \cos^2 \frac{1}{6}\pi = \left(\frac{1}{2}\sqrt{3}\right)^2 = \frac{3}{4}.$$

Therefore $\lim_{i\to\infty} \cos^2 i \neq 0$; in fact the limit doesn't exist. So $\sum \cos^2 i$ is divergent.

The next two rules are illustrated by Example 2.2.2. These are only true for series with all positive terms.

> If $\sum u_i$ is a series of positive terms, and if there is a number A such that all the partial sums S_n are less than A, then the series is convergent, and the sum to infinity is less than or equal to A.

You may be surprised by the words 'less than or equal to' in this rule. In Example 2.2.2 all the partial sums are less than 2, and the sum to infinity is less than 2. But if you take a series like the geometric series

$$1 + \tfrac{1}{2} + \left(\tfrac{1}{2}\right)^2 + \dots + \left(\tfrac{1}{2}\right)^{n-1},$$

all the partial sums are less than 2, but the sum to infinity is equal to 2. So in stating the general rule, the conclusion must be $S_\infty \leq A$ rather than $S_\infty < A$.

The inequality in Example 2.2.2 was obtained by comparing the terms of the series $\sum \frac{1}{i^2}$ with those of

$\sum \frac{1}{i^2 - \frac{1}{4}}$. This is an example of the **comparison test** for convergence.

> **The comparison test**   If $\sum u_i, \sum v_i$ are two series of positive terms such that, for all i, $u_i \leq v_i$, and if $\sum v_i$ converges to a limit S, then $\sum u_i$ converges to a limit less than or equal to S.

There is a corresponding test for divergence:

> If $\sum u_i, \sum v_i$ are two series of positive terms such that, for all i, $u_i \leq v_i$, and if $\sum u_i$ is divergent, then $\sum v_i$ is divergent.

For example, you know from Example 2.2.1 that $\sum \frac{1}{\sqrt{i}}$ is divergent. And if i is any number greater than 1, $\sqrt[4]{i} < \sqrt{i}$, so that $\frac{1}{\sqrt[4]{i}} > \frac{1}{\sqrt{i}}$. Taking $u_i = \frac{1}{\sqrt{i}}$ and $v_i = \frac{1}{\sqrt[4]{i}}$, it follows that $\sum \frac{1}{\sqrt[4]{i}}$ is divergent.

Exercise 2B

1   Give reasons why the following infinite series are divergent.

(a) $\sum \frac{i}{2i-1}$ (b) $\sum \frac{1}{\sqrt[3]{i}}$

2   Give reasons why the following infinite series are convergent.

(a) $\sum \frac{1}{i^{2.5}}$ (b) $\sum \frac{1}{i^2+1}$ (c) $\sum \frac{1}{2^i+1}$

3   (a)   Prove that, for $i > 1$, $\frac{1 \times 2 \times 3 \times \dots \times i}{i \times i \times i \times \dots \times i} \leq \frac{2}{i^2}$.

(b)   Prove that $\sum \frac{i!}{i^i}$ is convergent. Can you find a number M such that $\sum_{i=1}^{\infty} \frac{i!}{i^i} \leq M$?

(c)   Use a calculator to evaluate $\sum_{i=1}^{n} \frac{i!}{i^i}$ for as large a value of n as you can.

2 Infinite series   19

4 (a) Give a reason why $\sum \dfrac{1}{i^4}$ is convergent.

   (b) Use a calculator to find $\displaystyle\sum_{i=1}^{n} \dfrac{1}{i^4}$ for a large value of n.

   (c) It can be proved that $\displaystyle\sum_{i=1}^{\infty} \dfrac{1}{i^4} = \dfrac{1}{N} \pi^4$ where N is an integer. Use your answer to part (b) to identify the value of N.

5 (a) Give a reason why $\sum \dfrac{1}{i^3}$ is convergent.

   (b) Use a calculator to find $\displaystyle\sum_{i=1}^{n} \dfrac{1}{i^3}$ for a large value of n.

   (c) Show that, for $i \in \mathbb{Z}^+$, $i^3 > (i-1)i(i+1)$.

   (d) A student tries to find an upper bound to the value of $\displaystyle\sum_{i=1}^{\infty} \dfrac{1}{i^3}$ by comparing it with

   $\displaystyle\sum_{i=1}^{\infty} \dfrac{1}{(i-1)i(i+1)}$. What goes wrong?

   (e) Modify the method in part (d) to find an upper bound for $\displaystyle\sum_{i=1}^{\infty} \dfrac{1}{i^3}$. Compare this with your answer to part (b).

6 (a) The terms of the finite series $S_n = \displaystyle\sum_{i=1}^{n} \dfrac{1}{i}$ can be grouped as

   $$1 + \frac{1}{2} + \left(\frac{1}{3} + \frac{1}{4}\right) + \left(\frac{1}{5} + \frac{1}{6} + \frac{1}{7} + \frac{1}{8}\right) + \ldots + \left(\frac{1}{2^{j-1}+1} + \frac{1}{2^j}\right) + \frac{1}{2^j+1} + \ldots + \frac{1}{n},$$

   where j is the highest power of 2 less than or equal to n. Explain why the sum in each of the brackets is greater than $\frac{1}{2}$. Hence show that $S_n > 1 + \frac{1}{2} j$. What can you deduce about the infinite series $\sum \dfrac{1}{i}$?

   (b) Use part (a) to find a lower bound for the value of S_{1000}. By grouping the terms in a different way, prove that $S_{1000} < 10$.

   (c) Use a calculator to find S_{1000} correct to 6 decimal places.

7 (a) Prove that, for $i \in \mathbb{Z}^+$, $i! \ge 2^{i-1}$; for what values of i are the two sides equal? Hence prove that $\sum \dfrac{1}{i!}$ is convergent. What can you say about $\displaystyle\sum_{i=1}^{\infty} \dfrac{1}{i!}$?

   (b) Use an inequality similar to that in part (a) to prove that $\sum \dfrac{2^i}{i!}$ is convergent. Can you find a number M such that $\displaystyle\sum_{i=1}^{\infty} \dfrac{2^i}{i!} \le M$?

8 (a) Prove that, for $i > 1$, $\dfrac{(2i)!}{(i!)^2} > 2^i$.

(b) Prove that, if $u_i = \dfrac{1}{2^i C_i}$, $\sum u_i$ is convergent, and that $\sum\limits_{i=1}^{\infty} u_i \le 1$.

(c) Use a calculator to evaluate $\sum\limits_{i=1}^{n} u_i$ for as large a value of n as you can.

2.4 Some important limits

In Example 2.1.2 you needed to find the limit as $n \to \infty$ of $\dfrac{-\left(\frac{1}{2}\right)^n}{2n+1}$. This was simple, because the numerator of the fraction tends to 0 and the denominator tends to infinity, so $\dfrac{1}{2n+1}$ also tends to 0.

But what would happen if $(2n+1)$ had been in the numerator? You would then have the product of two factors, one tending to 0 and the other to infinity. Which would prevail?

You would have a similar problem if $\frac{1}{2}$ is replaced by 2. You would then have a fraction with both numerator and denominator tending to infinity. Will this tend to infinity, to 0, or somewhere in between?

The answer is that 'powers prevail over polynomials'. In the product $(2n+1) \times \left(\frac{1}{2}\right)^n$, the fact that $\left(\frac{1}{2}\right)^n$ tends to 0 is more powerful than that $(2n+1)$ tends to infinity. And the fact that 2^n tends to infinity is what determines the behaviour of the function $\dfrac{2^n}{2n+1}$.

You can easily check these statements numerically with a calculator, but they need to be proved algebraically. The basic results are:

If $a > 1$, then $\dfrac{a^n}{n} \to \infty$ as $n \to \infty$.

If $0 < b < 1$, then $nb^n \to 0$ as $n \to \infty$.

You can prove both of these by using the binomial theorem. For the first, since $a > 1$, you can write $a = 1 + c$, where $c > 0$. Then

$$a^n = 1 + nc + \frac{n(n-1)}{2}c^2 + \ldots + c^n,$$

and all the terms on the right are positive. So a^n is greater than any one of the terms. In particular,

$$a^n > \frac{n(n-1)}{2}c^2, \quad \text{so} \quad \frac{a^n}{n} > \frac{n-1}{2}c^2.$$

This inequality produces the desired result. Since c is constant, $\dfrac{n-1}{2}c^2$ tends to infinity as $n \to \infty$.

Therefore $\dfrac{a^n}{n}$, which is greater than $\dfrac{n-1}{2}c^2$, also tends to infinity.

The second result is proved in a similar way. If $0 < b < 1$, then $\dfrac{1}{b} > 1$, so write $\dfrac{1}{b} = 1 + c$.

Then

$$nb^n = \frac{n}{(1+c)^n} < \frac{n}{\dfrac{n(n-1)}{2}c^2} = \frac{2}{(n-1)c^2},$$

and since c is constant this tends to 0 as $n \to \infty$.

The next example shows how this can be used to find the sum of an infinite series.

Example 2.4.1

Show that $\sum i\left(\frac{1}{2}\right)^i$ is convergent, and find the sum to infinity.

If you can find a function f such that $f(i) - f(i-1) = i\left(\frac{1}{2}\right)^i$, you could sum the first n terms of the series. You would probably expect $f(i)$ to have $\left(\frac{1}{2}\right)^i$ as a factor, and perhaps another factor which is a linear polynomial in i. So try $f(i) = (Ai + B)\left(\frac{1}{2}\right)^i$ for some unknown coefficients A and B. These have to satisfy the identity

$$(Ai + B)\left(\tfrac{1}{2}\right)^i - (A(i-1) + B)\left(\tfrac{1}{2}\right)^{i-1} \equiv i\left(\tfrac{1}{2}\right)^i.$$

Dividing by $\left(\frac{1}{2}\right)^{i-1}$, A and B must satisfy

$$(Ai + B)\left(\tfrac{1}{2}\right) - A(i-1) - B \equiv i\left(\tfrac{1}{2}\right).$$

Equating coefficients of i and the constant term,

$$\tfrac{1}{2}A - A = \tfrac{1}{2} \quad \text{and} \quad \tfrac{1}{2}B + A - B = 0.$$

So $A = -1$ and $B = -2$.

Therefore $f(i) = -(i+2)\left(\frac{1}{2}\right)^i$, and the partial sum is

$$\sum_{i=1}^{n} i\left(\tfrac{1}{2}\right)^i = f(n) - f(0) = -(n+2)\left(\tfrac{1}{2}\right)^n + 2.$$

Now, since $\frac{1}{2}$ is between 0 and 1, $2 \times \left(\frac{1}{2}\right)^n \to 0$ and $n \times \left(\frac{1}{2}\right)^n \to 0$ as $n \to \infty$, so $(n+2)\left(\frac{1}{2}\right)^n \to 0$.

The series is therefore convergent, and $\displaystyle\sum_{i=1}^{\infty} i\left(\tfrac{1}{2}\right)^i = 2$.

A series like $\sum i\left(\frac{1}{2}\right)^i$ is sometimes described as 'arithmetico-geometric', because its terms are the product of an arithmetic sequence $u_i = i$ and a geometric sequence $v_i = \left(\frac{1}{2}\right)^i$.

The results in the previous shaded box can be generalised, with n raised to any positive power.

> If $a > 1$ and k is any positive number, then $\dfrac{a^n}{n^k} \to \infty$ as $n \to \infty$.
>
> If $0 < b < 1$ and k is any positive number, then $n^k b^n \to 0$ as $n \to \infty$.

To prove this, notice first that $\sqrt[k]{a} > 1$ and that $0 < \sqrt[k]{b} < 1$. So, applying the previous results with $a^{\frac{1}{k}} = \sqrt[k]{a}$ and $b^{\frac{1}{k}} = \sqrt[k]{b}$ in place of a and b, you can deduce that

$$\frac{\left(a^{\frac{1}{k}}\right)^n}{n} \to \infty \quad \text{and} \quad n\left(b^{\frac{1}{k}}\right)^n \to 0.$$

That is,

$$\frac{a^{\frac{n}{k}}}{n} \to \infty \quad \text{and} \quad nb^{\frac{n}{k}} \to 0 \quad \text{as } n \to \infty.$$

Now raise the expressions on the left to the power k. Since k is positive, the limits are still ∞ and 0 respectively, and

$$\left(\frac{a^{\frac{n}{k}}}{n}\right)^k = \frac{a^n}{n^k} \quad \text{and} \quad \left(nb^{\frac{n}{k}}\right)^k = n^k b^n.$$

So $\quad \dfrac{a^n}{n^k} \to \infty \quad$ and $\quad n^k b^n \to 0 \quad$ as $n \to \infty$.

Exercise 2C

1 Prove that, if $p(x)$ is a polynomial of any degree, and $0 < b < 1$, then $p(n) \times b^n \to 0$ as $n \to \infty$.

2 (a) Use the method of Example 2.4.1 to evaluate $\displaystyle\sum_{i=1}^{\infty} i\left(\frac{1}{3}\right)^i$.

   (b) Use the same method to prove that, if $0 < q < 1$, $\displaystyle\sum_{i=1}^{\infty} iq^i = \frac{q}{(1-q)^2}$.

3 Use a method similar to that in Example 2.4.1 to find $\displaystyle\sum_{i=1}^{\infty} i^2\left(\frac{1}{2}\right)^i$. Check your answer with a calculator.

3 Tests for convergence

There are a number of tests which you can use to investigate whether a series is convergent. Two of these are described in this chapter. When you have completed it, you should

- be able to use the ratio test to prove that an infinite series is convergent
- be able to use the limit comparison test to prove that an infinite series is either convergent or divergent.

3.1 The ratio test

You saw in Example 2.2.1 that, for a series of positive terms to converge, it is not sufficient for the terms to get steadily smaller and tend to 0. For the series $\sum u_i$, where $u_i = \dfrac{1}{\sqrt{i}}$, you know that $u_i < u_{i-1}$ and that $\lim_{i\to\infty} u_i = 0$, but $\sum u_i$ is divergent.

But suppose you have a series such that $u_i \leq \frac{1}{2} u_{i-1}$ for all values of i. Will this be sufficient to guarantee that $\sum u_i$ converges?

Putting $i = 2, 3, 4, \ldots$ in turn, you know that

$$u_2 \leq \tfrac{1}{2} u_1, \qquad u_3 \leq \tfrac{1}{2} u_2, \qquad u_4 \leq \tfrac{1}{2} u_3, \text{ and so on.}$$

By putting these inequalities together, you can find inequalities connecting all the terms $u_2, u_3, u_4, \ldots$ in terms of u_1. Thus

$$u_3 \leq \tfrac{1}{2} u_2 \leq \tfrac{1}{2}\left(\tfrac{1}{2} u_1\right) = \left(\tfrac{1}{2}\right)^2 u_1,$$

$$u_4 \leq \tfrac{1}{2} u_3 \leq \tfrac{1}{2}\left(\left(\tfrac{1}{2}\right)^2 u_1\right) = \left(\tfrac{1}{2}\right)^3 u_1,$$

and in general

$$u_i \leq \left(\tfrac{1}{2}\right)^{i-1} u_1.$$

Denote $\left(\tfrac{1}{2}\right)^{i-1} u_1$ by v_i, so that $u_i \leq v_i$ for all i. Then you have the situation of the comparison test in Section 2.3, since

$$\sum_{i=1}^{\infty} v_i = u_1 \sum_{i=1}^{\infty} \left(\tfrac{1}{2}\right)^{i-1}$$

is a convergent geometric series, with sum

$$u_1 \times \frac{1}{1 - \frac{1}{2}} = \frac{u_1}{\frac{1}{2}} = 2u_1.$$

It follows by the comparison test that $\sum u_i$ converges to a limit which is less than or equal to $2u_1$.

There is nothing special about the factor $\frac{1}{2}$. Any factor r less than 1 would do just as well, with $u_i \leq ru_{i-1}$ for all values of i. You would then define v_i as $r^{i-1}u_1$, so that $u_i \leq v_i$ for all i, and

$$\sum_{i=1}^{\infty} v_i = u_1 \sum_{i=1}^{\infty} r^{i-1} = u_1 \times \frac{1}{1-r}.$$

This is called the **ratio test**, because the condition $u_i \leq ru_{i-1}$ can be written in ratio form as $\dfrac{u_i}{u_{i-1}} \leq r$.

> **The ratio test**   If $\sum u_i$ is a series of positive terms such that, for all $i > 1$,
>
> $\dfrac{u_i}{u_{i-1}} \leq r$ where $r < 1$, then the series converges to a limit S_∞ such that
>
> $S_\infty \leq \dfrac{u_1}{1-r}.$

Example 3.1.1

Prove that the series $\sum \dfrac{1}{^{2i}C_i}$ is convergent. (See Exercise 2B Question 7.)

Since $^nC_r = \dfrac{n!}{r! \times (n-r)!}$ (see Higher Level Book 1 Section 3.6), $^{2i}C_i = \dfrac{(2i)!}{i! \times i!}$, and

$$u_i = \frac{1}{^{2i}C_i} = \frac{i! \times i!}{(2i)!}.$$

So

$$\frac{u_i}{u_{i-1}} = \frac{i! \times i!}{(2i)!} + \frac{(i-1)! \times (i-1)!}{(2i-2)!}$$

$$= \frac{i!}{(i-1)!} \times \frac{i!}{(i-1)!} \times \frac{(2i-2)!}{(2i)!}$$

$$= i \times i \times \frac{1}{(2i) \times (2i-1)}$$

$$= \frac{1}{2} \times \frac{i}{2i-1}.$$

Now if $i > 1$, $i < 2i - 1$, so $\dfrac{u_i}{u_{i-1}} \leq \frac{1}{2}$ for $i = 2,3,4,\dots$. Therefore, by the ratio test, $\sum \dfrac{1}{^{2i}C_i}$ is convergent, and

$$\sum_{i=1}^{\infty} \frac{1}{^{2i}C_i} \leq \frac{1}{^{2}C_1} \times \frac{1}{1-\frac{1}{2}} = \frac{1}{2} \times 2 = 1.$$

Example 3.1.2
Investigate the convergence of the infinite series $\sum \dfrac{1}{3^i - 2}$.

If $u_i = \dfrac{1}{3^i - 2}$, then $u_{i-1} = \dfrac{1}{3^{i-1} - 2}$, and

$$\frac{u_i}{u_{i-1}} = \frac{3^{i-1} - 2}{3^i - 2}.$$

It is not immediately obvious that this is always less than a number r less than 1. So try working out the first few values of the ratio:

$$\frac{u_2}{u_1} = \frac{3-2}{3^2-2} = \frac{1}{7} = 0.142..., \qquad \frac{u_3}{u_2} = \frac{3^2-2}{3^3-2} = \frac{7}{25} = 0.28,$$

$$\frac{u_4}{u_3} = \frac{3^3-2}{3^4-2} = \frac{25}{79} = 0.316..., \qquad \frac{u_5}{u_4} = \frac{3^4-2}{3^5-2} = \frac{79}{241} = 0.327.... \ .$$

It looks as if the ratio might always be less than $\frac{1}{3}$. So try working out

$$\begin{aligned}
\frac{1}{3} - \frac{u_i}{u_{i-1}} &= \frac{1}{3} - \frac{3^{i-1}-2}{3^i-2} \\
&= \frac{3^i - 2 - 3(3^{i-1} - 2)}{3(3^i - 2)} \\
&= \frac{3^i - 2 - 3^i + 6}{3(3^i - 2)} = \frac{4}{3(3^i - 2)}.
\end{aligned}$$

This is obviously positive, which proves that, for all $i > 1$, $\dfrac{u_i}{u_{i-1}} < \frac{1}{3}$. So the series converges.

Also, since $u_1 = \dfrac{1}{3^1 - 2} = 1$, $\quad \displaystyle\sum_{i=1}^{\infty} \frac{1}{3^i - 2} \le 1 \times \frac{1}{1 - \frac{1}{3}} = \frac{3}{2}.$

You can check this with a calculator. For example, $S_{50} = 1.2017...$. By the time that i reaches the value 50 the terms are very small indeed, so it is likely that the value of S_∞ is close to this.

3.2 Modifications of the ratio test

You often want to investigate the convergence of series for which the use of the ratio test doesn't exactly fit the wording in Section 3.1. This section discusses some possible modifications.

(i) Ignoring the early terms
If you want to know whether a series is convergent, what is important is the size of the terms u_i when i is large. It doesn't matter if some of the early terms don't fit the pattern.

So it isn't necessary to insist that the inequality $\dfrac{u_i}{u_{i-1}} \le r$ holds 'for all $i > 1$'. Provided that you can find a number m such that the inequality holds 'for all $i > m$', the series will still converge.

The only difference is that the inequality for S_∞ will have to be modified by detaching the first $m-1$ terms and summing them separately. It then becomes

$$S_\infty \le \sum_{i=1}^{m-1} u_i + \frac{u_m}{1-r}.$$

Example 3.2.1

Show that $\sum \frac{3^i}{i!}$ is convergent, and that the sum to infinity is not greater than $25\frac{1}{2}$.

If $u_i = \frac{3^i}{i!}$, then $\frac{u_i}{u_{i-1}} = \frac{3^i}{i!} \times \frac{(i-1)!}{3^{i-1}} = \frac{3}{i}$. So $\frac{u_2}{u_1} = \frac{3}{2}$, $\frac{u_3}{u_2} = \frac{3}{3} = 1$, $\frac{u_4}{u_3} = \frac{3}{4}, \dots$.

To prove convergence, the ratio of successive terms must be less than a number less than 1, and this happens from $i=4$ onwards; that is, for all $i > 3$. The ratio is then less than or equal to $\frac{3}{4}$, so the series is convergent, and

$$S_\infty \le \sum_{i=1}^{2} \frac{3^i}{i!} + \frac{3^3}{3!} \times \frac{1}{1-\frac{3}{4}}$$

$$\le \frac{3}{1!} + \frac{3^2}{2!} + \frac{3^3}{3!} \times 4$$

$$= 3 + \frac{9}{2} + \frac{27}{6} \times 4 = 25\frac{1}{2}.$$

(You will find in Section 9.3 that the exact sum to infinity is $e^3 - 1 = 19.08\dots$.)

(ii) A limit form of the ratio test

When you use the ratio test, it is sometimes rather tricky to find a suitable value of r and to obtain the inequality $\frac{u_i}{u_{i-1}} \le r$. But it quite often happens that $\frac{u_i}{u_{i-1}}$ tends to a limit as $i \to \infty$. If this limit is l, and if $l < 1$, then you can be sure that the ratio is as close as you like to l by making i large enough. So if you choose a number r between l and 1, you know that beyond some number m all the values of $\frac{u_i}{u_{i-1}}$ are less than r. This is illustrated in Fig. 3.1.

The conditions given in (i) above for $\sum u_i$ to converge are therefore satisfied. The ratio test then takes the form:

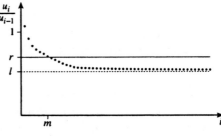

Fig. 3.1

The ratio test (limit form) If $\sum u_i$ is a series of positive terms such that

$\lim_{i \to \infty} \frac{u_i}{u_{i-1}} < 1$, then the series is convergent.

This is often a simpler form of the ratio test to use. The only drawback is that it requires the limit to exist. Occasionally you come across series for which $\dfrac{u_i}{u_{i-1}}$ doesn't tend to a limit, even though $\dfrac{u_i}{u_{i-1}} < r < 1$ for all $i > 1$.

Example 3.2.2

Investigate the convergence of the infinite series $\sum \dfrac{1}{3^i - 2}$.

This is a repeat of Example 3.1.2. In that example the most difficult part was to decide on a value for r and to prove the inequality. But it is quite easy to find the limit as $i \to \infty$ of $\dfrac{u_i}{u_{i-1}} = \dfrac{3^{i-1} - 2}{3^i - 2}$.

When you have a fraction where numerator and denominator have a similar form and both tend to infinity, a useful move is often to divide top and bottom by the same quantity so as to get expressions which tend to a finite limit. In this case, if you divide top and bottom by 3^{i-1}, you get

$$\frac{u_i}{u_{i-1}} = \frac{1 - \dfrac{2}{3^{i-1}}}{3 - \dfrac{2}{3^{i-1}}}.$$

Since $3^{i-1} \to \infty$ as $i \to \infty$, $\dfrac{2}{3^{i-1}} \to 0$. So

$$\lim_{i \to \infty} \frac{u_i}{u_{i-1}} = \frac{1 - 0}{3 - 0} = \frac{1}{3}.$$

And since $\frac{1}{3} < 1$, the limit form of the ratio test proves that $\sum \dfrac{1}{3^i - 2}$ is convergent.

(iii) A test for divergence?

In Section 3.1 the ratio test was proved by using the comparison test from Section 2.3. There was another part of the comparison test which could be used to prove a series divergent. So you might ask whether a ratio test can be used to prove a series divergent.

The answer is that it can, but there is not much point in doing so. For if $\dfrac{u_i}{u_{i-1}} > 1$ for all i, then $u_i > u_{i-1}$, so the terms are getting steadily larger as i increases. In that case, u_i can't tend to 0 as $i \to \infty$, so the series can't possibly converge. So rather than using a ratio test to prove the series divergent, it is usually simpler just to show that u_i doesn't tend to 0.

Finally, what happens if $\lim\limits_{i \to \infty} \dfrac{u_i}{u_{i-1}} = 1$?

In that case the ratio test is useless. To show this, look at the two examples in Section 2.2, $\sum \dfrac{1}{\sqrt{i}}$ and $\sum \dfrac{1}{i^2}$.

For the first series,

$$\frac{u_i}{u_{i-1}} = \frac{\sqrt{i-1}}{\sqrt{i}} = \sqrt{\frac{i-1}{i}} = \sqrt{1-\frac{1}{i}}, \qquad \text{so} \qquad \lim_{i\to\infty}\frac{u_i}{u_{i-1}} = \sqrt{1-0} = 1.$$

And for the second series,

$$\frac{u_i}{u_{i-1}} = \frac{(i-1)^2}{i^2} = \left(\frac{i-1}{i}\right)^2 = \left(1-\frac{1}{i}\right)^2, \qquad \text{so} \qquad \lim_{i\to\infty}\frac{u_i}{u_{i-1}} = (1-0)^2 = 1.$$

But the first series is divergent and the second is convergent.

> If $\lim_{i\to\infty}\dfrac{u_i}{u_{i-1}} = 1$, the ratio test tells you nothing about the convergence of $\sum u_i$.

Example 3.2.3

For what positive values of q is the infinite series $\sum \dfrac{q^i}{i^2}$ convergent?

If $u_i = \dfrac{q^i}{i^2}$,

$$\frac{u_i}{u_{i-1}} = \frac{q^i}{i^2} \times \frac{(i-1)^2}{q^{i-1}} = q \times \left(1-\frac{1}{i}\right)^2,$$

so $\lim_{i\to\infty}\dfrac{u_i}{u_{i-1}} = q(1-0)^2 = q.$

By the ratio test, the series converges if $q < 1$.

If $q > 1$, you know from Section 2.4 that $u_i = \dfrac{q^i}{i^2} \to \infty$ as $i \to \infty$. So the series is divergent if $q > 1$.

If $q = 1$, the series is $\sum \dfrac{1}{i^2}$. It was proved in Example 2.2.2 that this is convergent.

Therefore, if q is positive, $\sum \dfrac{q^i}{i^2}$ is convergent for $q \le 1$.

Notice that in this example a different argument has to be used for each of the three cases.

Exercise 3A

1   Use the ratio test to prove that the following series are convergent. Find an upper bound for the sum to infinity, and compare it with a suitable partial sum found with a calculator.

(a) $\sum \dfrac{1}{5^i - 1}$ (b) $\sum \dfrac{1}{2^{i^2}}$ (c) $\sum \dfrac{i^2}{2^i}$

2 Use the limit form of the ratio test to prove that the following series are convergent.

(a) $\displaystyle\sum \frac{1}{2^i - i}$ (b) $\displaystyle\sum \frac{1}{3^i - i^2}$

3 Prove that, if $u_i = \frac{1}{i}$, then $\frac{u_i}{u_{i-1}} < 1$ for all $i > 1$. Does this prove that $\sum \frac{1}{i}$ converges?

4 (a) Prove that $\displaystyle\frac{1}{\sqrt{i} + \sqrt{i-1}} = \sqrt{i} - \sqrt{i-1}$.

(b) Explain why you can't use the ratio test to investigate the convergence of $\displaystyle\sum \frac{1}{2^{\sqrt{i}}}$.

5 For what positive values of q are the following series convergent?

(a) $\displaystyle\sum \frac{q^i}{\sqrt{i}}$ (b) $\displaystyle\sum \frac{q^i}{i!}$ (c) $\displaystyle\sum i^3 q^i$

3.3 The limit comparison test

If $\sum u_i$ and $\sum v_i$ are infinite series and if, for all i, $v_i = k u_i$, where k is a positive constant, then if $\sum u_i$ is divergent, so is $\sum v_i$; and if $\sum u_i$ is convergent, so is $\sum v_i$.

This may seem trivial, but it is worth mentioning because of two possible modifications.

First, as already noted in Section 3.2(i), what is important is the size of the terms when i is large. It doesn't matter if the early terms don't fit the pattern. So in the statement in the first paragraph, you can replace 'for all i' by 'for all $i > m$' where m is some fixed number.

Secondly, the multiplier k doesn't have to be 'absolutely constant', provided that it is not very different from k. If you choose two numbers, one above k and one below, as close as you like to k, and if the ratio $\frac{v_i}{u_i}$ is always between these two numbers when i is large enough, it would still be true that the two series diverge together, or converge together.

Putting these two modifications together, the multiplier has to be very close to k for values of i greater than m. What this means is that the multiplier can be different for each value of i, but it has to tend to k as a limit as $i \to \infty$.

So denote the multiplier by k_i, where $\lim_{i \to \infty} k_i = k$ is a positive constant. Then you can amend the statement in the first paragraph as follows.

> If $\sum u_i$ and $\sum v_i$ are infinite series and if $v_i = k_i u_i$, where $\lim_{k \to \infty} k_i = k > 0$, then if $\sum u_i$ is divergent, so is $\sum v_i$; and if $\sum u_i$ is convergent, so is $\sum v_i$.
>
> This is called the **limit comparison test**.

You can use the limit comparison test when you have a series whose terms v_i are given by a rather complicated expression. The idea is to compare this with a series with simpler terms u_i which have the same order of magnitude as v_i.

Example 3.3.1

Prove that $\sum \dfrac{1}{i^2 - i + 1}$ is convergent.

When i is large, the dominant term in $i^2 - i + 1$ is the quadratic term i^2, since

$$i^2 - i + 1 = i^2\left(1 - \frac{1}{i} + \frac{1}{i^2}\right),$$

and both $\frac{1}{i}$ and $\frac{1}{i^2}$ are small when i is large. So you can write

$$\frac{1}{i^2 - i + 1} = \frac{1}{1 - \frac{1}{i} + \frac{1}{i^2}} \times \frac{1}{i^2} \quad \text{as} \quad k_1 \times \frac{1}{i^2}, \quad \text{where} \quad \lim_{i \to \infty} k_1 = 1.$$

You already know from Example 2.2.2 that $\sum \dfrac{1}{i^2}$ is convergent. It follows, by the limit comparison test, that $\sum \dfrac{1}{i^2 - i + 1}$ is convergent.

By now you are familiar with a number of convergent series, for example:

$$\sum \frac{1}{i^2}, \ \sum \frac{1}{i^3}, \ \sum \frac{1}{i^4}, \ \dots \ ; \ \sum \frac{1}{i(i+1)}, \ \sum \frac{1}{i(i+1)(i+2)}, \ \dots \ ; \ \sum ar^{i-1} \quad \text{for} \ \ 0 < r < 1.$$

You also know some divergent series:

$$\sum \frac{1}{\sqrt{i}}, \ \sum \frac{1}{\sqrt[3]{i}}, \ \sum \frac{1}{\sqrt[4]{i}}, \ \dots \ ; \ \sum i, \ \sum i(i+1), \ \sum i(i+1)(i+2), \ \dots \ ; \ \sum ar^{i-1} \quad \text{for} \ \ r > 1.$$

And you have met some sequences which tend to a positive limit. A good way of finding such limits is to notice that, as $i \to \infty$, $\frac{1}{i} \to 0$. If you can express a sequence k_i in terms of $\frac{1}{i}$, then you can usually find the limit of the sequence by replacing $\frac{1}{i}$ by 0. Here are some examples.

$$\frac{ai + b}{pi + q} \quad \text{can be written as} \quad \frac{a + \frac{b}{i}}{p + \frac{q}{i}}, \text{ so } \lim_{i \to \infty} \frac{ai + b}{pi + q} = \frac{a + 0}{p + 0} = \frac{a}{p}.$$

If a is a positive number, $\lim_{i \to \infty} \sqrt[i]{a} = \lim_{i \to \infty} a^{\frac{1}{i}} = a^0 = 1.$

Since $\lim_{x\to 0}\dfrac{\sin x}{x}=1$ (see Higher Level Book 2 Section 21.1), $\lim_{i\to\infty} i\sin\left(\dfrac{1}{i}\right)=\lim_{i\to\infty}\dfrac{\sin\left(\frac{1}{i}\right)}{\frac{1}{i}}=1$.

So if you take one of the series as $\sum u_i$, and one of the sequences as the multiplier k_i, then you get another series $\sum v_i$ which diverges if $\sum u_i$ diverges, and converges if $\sum u_i$ converges.

Example 3.3.2
Investigate whether the following series are convergent or divergent.

(a) $\sum\dfrac{\sqrt{i}}{2i-1}$ (b) $\sum\dfrac{1}{i}\sin\left(\dfrac{1}{i}\right)$ (c) $\sum 2^{\frac{1}{i}}\times\left(\dfrac{1}{2}\right)^{i}$

   (a)   You can write $\dfrac{\sqrt{i}}{2i-1}$ as $\dfrac{i}{2i-1}\times\dfrac{1}{\sqrt{i}}$, and

$$\lim_{i\to\infty}\frac{i}{2i-1}=\lim_{i\to\infty}\frac{1}{2-\frac{1}{i}}=\frac{1}{2-0}=\tfrac{1}{2}.$$

   Since $\sum\dfrac{1}{\sqrt{i}}$ is divergent, the limit comparison test shows that $\sum\dfrac{\sqrt{i}}{2i-1}$ is divergent.

   (b)   You can write $\dfrac{1}{i}\sin\left(\dfrac{1}{i}\right)$ as $i\sin\left(\dfrac{1}{i}\right)\times\dfrac{1}{i^2}$.

   Since $\lim_{i\to\infty} i\sin\left(\dfrac{1}{i}\right)=1$ and $\sum\dfrac{1}{i^2}$ is convergent, it follows by the limit comparison test that $\sum\dfrac{1}{i}\sin\left(\dfrac{1}{i}\right)$ is convergent.

   (c)   Since $\lim_{i\to\infty} 2^{\frac{1}{i}}=2^0=1$ and $\sum\left(\dfrac{1}{2}\right)^{i}$ is convergent, $\sum 2^{\frac{1}{i}}\times\left(\dfrac{1}{2}\right)^{i}$ is convergent.

Exercise 3B

1   Find the limits as $i\to\infty$ of

   (a) $\cos\left(\dfrac{1}{i}\right)$,   (b) $\dfrac{2i^2+3i+4}{4i^2+3i+2}$.

2   Use the limit comparison test to prove the results in Exercise 3A Question 2.

3   Investigate whether the following infinite series are convergent or divergent.

   (a) $\sum\sin^2\left(\dfrac{1}{i}\right)$ (b) $\sum\dfrac{i+2}{i(i+1)^2}$ (c) $\sum\sqrt{\dfrac{(i+1)(i+3)}{i(i+2)(i+4)}}$

   (d) $\sum\dfrac{1}{i^2}\cos\left(\dfrac{1}{i}\right)$ (e) $\sum\dfrac{i(i+2)}{i+1}$ (f) $\sum\dfrac{2^i+3}{3^i+4}$

4 Series and integrals

This chapter introduces definite integrals and their links with finite series. When you have completed it, you should

- know how to define a definite integral in terms of lower and upper sums
- be able to use lower and upper sums to find bounds for the sums of finite series.

4.1 Defining a definite integral

If you were asked to say what you mean by $\int_a^b f(x)\,dx$, you would probably begin by describing how to find it. You might say something like 'find a function $I(x)$ whose derivative is $f(x)$, then $\int_a^b f(x)\,dx$ is $I(b)-I(a)$'.

That may do well enough for a function like $f(x)=x^3$, for which you can take $I(x)$ to be $\frac{1}{4}x^4$. But it doesn't help for a function like $f(x)=\sqrt{1+x^3}$, because you don't know any function $I(x)$ such that $I'(x)=\sqrt{1+x^3}$, or even that such a function exists.

In fact such a function does exist, and it is $\int_0^x \sqrt{1+t^3}\,dt$. But that doesn't help with the problem of defining a definite integral, because it is itself a definite integral! You are just chasing yourself round in circles.

The reason for using the letter t rather than x inside the integral is to avoid using x in two different senses in the same expression. Inside a definite integral it doesn't matter what letter you use; $\int_a^b t^3\,dt$ is the same as $\int_a^b x^3\,dx$, that is $\frac{1}{4}\left(b^4-a^4\right)$. So $\int_0^x t^3\,dt=\frac{1}{4}x^4$ is a function of x, whose derivative is x^3.

So what you need is a way of defining a definite integral that doesn't depend on the idea of differentiation. The way to do this is to go back to the idea of $\int_a^b f(x)\,dx$ as the area under the graph of $y=f(x)$ over the interval $[a,b]$.

Begin by trying to fill the region under the graph as well as you can with rectangles, as in Fig. 4.1. Each rectangle must be completely inside the region, but as tall as possible. If there are n rectangles in all, what you are doing is in effect to split the interval $[a,b]$ on the x-axis into n small subintervals, and then to make the height of each rectangle equal to the smallest value which $f(x)$ takes in that subinterval.

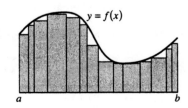

Fig. 4.1

This is called the 'lower bound' of $f(x)$ in the subinterval.

You need a notation to express this. First, since a is at the left end of the first subinterval and b is at the right end of the last, nth, subinterval, it is useful to write $a = x_0$ and $b = x_n$. You can then denote the ith subinterval by $[x_{i-1}, x_i]$, and its width by $w_i = x_i - x_{i-1}$. There is no need for all the rectangles to have the same width, but there is no reason why they shouldn't if you choose. If they do, then this width can be denoted by w, where

$$w = \frac{b-a}{n},$$

and $x_i - x_{i-1} = w$ for each i. Then $b = a + nw$ and

$$x_i = x_0 + iw = a + iw.$$

The height of the ith rectangle is the lower bound of $f(x)$ in the subinterval. Denoting this by m_i,

$$x_{i-1} \le x \le x_i \quad \Rightarrow \quad f(x) \ge m_i.$$

The notation is illustrated in Fig. 4.2.

The total area of all the rectangles is then

$$s = m_1 w_1 + m_2 w_2 + \ldots + m_n w_n$$
$$= \sum_{i=1}^{n} m_i (x_i - x_{i-1}).$$

Fig. 4.2

This is called the **lower sum** for this particular subdivision.

It is sometimes called the lower Riemann sum, after Bernhard Riemann (1826–1866), who was a professor at the University of Göttingen in Germany. The basic idea goes back to Archimedes (3rd century BC), but Riemann developed it into a general and mathematically rigorous definition.

This particular lower sum is of course not greater than the actual area of the region under the graph. But if you imagine every possible way of subdividing the interval $[a,b]$ into any number of subintervals, you could get some for which the corresponding lower sum is as close as you like to the area under the graph. That is, the area can be found as the limit of all the possible lower sums as the width of the subintervals tends to 0.

Will this always work? Might there be some functions, perhaps with very spiky graphs, for which the limit doesn't exist, or doesn't give the area you want?

To be quite sure, you can try another way of finding the area. Instead of drawing rectangles which fit inside the region, you could draw rectangles which completely cover the region but are as short as possible. To do this, begin by splitting the interval $[a,b]$ into subintervals as before, but then construct rectangles whose height is the upper bound of $f(x)$ in each subinterval. If this height is denoted by M_i, then

$$x_{i-1} \le x \le x_i \quad \Rightarrow \quad f(x) \le M_i.$$

This is illustrated in Fig. 4.3. The total area of all these rectangles is the **upper sum**,

$$S = M_1 w_1 + M_2 w_2 + \ldots + M_n w_n$$

$$= \sum_{i=1}^{n} M_i (x_i - x_{i-1}).$$

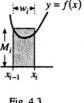

Fig. 4.3

Fig. 4.4 shows the upper sum, which is certainly not less than the actual area of the region under the graph.

Taking the limit of all possible upper sums as the width of the subintervals tends to 0 gives another way of finding the area you want. For any subdivision of $[a,b]$,

$s \leq$ area under the graph $\leq S$.

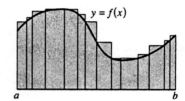

Fig. 4.4

So if the limit of the lower sums is equal to the limit of the upper sums, there can be no doubt that the area under the graph is equal to this common limit.

The first example illustrates the idea with a numerical calculation.

Example 4.1.1

Find $\displaystyle\int_0^2 \sqrt{1+x^3}\,\mathrm{d}x$ correct to 3 significant figures.

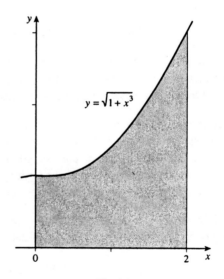

Since $\sqrt{1+x^3}$ is an increasing function (see Fig. 4.5), the lower bound for each subinterval is the value at the left end of the subinterval and the upper bound is the value at the right end.

Try splitting the interval $[0,2]$ into 100 equal subintervals, each of width 0.02. The ith subinterval runs from $0.02(i-1)$ to $0.2i$, so

$$m_i = \sqrt{1 + (0.02(i-1))^3}$$

and

$$M_i = \sqrt{1 + (0.02i)^3}.$$

Fig. 4.5

The lower and upper sums are then

$$s = \sum_{i=1}^{100} \sqrt{1 + (0.02(i-1))^3} \times 0.02 \qquad \text{and} \qquad S = \sum_{i=1}^{100} \sqrt{1 + (0.02i)^3} \times 0.02$$
$$= 3.221\ldots \qquad\qquad\qquad\qquad\qquad = 3.261\ldots \ ,$$

using a calculator to find the sums.

These values are not close enough to give the area correct to 3 significant figures, so you will need to split the interval $[0,2]$ into a larger number of narrower intervals. If you take 800 intervals, each of width 0.0025, then the ith subinterval runs from $0.0025(i-1)$ to $0.0025i$. Reasoning as before, the lower and upper sums are then

$$s = \sum_{i=1}^{800} \sqrt{1 + (0.0025(i-1))^3} \times 0.0025 \quad \text{and} \quad S = \sum_{i=1}^{800} \sqrt{1 + (0.0025i)^3} \times 0.0025$$

$$= 3.2388\ldots \qquad\qquad\qquad\qquad = 3.2438\ldots\ .$$

Correct to 3 significant figures both of these are 3.24, so the area under the graph must also be 3.24, correct to 3 significant figures.

Notice how in Example 4.1.1 the increase in the number of subintervals from 100 to 800 brings the lower sum and upper sum closer together, and therefore closer to the limiting value. In the second calculation there are 8 new subintervals for each of the subintervals in the first calculation. Fig. 4.6 shows how the effect of this is to increase the lower sum and decrease the upper sum.

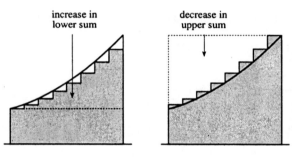

Fig. 4.6

But the numerical calculation doesn't by itself prove that s and S are tending to the same limit. To do this, you can use the fact that $\sqrt{1 + x^3}$ is an increasing function. This means that the height of the ith rectangle contributing to the lower sum is the same as the height of the $(i-1)$th rectangle contributing to the upper sum. So the 2nd, 3rd, ... , nth terms in the sum for s are the same as the 1st, 2nd, ... , $(n-1)$th terms in the sum for S. This is illustrated by Fig. 4.7; because the function is increasing, the rectangles for the upper sum are just the same as the rectangles for the lower sum, but translated to the left by the width of one subinterval.

So the only difference between the sums for s and S is that the first term of s is replaced by the last term of S.

That is, with n subintervals each of width $\frac{2}{n}$,

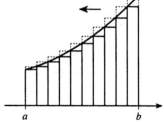

Fig. 4.7

$$S - s = \sqrt{1 + 2^3} \times \frac{2}{n} - \sqrt{1 + 0^3} \times \frac{2}{n}$$

$$= (3 - 1) \times \frac{2}{n} = \frac{4}{n}.$$

And since $\lim\limits_{n\to\infty} \dfrac{4}{n} = 0$, it follows that s and S tend to the same limit, which is $\displaystyle\int_0^2 \sqrt{1+x^3}\,dx$.

But you can't find the value of this limit precisely, because you can't find a formula for a sum like

$\displaystyle\sum_{i=1}^{n}\sqrt{1+\left(\dfrac{2}{n}i\right)^3}$. If you could sum the series, you could then find a formula for the definite integral. This is what happens in the next example.

Example 4.1.2

Use the summation method to find $\displaystyle\int_0^a x^3\,dx$, where $a>0$.

The function x^3 is increasing in the interval $[0,a]$, so as in Example 4.1.1 the lower bound in each subinterval is on the left and the upper bound is on the right.

Split the interval $[0,a]$ into n subintervals, each of width $\dfrac{a}{n}$. The ith subinterval runs from $x = (i-1)\dfrac{a}{n}$ to $x = i\dfrac{a}{n}$, so for this subinterval

$$m_i = (i-1)^3\dfrac{a^3}{n^3} \quad\text{and}\quad M_i = i^3\dfrac{a^3}{n^3}.$$

The upper and lower sums are then

$$s = \sum_{i=1}^{n}(i-1)^3\dfrac{a^3}{n^3}\times\dfrac{a}{n} \qquad S = \sum_{i=1}^{n}i^3\dfrac{a^3}{n^3}\times\dfrac{a}{n}$$

$$\text{and}$$

$$= \dfrac{a^4}{n^4}\sum_{i=1}^{n}(i-1)^3 \qquad\qquad = \dfrac{a^4}{n^4}\sum_{i=1}^{n}i^3.$$

Now you know that $\displaystyle\sum_{i=1}^{n}i^3 = \tfrac{1}{4}n^2(n+1)^2$ (see Example 1.1.3). Also

$$\sum_{i=1}^{n}(i-1)^3 = 0^3 + 1^3 + \ldots + (n-1)^3$$

$$= 0 + \sum_{i=1}^{n-1}i^3 = \tfrac{1}{4}(n-1)^2 n^2.$$

So

$$s = \dfrac{a^4}{n^4}\times\tfrac{1}{4}(n-1)^2 n^2 \qquad\qquad S = \dfrac{a^4}{n^4}\times\tfrac{1}{4}n^2(n+1)^2$$

$$= \tfrac{1}{4}a^4\times\dfrac{(n-1)^2}{n^2} \qquad\text{and}\qquad = \tfrac{1}{4}a^4\times\dfrac{(n+1)^2}{n^2}$$

$$= \tfrac{1}{4}a^4\left(1-\dfrac{1}{n}\right)^2 \qquad\qquad = \tfrac{1}{4}a^4\times\left(1+\dfrac{1}{n}\right)^2.$$

Since $\lim\limits_{n\to\infty}\dfrac{1}{n}=0$, it follows that

$$\lim_{n\to\infty} s = \tfrac{1}{4}a^4(1-0)^2 = \tfrac{1}{4}a^4 \quad \text{and} \quad \lim_{n\to\infty} S = \tfrac{1}{4}a^4(1+0)^2 = \tfrac{1}{4}a^4.$$

And since these limits are the same, both are equal to the definite integral,

$$\int_0^a x^3\,\mathrm{d}x = \tfrac{1}{4}a^4.$$

Of course, it is much easier to get the result in Example 4.1.2 by the anti-differentiation method than by the summation method. And the latter only works because you know how to sum $\sum\limits_{i=1}^{n} i^3$. You couldn't use the summation method to find $\int_0^a \sqrt{x}\,\mathrm{d}x$, for example, because you don't know how to sum $\sum\limits_{i=1}^{n} \sqrt{i}$; but it is simple by anti-differentiation. In fact, the great breakthrough by Newton and Leibniz was to show that the anti-differentiation method provides a far more powerful way of finding areas than the summation method initiated by Archimedes.

So the purpose of this section is to find a *definition* for $\int_a^b f(x)\,\mathrm{d}x$, not to suggest a new way of calculating it. Once you know that the definition is secure, you can go on to prove, just as in Higher Level Book 1 Section 29.4, that $\dfrac{\mathrm{d}}{\mathrm{d}x}\int_a^x f(t)\,\mathrm{d}t = f(x)$. And once you have done that, this is the property which you use to find definite integrals.

But the summation method does have one other advantage. It provides you with a way of finding a numerical value for definite integrals when you can't find a function $I(x)$ such that $I'(x)=f(x)$. You can then use the method of Example 4.1.1 to find bounds within which the value of $\int_a^b f(x)\,\mathrm{d}x$ must lie.

Exercise 4A

1   Areas under the following graphs over the given intervals are estimated by lower and upper sums with subintervals of equal widths. Calculate these sums for the stated widths, and compare them with the exact values of the areas.

(a) $y = 2x+3$, $0 \le x \le 1$; widths 0.5, 0.1, 0.01

(b) $y = 3x^2$, $1 \le x \le 2$; widths 0.5, 0.1, 0.01

(c) $y = \sqrt{x}$, $1 \le x \le 4$; widths 1, 0.1, 0.01

(d) $y = 12x - x^3$, $0 \le x \le 3$; widths 1, 0.5

2   By finding lower and upper sums, with n intervals of equal width, find the following integrals.

(a) $\displaystyle\int_0^{10} x\,dx$ (b) $\displaystyle\int_0^a x^2\,dx$ (c) $\displaystyle\int_0^1 e^x\,dx$

(In part (c), remember that, from the definition of e, $\displaystyle\lim_{h\to0}\frac{e^h-1}{h}=1$. See Higher Level Book 2 Section 13.2.)

3   A value for $\displaystyle\int_0^1 2^x\,dx$ is estimated by finding lower and upper sums with subintervals of equal width. Find the difference between the lower and upper sums if the number of subintervals is

(a) 5,   (b) 100,   (c) n.

4   Repeat Question 3 for the integral $\displaystyle\int_1^4 \frac{1}{\sqrt{x}}\,dx$.

5   A function f is increasing over the interval $[a,b]$. A value for $\displaystyle\int_a^b f(x)\,dx$ is obtained by finding the lower sums s and the upper sum S when the interval $[a,b]$ is split into n subintervals of equal width. Prove that

$$S-s=\frac{(f(b)-f(a))(b-a)}{n}.$$

Deduce that $\displaystyle\lim_{n\to\infty} S = \lim_{n\to\infty} s = \int_a^b f(x)\,dx.$

What would be the corresponding result if f were a decreasing function over $[a,b]$?

4.2   Finding bounds for the sums of series

The idea of lower and upper sums can be adapted to find upper and lower bounds for the sums of finite series which cannot be summed exactly. By representing each term as the area of a rectangle of width 1, the sum can be compared with an integral over the same interval.

Example 4.2.1
Find upper and lower bounds for $\sqrt{1}+\sqrt{2}+\sqrt{3}+\ldots+\sqrt{10}$.

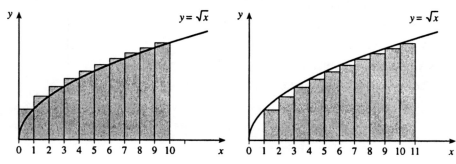

Fig. 4.8

In the left diagram of Fig. 4.8 the sum is represented as the area of a set of 10 rectangles, each having width 1 and with heights $\sqrt{1}$, $\sqrt{2}$, $\sqrt{3}$, ... , $\sqrt{10}$. These cover the interval $0 \le x \le 10$ of the x-axis.

The top right corners of these rectangles have coordinates $\left(1,\sqrt{1}\right)$, $\left(2,\sqrt{2}\right)$, $\left(3,\sqrt{3}\right)$, ... , $\left(10,\sqrt{10}\right)$ all of which lie on the curve $y = \sqrt{x}$.

Clearly the sum of the areas of the rectangles is greater than the area under the curve, so that

$$\sum_{i=1}^{10} \sqrt{i} > \int_0^{10} \sqrt{x}\, dx$$
$$= \left[\tfrac{2}{3} x^{\frac{3}{2}} \right]_0^{10}$$
$$= \tfrac{2}{3} \times 10\sqrt{10} = \tfrac{20}{3} \sqrt{10},$$

giving

$$\tfrac{20}{3} \sqrt{10} < \sum_{i=1}^{10} \sqrt{i}.$$

This gives a lower bound for the sum.

To find an upper bound, push all the rectangles to the right by 1 unit, so that they cover the interval $1 \le x \le 11$. The right diagram of Fig. 4.8 shows that the top left corners of the rectangles now lie on $y = \sqrt{x}$, and it is easy to see that

$$\sum_{i=1}^{n} \sqrt{i} < \int_1^{11} \sqrt{x}\, dx$$
$$= \left[\tfrac{2}{3} x^{\frac{3}{2}} \right]_1^{11}$$
$$= \tfrac{2}{3}\left(11\sqrt{11} - 1\right) = \tfrac{22}{3}\sqrt{11} - \tfrac{2}{3},$$

giving

$$\sum_{i=1}^{n} \sqrt{i} < \tfrac{22}{3}\sqrt{11} - \tfrac{2}{3}.$$

as an upper bound for the sum.

So $\tfrac{20}{3}\sqrt{10} < \sum_{i=1}^{n} \sqrt{i} < \tfrac{22}{3}\sqrt{11} - \tfrac{2}{3}$

You could of course find $\sqrt{1} + \sqrt{2} + ... + \sqrt{10}$ with a calculator. But you can use the same method to find a general inequality for the sum of the first n square roots, as in the next example.

Example 4.2.2

Find lower and upper bounds for the sum $\sqrt{1}+\sqrt{2}+\sqrt{3}+\ldots+\sqrt{n}$.

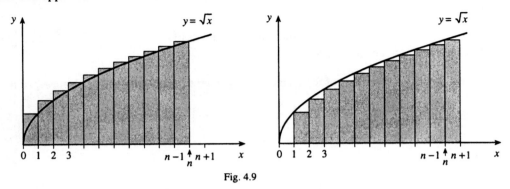

Fig. 4.9

In the left diagram of Fig. 4.9 the sum is represented as the area of a set of n rectangles, each having width 1 and with heights $\sqrt{1}$, $\sqrt{2}$, $\sqrt{3}$, ... , $\sqrt{n}$. These cover the interval $0 \le x \le n$ of the x-axis.

The top right corners of these rectangles have coordinates $(1,\sqrt{1})$, $(2,\sqrt{2})$, $(3,\sqrt{3})$, ... , $(n,\sqrt{n})$ all of which lie on the curve $y=\sqrt{x}$.

Clearly the sum of the areas of the rectangles is greater than the area under the curve, so that

$$\sum_{i=1}^{n}\sqrt{i} > \int_{0}^{n}\sqrt{x}\,dx$$
$$=\left[\tfrac{2}{3}x^{\frac{3}{2}}\right]_{0}^{n}=\tfrac{2}{3}n\sqrt{n},$$

giving

$$\tfrac{2}{3}n\sqrt{n} < \sum_{i=1}^{n}\sqrt{i}.$$

This gives a lower bound for the sum.

To find an upper bound, push all the rectangles to the right by 1 unit, so that they cover the interval $1 \le x \le n+1$. The right diagram of Fig. 4.9 shows that the top left corners of the rectangles now lie on $y=\sqrt{x}$, and it is easy to see that

$$\sum_{i=1}^{n}\sqrt{i} < \int_{1}^{n+1}\sqrt{x}\,dx$$
$$=\left[\tfrac{2}{3}x^{\frac{3}{2}}\right]_{1}^{n+1}=\tfrac{2}{3}\left((n+1)\sqrt{n+1}-1\right),$$

giving

$$\sum_{i=1}^{n}\sqrt{i} < \tfrac{2}{3}\left((n+1)\sqrt{n+1}-1\right)$$

as an upper bound.

So $\frac{2}{3}n\sqrt{n} < \sum_{i=1}^{n}\sqrt{i} < \frac{2}{3}\left((n+1)\sqrt{n+1}-1\right).$

This method gives remarkably good approximations. For example, if you put $n = 100$ in Example 4.2.2, you find that the sum of the square roots of the first 100 natural numbers lies between

$$\frac{2}{3}\times 100\sqrt{100} = 666.66\ldots \qquad \text{and} \qquad \frac{2}{3}\times\left(101\sqrt{101}-1\right) = 676.02\ldots.$$

The correct value of the sum is $671.46\ldots$. Both bounds are within 1% of this.

Things are slightly different if the graph of the function is decreasing.

Example 4.2.3

Show that $\ln 101 < 1 + \dfrac{1}{2} + \dfrac{1}{3} + \ldots + \dfrac{1}{100} < 1 + \ln 100.$

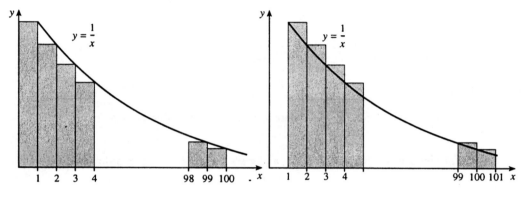

Fig. 4.10

The right diagram of Fig. 4.10 shows the sum $1 + \dfrac{1}{2} + \dfrac{1}{3} + \ldots + \dfrac{1}{100}$ represented as a set of 100

rectangles, each having width 1 and heights $1, \dfrac{1}{2}, \dfrac{1}{3}, \ldots, \dfrac{1}{100}$. These cover the interval $1 \le x \le 101$

of the x-axis. The top left corners of these rectangles have coordinates $(1,1)$, $\left(2,\dfrac{1}{2}\right)$, $\left(3,\dfrac{1}{3}\right)$, $\ldots$,

$\left(100,\dfrac{1}{100}\right)$ all of which lie on the curve $y = \dfrac{1}{x}$. Clearly the sum of the areas of the rectangles is

greater than the area under the curve, so that

$$1 + \frac{1}{2} + \frac{1}{3} + \ldots + \frac{1}{100} > \int_{1}^{101}\frac{1}{x}\,\mathrm{d}x$$
$$= [\ln x]_{1}^{101}$$
$$= \ln 101,$$

or $\ln 101 < 1 + \dfrac{1}{2} + \dfrac{1}{3} + \ldots + \dfrac{1}{100}.$

The left diagram shows all the shaded rectangles having moved to the left by 1 unit.

However, there is a problem, because you cannot have 0 as the lower limit of this integral which would then not exist. The solution is to ignore the first rectangle: the area under the curve between 1 and 100 is greater than the sum of the areas of the remaining rectangles, so

$$\frac{1}{2} + \frac{1}{3} + \ldots + \frac{1}{100} < \int_1^{100} \frac{1}{x} dx$$

$$= [\ln x]_1^{100} = \ln 100,$$

giving

$$\frac{1}{2} + \frac{1}{3} + \ldots + \frac{1}{100} < \ln 100.$$

Therefore, adding 1 (the area of the first rectangle) to both sides,

$$1 + \frac{1}{2} + \frac{1}{3} + \ldots + \frac{1}{100} < 1 + \ln 100.$$

So $\ln 101 < 1 + \frac{1}{2} + \frac{1}{3} + \ldots + \frac{1}{100} < 1 + \ln 100.$

Example 4.2.4

Find lower and upper bounds for $\sum\limits_{i=m}^{n} \frac{1}{i^2}$, where $n > m \geq 2$. Hence find bounds for $\sum\limits_{i=m}^{\infty} \frac{1}{i^2}$.

Sketch for yourself the graph of $y = \frac{1}{x^2}$, and mark on it points with coordinates $\left(m, \frac{1}{m^2}\right)$, $\left(m+1, \frac{1}{(m+1)^2}\right), \left(m+2, \frac{1}{(m+2)^2}\right), \ldots, \left(n, \frac{1}{n^2}\right)$.

Since $\frac{1}{x^2}$ is a decreasing function, you will get a lower bound by representing the sum by rectangles with these points at the top left corners, so that they cover the interval $m \leq x \leq n+1$.

The curve then lies inside the rectangles, so the sum of the areas of the rectangles is greater than the area under the curve, that is

$$\sum_{i=m}^{n} \frac{1}{i^2} > \int_m^{n+1} \frac{1}{x^2} dx$$

$$= \left[-\frac{1}{x}\right]_m^{n+1}$$

$$= \frac{1}{m} - \frac{1}{n+1},$$

which gives

$$\frac{1}{m} - \frac{1}{n+1} < \sum_{i=m}^{n} \frac{1}{i^2}.$$

To get an upper bound, push all the rectangles to the left by 1 unit. They then cover the interval $m-1 \le x \le n$, and have their top right corners on the curve, so that the curve lies above the rectangles. (Since $m \ge 2$, the interval does not include the awkward value $x = 0$.)

Therefore

$$\sum_{i=m}^{n} \frac{1}{i^2} < \int_{m-1}^{n} \frac{1}{x^2} dx$$

$$= \left[-\frac{1}{x} \right]_{m-1}^{n}$$

$$= \frac{1}{m-1} - \frac{1}{n},$$

giving

$$\sum_{i=m}^{n} \frac{1}{i^2} < \frac{1}{m-1} - \frac{1}{n}.$$

Combining these results,

$$\frac{n-m+1}{m(n+1)} < \sum_{i=m}^{n} \frac{1}{i^2} < \frac{n-m+1}{(m-1)n}.$$

By letting $n \to \infty$ you can find bounds for the sum of the infinite series $\sum_{i=m}^{\infty} \frac{1}{i^2}$. Since

$$\lim_{n \to \infty} \frac{n-m+1}{n+1} = \lim_{n \to \infty} \frac{1 - \frac{m-1}{n}}{1 + \frac{1}{n}} = \frac{1-0}{1+0} = 1 \quad \text{and} \quad \lim_{n \to \infty} \frac{n-m+1}{n} = \lim_{n \to \infty} \left(1 - \frac{m-1}{n} \right) = 1 - 0 = 1,$$

it follows that

$$\frac{1}{m} \le \sum_{i=m}^{\infty} \frac{1}{i^2} \le \frac{1}{m-1}.$$

When you reason by taking limits as $n \to \infty$, $<$ must be replaced by $\le$. See Section 2.3. But you should be able to see from your figure that in this example the strong inequality $<$ is in fact valid.

Exercise 4B

1   Establish the following upper and lower bounds for the given sums.

   (a) $4 - \ln 3 < \frac{2}{3} + \frac{3}{4} + \frac{4}{5} + \frac{5}{6} < 4 - \ln\left(\frac{7}{3}\right)$

   (b) $2 - \frac{2}{\sqrt{5}} < \frac{1}{1\sqrt{1}} + \frac{1}{2\sqrt{2}} + \frac{1}{3\sqrt{3}} + \frac{1}{4\sqrt{4}} < 2$

   (c) $20 - 2\sqrt{10} < \frac{1}{\sqrt{10}} + \frac{1}{\sqrt{11}} + \frac{1}{\sqrt{12}} + \dots + \frac{1}{\sqrt{99}} < 6\sqrt{11} - 6$

2 Find upper and lower bounds for the following sums. Give your answers in decimal form to 4 significant figures, rounding upper bounds up and lower bounds down.

(a) $\sqrt[4]{100} + \sqrt[4]{101} + \sqrt[4]{102} + \ldots + \sqrt[4]{999}$

(b) $\dfrac{1}{101} + \dfrac{2}{102} + \dfrac{3}{103} + \ldots + \dfrac{99}{199}$

(c) $\displaystyle\sum_{i=1}^{89} \sin i°$

(d) $\displaystyle\sum_{i=1}^{100} \dfrac{1}{100^2 + i^2}$

3 If $n > m > 1$, find upper and lower bounds for

(a) $\displaystyle\sum_{i=m}^{n} \dfrac{1}{i^3}$

(b) $\displaystyle\sum_{i=m}^{n} \dfrac{i}{1 + i^2}$

(c) $\dfrac{n!}{m!}$

4 (a) Use your answer to Question 3(a) to prove that $\displaystyle\sum_{i=1}^{\infty} \dfrac{1}{i^3} \leq 1\tfrac{1}{2}$.

(b) Use your answer to Question 3(b) to prove that $\displaystyle\sum_{i=1}^{\infty} \dfrac{i}{1 + i^2}$ is divergent.

5 (a) By considering a suitable integral, show that $12 < \sqrt[3]{1} + \sqrt[3]{2} + \sqrt[3]{3} + \ldots + \sqrt[3]{8}$.

(b) Find an upper bound for $\displaystyle\sum_{i=1}^{8} \sqrt[3]{i}$.

(c) Use a similar method to find upper and lower bounds for $\displaystyle\sum_{i=101}^{200} \sqrt[3]{i}$.

6 Show that $\displaystyle\int_{n}^{2n} \dfrac{1}{x}\,dx - \dfrac{1}{2n} < \dfrac{1}{n+1} + \dfrac{1}{n+2} + \ldots + \dfrac{1}{2n} < \int_{n}^{2n} \dfrac{1}{x}\,dx$.

Hence prove that $\displaystyle\lim_{n \to \infty} \left(\dfrac{1}{n+1} + \dfrac{1}{n+2} + \ldots + \dfrac{1}{2n} \right) = \ln 2$.

5 Infinite integrals and infinite series

You already know how to find the sum of an infinite series as the limit of a finite sum. This chapter describes how, in a similar way, you can define an infinite integral as a limit. When you have completed it, you should

- know the definition of an infinite integral, and be able to calculate infinite integrals
- know how to use infinite integrals to determine whether an infinite series is convergent or divergent
- know what is meant by a p-series, and for what values of p it is convergent
- be able to use infinite integrals to find approximations to the sums of infinite series.

5.1 Infinite integrals

In the definition of a definite integral in Section 4.1 it seemed hardly necessary to mention that the interval $[a,b]$ has to be finite. You can't split an interval $[a,\infty]$ into n subintervals whose width tends to 0 as $n \to \infty$.

But provided that b remains a real number, it can be as large as you like. The definition of integral can be used to find integrals such as $\displaystyle\int_0^{10^6} f(x)\,dx$.

And if you write $\displaystyle\int_a^b f(x)\,dx$ as $I(b) - I(a)$, where $I'(x) = f(x)$, it may happen that $I(b)$ tends to a limit as $b \to \infty$. If so, then

$$\lim_{b\to\infty}\int_a^b f(x)\,dx = \left(\lim_{b\to\infty} I(b)\right) - I(a).$$

This is called an **infinite** (or **improper**) **integral**, and it is denoted by $\displaystyle\int_a^\infty f(x)\,dx$. The integral $\displaystyle\int_a^b f(x)\,dx$ is said to be **convergent** as $b \to \infty$.

The description 'improper' is sometimes reserved for a different kind of definite integral, in which the integrand is unbounded within the interval of integration.

Example 5.1.1
Show that $\displaystyle\int_0^b e^{-2x}\,dx$ is convergent, and find $\displaystyle\int_0^\infty e^{-2x}\,dx$.

The integral is found in the usual way, as

$$\int_0^b e^{-2x}\,dx = \left[-\tfrac{1}{2}e^{-2x}\right]_0^b = -\tfrac{1}{2}e^{-2b} + \tfrac{1}{2}.$$

Since $\lim\limits_{b\to\infty} e^{-2b} = 0$, this integral is convergent, and

$$\int_0^\infty e^{-2x}\,dx = \lim_{b\to\infty} \int_0^b e^{-2x}\,dx = -\tfrac{1}{2}\times 0 + \tfrac{1}{2} = \tfrac{1}{2}.$$

Fig. 5.1 shows the graph of $y = e^{-2x}$.
However large the value of b, the shaded area
is less than $\tfrac{1}{2}$, and it tends to $\tfrac{1}{2}$ as $b\to\infty$.

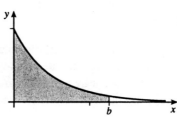

Fig. 5.1

Exercise 5A

1 Find which of the following integrals converge as $b\to\infty$. For those which do, give the
values of the infinite integral.

(a) $\displaystyle\int_1^b \frac{1}{x^2}\,dx$ 　　(b) $\displaystyle\int_0^b \frac{1}{1+x}\,dx$ 　　(c) $\displaystyle\int_0^b e^{-\frac{1}{3}x}\,dx$

(d) $\displaystyle\int_0^b \frac{1}{(2x+1)^{\frac{3}{2}}}\,dx$ 　　(e) $\displaystyle\int_0^b \frac{1}{\sqrt{x+1}}\,dx$ 　　(f) $\displaystyle\int_0^b xe^{-x}\,dx$

2 Find for what values of p the following infinite integrals exist.

(a) $\displaystyle\int_0^\infty e^{px}\,dx$ 　　(b) $\displaystyle\int_1^\infty x^p\,dx$

3 Find the values of the following infinite integrals.

(a) $\displaystyle\int_1^\infty \frac{1}{x^3}\,dx$ 　　(b) $\displaystyle\int_0^\infty xe^{-\frac{1}{2}x^2}\,dx$ 　　(c) $\displaystyle\int_0^\infty \frac{1}{1+x^2}\,dx$

(d) $\displaystyle\int_0^\infty \frac{x}{\left(1+x^2\right)^2}\,dx$ 　　(e) $\displaystyle\int_0^\infty \frac{x}{(x+2)^3}\,dx$ 　　(f) $\displaystyle\int_1^\infty \frac{1}{\sqrt{x}}e^{-\sqrt{x}}\,dx$

4 If $f(x)$ tends to a limit L as $x\to\infty$, prove that $\displaystyle\int_a^\infty f(x)\,dx$ can only exist if $L = 0$.

Is it true that, if $L = 0$, then $\displaystyle\int_a^\infty f(x)\,dx$ exists? Give a reason for your answer.

5 If $0 < f(x) < g(x)$ for all $x > a$, and if $\displaystyle\int_a^\infty g(x)\,dx$ exists, show that $\displaystyle\int_a^\infty f(x)\,dx$ exists.

5.2   The integral test

Infinite integrals and infinite series have a lot in common. For example, Question 4 in Exercise 5A will have reminded you of the property in Section 2.3 that, if $\sum u_i$ is convergent, then $\lim_{n \to \infty} u_n = 0$, but the converse is not true. And Question 5 is a comparison test for infinite integrals similar to the comparison test for infinite series in Section 2.3.

The links are not confined to general properties like this. In Section 4.2 the value of $\sum_{i=1}^{n} f(i)$ was found by

sandwiching it between $\int_{0}^{n} f(x)\,dx$ and $\int_{1}^{n+1} f(x)\,dx$. This section extends this idea, and gives a way of

comparing $\sum_{i=1}^{\infty} f(i)$ with $\int_{1}^{\infty} f(x)\,dx$, where these exist.

Suppose that f is a function defined for $x > 0$ which has the two properties

• $f(x)$ is a decreasing function
• $f(x)$ tends to 0 as $x \to \infty$.

You know many functions with these properties, such as $\dfrac{1}{x}$, $\dfrac{1}{\sqrt{x}}$, e^{-x}, $\dfrac{1}{x^2 + 1}$. Obviously such a function

must have $f(x) > 0$.for all $x > 0$.

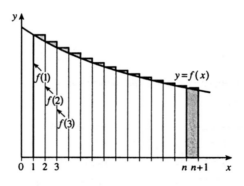

Fig. 5.2

Fig. 5.2 shows the graph of such a function, and a set of n rectangles of width 1 whose area represents

the sum $\sum_{i=1}^{n} f(i)$. These rectangles cover the interval $1 \le x \le n+1$ on the x-axis. It is clear from Fig. 5.2

that this sum is greater than the area under the curve from $x = 1$ to $x = n$. The shaded regions have an area which represents the difference

$$d_n = \sum_{i=1}^{n} f(i) - \int_{1}^{n} f(x)\,dx,$$

so $d_n > 0$.

Now d_n is also a sequence. Notice that

$$d_1 = f(1) - 0 = f(1).$$

The term of the sequence after d_n is

$$d_{n+1} = \sum_{i=1}^{n+1} f(i) - \int_1^{n+1} f(x)\,dx,$$

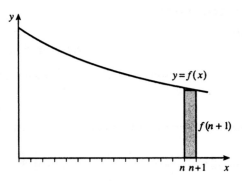

Fig. 5.3

so $$d_{n+1} - d_n = f(n+1) - \int_n^{n+1} f(x)\,dx.$$

The quantity on the right side of this equation is the difference between the area of the rectangle and the area under the curve in Fig. 5.3, and this shows that $d_{n+1} - d_n < 0$, that is $d_{n+1} < d_n$.

You now know three things about the sequence d_n:

- $d_1 = f(1)$
- $d_n > 0$ for all n
- the terms of the sequence decrease as n increases.

Example 5.2.1

Demonstrate these properties of the sequence d_n when $f(x) = \dfrac{1}{x}$.

Table 5.4 gives the values of $S_n = \sum_{i=1}^n \dfrac{1}{i}$ and of $\int_1^n \dfrac{1}{x}\,dx = \ln n$ for values of $n = 10^k$ for $k = 0, 1, 2, 3, 4, 5$ and 6. The last line gives the difference $d_n = S_n - \ln n$. All entries are rounded correct to 5 decimal places.

n	1	10	10^2	10^3	10^4	10^5	10^6
S_n	1	2.928 97	5.187 38	7.485 47	9.787 61	12.090 15	14.392 73
$\ln n$	0	2.302 59	4.605 17	6.907 76	9.210 34	11.512 93	13.815 51
d_n	1	0.626 38	0.582 21	0.577 72	0.577 27	0.577 22	0.577 22

Table 5.4

You can see from the last line of the table that the values of $d_n = S_n - \ln n$ tend to a limit of about 0.577 22 as $n \to \infty$. This limit is called **Euler's constant**, after the 18th-century Swiss mathematician who first discovered it; it is usually denoted by γ, the Greek letter gamma.

The fact that d_n tends to a limit as $n \to \infty$, shown in this example for the function $f(x) = \dfrac{1}{x}$, is an inevitable consequence of the properties of d_n listed above. If a sequence is decreasing and positive, it must tend to a limit.

These results can be summed up as follows:

If a function $f(x)$ is decreasing for $x > 0$ and $f(x)$ tends to 0 as $x \to \infty$, then

$$\sum_{r=1}^{n} f(r) - \int_{1}^{n} f(x)\,dx \quad \text{tends to a limit between 0 and } f(1) \text{ as } n \to \infty.$$

Now suppose that the infinite integral $\int_{1}^{\infty} f(x)\,dx$ exists. Then, by letting $n \to \infty$ in the equation

$$\sum_{i=1}^{n} f(i) = d_n + \int_{1}^{n} f(x)\,dx,$$

it follows that the sum of the series tends to a limit as $n \to \infty$. On the other hand, if $\int_{1}^{n} f(x)\,dx$ diverges to infinity, then so does the sum of the series. This is called the **integral test**.

The integral test   If a function $f(x)$ is decreasing for $x > 0$ and $f(x)$ tends to 0 as $x \to \infty$, then the infinite series $\sum f(i)$ converges if and only if

$$\int_{1}^{\infty} f(x)\,dx \quad \text{exists, and then}$$

$$\int_{1}^{\infty} f(x)\,dx < \sum_{i=1}^{\infty} f(i) < f(1) + \int_{1}^{\infty} f(x)\,dx.$$

Example 5.2.2

Prove that $\displaystyle\sum_{i=1}^{\infty} \frac{1}{i(3i-1)}$ exists, and find bounds for its value.

You found the sums of some series like this in Chapter 2. A useful first step is to express the terms in partial fractions. So begin by writing

$$\frac{1}{i(3i-1)} \equiv \frac{3}{3i-1} - \frac{1}{i}.$$

Substituting $i = 1, 2, 3, \ldots$ you get

$$\frac{1}{1 \times 2} = \frac{3}{2} - \frac{1}{1}, \quad \frac{1}{2 \times 5} = \frac{3}{5} - \frac{1}{2}, \quad \frac{1}{3 \times 8} = \frac{3}{8} - \frac{1}{3}, \ldots .$$

If you write $\dfrac{1}{1}$ as $\dfrac{3}{3}$, $\dfrac{1}{2}$ as $\dfrac{3}{6}$, $\dfrac{1}{3}$ as $\dfrac{3}{9}$, $\ldots$, the sum is

$$\sum_{i=1}^{\infty} \frac{1}{i(3i-1)} = \left(\frac{3}{2} - \frac{3}{3}\right) + \left(\frac{3}{5} - \frac{3}{6}\right) + \left(\frac{3}{8} - \frac{3}{9}\right) + \cdots$$

$$= 3\left(\frac{1}{2} - \frac{1}{3} + \frac{1}{5} - \frac{1}{6} + \frac{1}{8} - \frac{1}{9} + \cdots \right).$$

Unfortunately none of these fractions cancel out as they did in the examples in Chapter 2, so you can't get any further along this route.

But you can find an exact expression for the infinite integral $\int_1^\infty \frac{1}{x(3x-1)}\,dx$. Using the same partial fractions as before,

$$\int_1^n \frac{1}{x(3x-1)}\,dx = \int_1^n \left(\frac{3}{3x-1} - \frac{1}{x}\right)dx$$
$$= \left[\ln(3x-1) - \ln x\right]_1^n$$
$$= (\ln(3n-1) - \ln n) - (\ln 2 - \ln 1)$$
$$= \ln\left(\frac{3n-1}{2n}\right) = \ln\left(\frac{3}{2} - \frac{1}{2n}\right).$$

As $n \to \infty$, $\frac{1}{2n} \to 0$, so $\lim_{n\to\infty} \ln\left(\frac{3}{2} - \frac{1}{2n}\right) = \ln\frac{3}{2}$. Therefore

$$\int_1^\infty \frac{1}{x(3x-1)}\,dx = \ln\frac{3}{2}.$$

Also $f(1) = \frac{1}{1\times 2} = \frac{1}{2}$. Therefore, by the integral test, $\sum \frac{1}{i(3i-1)}$ converges, and

$$\ln\frac{3}{2} < \sum_{i=1}^\infty \frac{1}{i(3i-1)} < \frac{1}{2} + \ln\frac{3}{2}.$$

As a check, the calculator gives for this series $S_{999} = 0.7406\ldots$, so S_∞ will be a little greater than this. The bounds for the sum to infinity are $\ln\frac{3}{2} = 0.4054\ldots$ and $\frac{1}{2} + \ln\frac{3}{2} = 0.9054\ldots$.

5.3   The p-series

An important application of the integral test is to the series

$$\sum \frac{1}{i^p} = \frac{1}{1^p} + \frac{1}{2^p} + \frac{1}{3^p} + \ldots, \qquad \text{where } p > 0, \text{ which is known as the } p\text{-series.}$$

It was shown in Section 2.2 that $\sum \frac{1}{i^2}$ is convergent, and that $\sum \frac{1}{\sqrt{i}} = \sum \frac{1}{i^{\frac{1}{2}}}$ is divergent. So whether the series converges or diverges depends on the value of p. There is no easy way to sum the series exactly for a general value of p.

But the infinite integral $\int_1^\infty \frac{1}{x^p}\,dx$, where it exists, can be found exactly. It helps to consider three cases separately.

If $p < 1$,

$$\int_1^n x^{-p}\,dx = \left[\frac{1}{1-p} x^{1-p}\right]_1^n = \frac{1}{1-p}\left(n^{1-p} - 1\right).$$

Since $1-p>0$, n^{1-p} increases without limit as $n\to\infty$, so the infinite integral doesn't exist.

If $p=1$,

$$\int_1^n x^{-1}\,dx = [\ln x]_1^n = \ln n.$$

This also increases without limit as $n\to\infty$, so the infinite integral doesn't exist.

If $p>1$,

$$\int_1^n x^{-p}\,dx = \left[-\frac{1}{p-1}x^{-(p-1)}\right]_1^n = \frac{1}{p-1}\left(-n^{-(p-1)}+1\right).$$

Since $p-1>0$, $n^{-(p-1)}\to 0$ as $n\to\infty$, so the integral converges to $\frac{1}{p-1}(-0+1)$, and

$$\int_1^\infty \frac{1}{x^p}\,dx = \frac{1}{p-1}.$$

The infinite integral $\int_1^n \frac{1}{x^p}\,dx$ converges as $n\to\infty$ if $p>1$, and

$$\int_1^\infty \frac{1}{x^p}\,dx = \frac{1}{p-1}.$$

You can now apply the integral test to $\sum\frac{1}{i^p}$. Note that the function $\frac{1}{x^p}$ with $p>0$ is decreasing for $x>0$, and tends to 0 as $x\to\infty$, so the conditions for the test are satisfied.

The infinite series $\sum\frac{1}{i^p}$ is convergent if $p>1$, and

$$\frac{1}{p-1} < \sum_{i=1}^\infty \frac{1}{i^p} < 1+\frac{1}{p-1}.$$

The series is divergent if $p\le 1$.

This shows that $\sum_{i=1}^\infty \frac{1}{i^p}$ is a function of p with domain $p>1$. It is usually denoted by $\zeta(p)$, and is called *Riemann's zeta-function*. (ζ (zeta) is the Greek letter z.)

When $p=1$ the series becomes $1+\frac{1}{2}+\frac{1}{3}+\frac{1}{4}+\dots$, which is known as the *harmonic series*.

![Exercise 5B]

Exercise 5B

1 Use the integral test to prove that the following series are divergent.

(a) $\sum \dfrac{i}{i^2 + 3}$ (b) $\sum \dfrac{i^2}{(i+1)^3}$ (c) $\sum \dfrac{i}{(i+1)(2i-1)}$

Keep your solutions to Question 2 for use in Exercise 5C Question 2.

2 Use the integral test to prove that the following series $\sum f(i)$ are convergent, and find lower and upper bounds for the value of $\displaystyle\sum_{i=1}^{\infty} f(i)$. Check these by finding approximations to the sum to infinity with a calculator.

(a) $\sum \dfrac{1}{i(2i-1)}$ (b) $\sum \dfrac{1}{i^2 + 9}$ (c) $\sum \dfrac{1}{(2i-1)(3i-2)}$

(d) $\sum \dfrac{1}{i^2} \cos\left(\dfrac{1}{i}\right)$ (e) $\sum \dfrac{i}{\left(i^2 + 24\right)^{\frac{3}{2}}}$

3 Prove that the infinite series

$$\frac{1}{2(\ln 2)^p} + \frac{1}{3(\ln 3)^p} + \frac{1}{4(\ln 4)^p} + \dots$$

is convergent for $p > 1$ and divergent for $p \le 1$.

4 Find $\dfrac{d}{dx} \ln\left(x + \sqrt{1 + x^2}\right)$ and $\dfrac{d}{dx} \dfrac{x}{\sqrt{1 + x^2}}$. Hence show that $\sum \dfrac{1}{\left(1 + i^2\right)^{\frac{1}{2}}}$ is divergent and that

$\sum \dfrac{1}{\left(1 + i^2\right)^{\frac{3}{2}}}$ is convergent. Find lower and upper bounds for the value of $\displaystyle\sum_{i=1}^{\infty} \dfrac{1}{\left(1 + i^2\right)^{\frac{3}{2}}}$.

5 Use the integral test to prove that the infinite integral $\displaystyle\int_{1}^{\infty} r^x \, dx$ exists if $0 < r < 1$.

5.4 Calculating sums to infinity

The integral test is a useful way of proving that an infinite series is convergent, but the lower and upper bounds are too far apart to give an accurate value of the sum to infinity. This is because they differ by $f(1)$, and since the terms of the series are decreasing the first term will usually be comparatively large.

You will probably have experienced occasional difficulties in using a calculator to estimate the sum to infinity of a series. These are of two kinds.

- The program for finding sums may impose a restriction on the number of terms that can be added. For the calculator used in writing this book the largest permitted number of terms is 999.
- There is a ceiling over the size of numbers that the calculator can handle. On many calculators this is 10^{100}. If the expression for the terms involves a function such as $i!$ or i^i this ceiling will soon be reached. For example, $70!$ and 57^{57} both exceed it.

However, by combining the use of a calculator with the integral test inequalities you can often find the sum to infinity of a series to a high degree of accuracy.

In Section 5.2 the series and the integral started at $i = 1$ and $x = 1$, but they could have started at any integer m. The argument would be exactly the same, but the inequalities in the shaded box at the end of the section would then become

$$\int_m^\infty f(x)\,dx < \sum_{i=m}^\infty f(i) < f(m) + \int_m^\infty f(x)\,dx.$$

The important change is that the difference between the upper and lower bounds is now $f(m)$ instead of $f(1)$. Since $f(x)$ is a decreasing function, the difference between the upper and lower bounds gets smaller as m gets larger.

Now the sum to infinity of the series can be split into two parts, as

$$\sum_{i=1}^\infty f(i) = \sum_{i=1}^{m-1} f(i) + \sum_{i=m}^\infty f(i).$$

So, adding $\sum\limits_{i=1}^{m-1} f(i)$ to the expressions in the inequality, you get

$$\sum_{i=1}^{m-1} f(i) + \int_m^\infty f(x)\,dx < \sum_{i=1}^\infty f(i) < f(m) + \sum_{i=1}^{m-1} f(i) + \int_m^\infty f(x)\,dx.$$

The method is to use a calculator to find $\sum\limits_{i=1}^{m-1} f(i)$, taking as large a value for m as you can, and to add to this the infinite integral $\int_m^\infty f(x)\,dx$. You can then be sure that you have a value for $\sum\limits_{i=1}^\infty f(i)$, with a maximum possible error of $f(m)$.

Example 5.4.1

Find $\sum\limits_{i=1}^\infty \dfrac{1}{i(3i-1)}$ correct to as many decimal places as you can. (See Example 5.2.2.)

If the calculator program for summing series is restricted to 999 terms, take $m = 1000$. Then, from the calculator,

$$\sum_{i=1}^{999} \frac{1}{i(3i-1)} = 0.740\,685\,195, \quad \text{correct to 9 decimal places.}$$

You have to add to this the infinite integral $\int_{1000}^\infty \dfrac{1}{x(3x-1)}\,dx$, using partial fractions to do the integration as in Example 5.2.2. Begin by finding the integral from 1000 to n, as

$$\int_{1000}^n \frac{1}{x(3x-1)}\,dx = \left[\ln(3x-1) - \ln x\right]_{1000}^n$$

$$= \ln\!\left(\frac{3n-1}{n}\right) - \ln\tfrac{2999}{1000} = \ln\!\left(3 - \frac{1}{n}\right) - \ln\tfrac{2999}{1000}.$$

The limit as $n \to \infty$ is

$$\int_{1000}^{\infty} \frac{1}{x(3x-1)}\,dx = \ln 3 - \ln \frac{2999}{1000} = \ln \frac{3000}{2999}$$

$$= 0.000\ 333\ 389.$$

So the lower bound is

$$\sum_{i=1}^{999} \frac{1}{i(3i-1)} + \int_{1000}^{\infty} \frac{1}{x(3x-1)}\,dx = 0.740\ 685\ 195\ldots + 0.000\ 333\ 389\ldots$$

$$= 0.741\ 018\ 583\ldots\ .$$

For the upper bound you have to add on the value of the 1000th term, which is

$$\frac{1}{1000(3\times 1000 - 1)} = \frac{1}{1000 \times 2999} = 0.000\ 000\ 333.$$

So the upper bound is $0.741\ 018\ 916$.

It follows that

$$0.741\ 018\ 583 < \sum_{i=1}^{\infty} \frac{1}{i(3i-1)} < 0.741\ 018\ 916.$$

The sum to infinity is $0.741\ 019$, correct to 6 decimal places.

Exercise 5C

1 Find lower and upper bounds for

(a) $\displaystyle\sum_{i=1}^{\infty} \frac{1}{i^2}$, (b) $\displaystyle\sum_{i=1}^{\infty} \frac{1}{(4i-3)(4i-1)}$,

keeping as many decimal places in your answers as the calculator allows.

The exact values of these sums are (a) $\frac{1}{6}\pi^2$ and (b) $\frac{1}{8}\pi$. Check that these lie within the bounds you have calculated.

2 For the series in Exercise 5B Question 2 find the sum to infinity correct to as many decimal places as you can.

6 Series with positive and negative terms

This chapter extends the study of infinite series to series with some positive and some negative terms. When you have completed it, you should

- know what is meant by an alternating series, and that alternating series with terms decreasing in absolute value with limit 0 are convergent
- be familiar with the various ways in which a series may diverge
- be able to distinguish between absolutely convergent and conditionally convergent series.

6.1 Alternating series

So far in this book all the infinite series have had only positive terms. The only exceptions you have seen have been geometric series with a negative common ratio. Fig. 6.1 is a copy of the graph in Higher Level Book 1 Section 30.4, and shows the sum sequence for the series $\sum 10 \times (-0.9)^{i-1}$, that is, $\sum u_i$ defined by

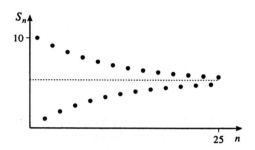

$$u_1 = 10, \quad u_i = -0.9u_{i-1} \quad \text{for } i > 1.$$

The partial sum of n terms for this series is

$$S_n = 10 \times \frac{1-(-0.9)^n}{1-(-0.9)}$$
$$= \tfrac{100}{19} - \tfrac{100}{19} \times (-0.9)^n.$$

Fig. 6.1

The sum to infinity is $\tfrac{100}{19}$; S_n is greater than $\tfrac{100}{19}$ when n is odd and less than $\tfrac{100}{19}$ when n is even.

Series like this, whose terms are alternately positive and negative, are called **alternating series**. They are an important special case of infinite series with both positive and negative terms.

There are a lot of series whose sum series have graphs similar to Fig. 6.1. For example, Fig. 6.2 shows the graph of S_n for the series $1 - \tfrac{1}{2} + \tfrac{1}{3} - \tfrac{1}{4} + \dots$, with $u_i = \frac{(-1)^{i-1}}{i}$.

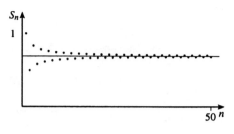

As in Fig. 6.1, the sequence $S_1, S_3, S_5, \dots$ of partial sums for odd n is decreasing. This is because in absolute value the terms are getting steadily smaller: for all i, $|u_i| < |u_{i-1}|$. So to get from S_1 to S_3 you go down by $|u_2| = \tfrac{1}{2}$ and then up by $|u_3| = \tfrac{1}{3}$, so $S_3 < S_1$. Similarly $S_5 < S_3$, $S_7 < S_5$ and so on.

Fig. 6.2

A similar argument shows that the sequence of partial sums for even n is increasing.

But also the odd-suffix partial sums are all greater than the even-suffix ones. For example, to show that $S_{11} > S_6$, you have only to remark that $S_6 < S_8 < S_{10}$ because the even-suffix sequence is increasing, and $S_{11} > S_{10}$ because $S_{11} = S_{10} + u_{11}$ and u_{11} is positive.

It follows that the sequence of odd-suffix partial sums tends to a limit, and so does the even-suffix sequence. And because $\lim_{i \to \infty} u_i = 0$, these limits must be the same. So S_n tends to a limit as $n \to \infty$; that is, $\sum u_i$ is convergent.

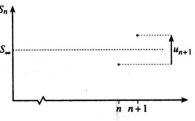

You can also say something about the value of the sum to infinity S_∞.

Fig. 6.3 illustrates the case in which n is even, so that $S_n < S_\infty$. Also $n+1$ is odd, so $S_{n+1} > S_\infty$. And $S_{n+1} = S_n + u_{n+1}$, so

$$S_\infty - S_n < S_{n+1} - S_n = u_{n+1}.$$

Fig. 6.3

If n is odd (Fig. 6.4) then the corresponding inequalities are $S_n > S_\infty$ and $S_{n+1} < S_\infty$, so

$$S_n - S_\infty < S_n - S_{n+1} = -u_{n+1},$$

and $-u_{n+1} = |u_{n+1}|$ because $u_{n+1} < 0$.

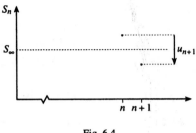

These inequalities show that, in either case, the error in using S_n as an approximation to S_∞ is less than the absolute value of the next term. This is called the **truncation error**.

Fig. 6.4

For example, you can calculate for the series $\sum \frac{(-1)^{i-1}}{i}$ in Fig. 6.2 that $S_{999} = 0.6936\ldots$ and $S_{1000} = 0.6926\ldots$. In Section 6.3 you will find that the sum to infinity of this series is $\ln 2 = 0.6931\ldots$. The error in using S_{999} as an approximation to $\ln 2$ is about 0.0005, which is less than the absolute value of the 1000th term, which is $\left| -\frac{1}{1000} \right| = 0.001$.

The argument above depends on just three properties: that the terms are alternately positive and negative, that they get steadily smaller in absolute value, and that they tend to 0. So you can sum it up in a general statement.

If an infinite series $\sum u_i$ has

- terms which are alternately positive and negative

- for all $i > 1$, $|u_i| < |u_{i-1}|$

- $\lim_{i \to \infty} u_i = 0$,

then the series is convergent.

The error in taking the sum of n terms as an approximation to the sum to infinity (the truncation error) is less than the absolute value of the $(n+1)$th term.

Example 6.1.1

How many terms of the series $\dfrac{1}{1^2} - \dfrac{1}{2^2} + \dfrac{1}{3^2} - \ldots$ should you take to be sure of finding the sum to infinity with truncation error whose absolute value is less than 0.001?

This series satisfies the three conditions listed in the shaded box. The absolute value of the $(n+1)$ th term is $\dfrac{1}{(n+1)^2}$, so the magnitude of the truncation error is less than this. To be sure that the absolute error is less than 0.001, you should choose n to satisfy the inequality

$$\frac{1}{(n+1)^2} < 0.001,$$

so that $(n+1)^2 > 1000$, that is $n > \sqrt{1000} - 1 = 30.6\ldots$. Since n must be an integer, you should take 31 terms.

If you work out the sum of 31 terms in this example you get $S_{31} = 0.822\,97\ldots$. The exact sum to infinity is in fact $\frac{1}{12}\pi^2 = 0.822\,46\ldots$, so the absolute value of the truncation error is $0.000\,51\ldots$, considerably less than the 0.001 required. To get an error less than 0.001 you need only 22 terms, since $S_{22} = 0.821\,48\ldots$ and $S_{23} = 0.823\,37\ldots$, with truncation errors of absolute value $0.000\,98\ldots$ and $0.000\,90\ldots$ respectively. Any subsequent partial sums are closer than this to the sum to infinity. But the critical words in the question asked are 'to be *sure*'; and for this, using the methods of this section, you must take 31 terms.

6.2 Different forms of divergence

If all the terms of an infinite series are positive, there are only two possibilities: either the series converges, or it diverges to infinity.

But if some terms are positive and some are negative, there are other possibilities. Some of these are illustrated by the examples in this section.

Example 6.2.1

Display the graph of the partial sums S_n for the infinite geometric series $\sum 10 \times (-1.1)^{i-1}$.

This series cannot converge, because the terms do not tend to 0 as $i \to \infty$.

If you compare the graph in Fig. 6.5 with Fig. 6.1, you will see that the odd-suffix partial sums form an increasing sequence which tends to ∞, and the even-suffix partial sums form a decreasing sequence which tends to $-\infty$. This is because the absolute value of the terms increases as i increases, so each jump (up or down) from S_{n-1} to S_n is larger than the one before.

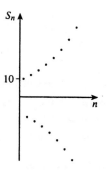

Fig. 6.5

A sequence like the one in Example 6.2.1 is said to **oscillate**. Because there are no bounds for the values of S_n, it is described as 'oscillating infinitely'.

Example 6.2.2

Describe the behaviour of the sequence of partial sums for the infinite series $\sum \left(1 + 2 \times (-1)^{i-1}\right) \times i$.

The expression in brackets, $1 + 2 \times (-1)^{i-1}$, takes alternately the values 3 when i is odd and -1 when i is even. So successive terms of the series are

$$3 \times 1, \quad -1 \times 2, \quad 3 \times 3, \quad -1 \times 4, \quad 3 \times 5, \quad -1 \times 6, \quad \dots$$

and the partial sums are

$$3, \quad 1, \quad 10, \quad 6, \quad 21, \quad 15, \quad \dots .$$

You can write separate formulae for the partial sum S_n according as n is an even or an odd number.

If $n = 2m$, then

$$S_n = 3 \times (1 + 3 + 5 + \dots + (2m-1)) - (2 + 4 + 6 + \dots + 2m).$$

Both brackets contain arithmetic series, with sums $\frac{1}{2}m(1 + (2m-1)) = m^2$ and $2\left(\frac{1}{2}m(m+1)\right) = m(m+1)$ respectively. So

$$S_n = 3m^2 - m(m+1) = 2m^2 - m$$
$$= 2\left(\tfrac{1}{2}n\right)^2 - \tfrac{1}{2}n = \tfrac{1}{2}n(n-1).$$

If $n = 2m - 1$, then

$$S_n = 3 \times (1 + 3 + 5 + \dots + (2m-1)) - (2 + 4 + 6 + \dots + 2(m-1))$$
$$= 3m^2 - (m-1)m = 2m^2 + m$$
$$= 2\left(\tfrac{1}{2}(n+1)\right)^2 + \tfrac{1}{2}(n+1) = \tfrac{1}{2}(n+1)(n+2).$$

So

$$S_n = \begin{cases} \frac{1}{2}(n+1)(n+2) & \text{if } n \text{ is odd,} \\ \frac{1}{2}n(n-1) & \text{if } n \text{ is even.} \end{cases}$$

Although the terms alternate in sign, so that the values of S_n successively increase and decrease, this series does *not* oscillate. The expressions for S_n both tend to infinity as $n \to \infty$, so this series diverges to infinity. This is shown graphically in Fig. 6.6.

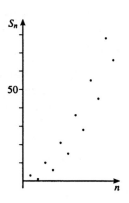

Fig. 6.6

All the series so far in this chapter have been alternating series, but the third example in this section is more erratic. Positive and negative terms occur in blocks, mostly of 3 terms but occasionally of 4.

Example 6.2.3

For the infinite series $\sum \cos i$, display graphs of $u_i = \cos i$ and $S_n = \sum_{i=1}^{n} \cos i$.

This series cannot converge because $\cos i$ doesn't tend to 0 as $i \to \infty$.

In Exercise 1A Question 9 you found that

$$\sum_{i=1}^{n} \cos i\theta = \frac{\sin\left(n + \frac{1}{2}\right)\theta}{2\sin\frac{1}{2}\theta} - \frac{1}{2}.$$

So, putting $\theta = 1$,

$$S_n = \sum_{i=1}^{n} \cos i = \frac{1}{2}\left(\frac{\sin\left(n + \frac{1}{2}\right)}{\sin\frac{1}{2}} - 1\right).$$

Figs. 6.7 and 6.8 are the graphs of u_i and S_n respectively. They consist of the points for which

$x \in \mathbb{Z}^+$ on the graphs of $y = \cos x$ and $y = \frac{1}{2}\left(\dfrac{\sin\left(x + \frac{1}{2}\right)}{\sin\frac{1}{2}} - 1\right)$, which are shown grey in the figures.

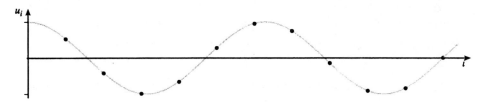

Fig. 6.7

Fig. 6.8

The values of u_i are all between -1 and $+1$. They never equal these bounding values (because π is an irrational number) but they sometimes get very close; for example, $u_{22} = -0.999\,96\ldots$. Since

$\sin\left(n + \frac{1}{2}\right)$ is always between -1 and $+1$, the values of S_n lie between $\frac{1}{2}\left(-\dfrac{1}{\sin\frac{1}{2}} - 1\right) = -1.5429\ldots$

and $\frac{1}{2}\left(\dfrac{1}{\sin\frac{1}{2}} - 1\right) = 0.5429\ldots$.

In Example 6.2.3 the series oscillates as $n \to \infty$, but it differs from Example 6.2.1 in that the values of S_n always lie within fixed bounds. The series is said to 'oscillate finitely'.

> If an infinite series has some positive and some negative terms, then it may converge, diverge to $+\infty$ or to $-\infty$, or oscillate (finitely or infinitely).

6.3 Absolute and conditional convergence

The two series $\sum 10 \times (-0.9)^{i-1}$ and $\sum \frac{(-1)^{i-1}}{i}$, whose graphs are drawn in Fig. 6.1 and Fig. 6.2, could both be proved convergent by using the alternating series property in the shaded box in Section 6.1. But although they are similar in this respect, in other ways they are very different.

The essential distinction between the two is that if you make new series by taking the absolute value of each term, the first series becomes $\sum 10 \times 0.9^{i-1}$, which is just another convergent geometric series with common ratio 0.9 rather than –0.9; but the second becomes $\sum \frac{1}{i}$, which was shown in Section 5.3 to be divergent.

> If $\sum u_i$ is a series with a mixture of positive and negative terms, and if $\sum |u_i|$ is convergent, then $\sum u_i$ is said to be **absolutely convergent**; however, if $\sum |u_i|$ is divergent but $\sum u_i$ is convergent, then $\sum u_i$ is **conditionally convergent**.

So with these definitions $\sum 10 \times (-0.9)^{i-1}$ is absolutely convergent, but $\sum \frac{(-1)^{i-1}}{i}$ is conditionally convergent.

With conditionally convergent series it is possible to reach absurd conclusions when you carry out what seem to be quite normal algebraic procedures. Here are two examples.

Example 6.3.1
A 'proof' that $0 > \frac{1}{2}$.

It is clear from Fig. 6.2 that $\sum \frac{(-1)^{i-1}}{i}$ converges to a limit which is certainly greater than $\frac{1}{2}$. But

$$1 - \tfrac{1}{2} + \tfrac{1}{3} - \tfrac{1}{4} + \tfrac{1}{5} - \tfrac{1}{6} + \tfrac{1}{7} - \tfrac{1}{8} + \ldots = \left(1 + \tfrac{1}{2} + \tfrac{1}{3} + \tfrac{1}{4} + \tfrac{1}{5} + \tfrac{1}{6} + \tfrac{1}{7} + \tfrac{1}{8} + \ldots\right) - 2 \times \left(\tfrac{1}{2} + \tfrac{1}{4} + \tfrac{1}{6} + \tfrac{1}{8} + \ldots\right)$$
$$= \left(1 + \tfrac{1}{2} + \tfrac{1}{3} + \tfrac{1}{4} + \ldots\right) - \left(1 + \tfrac{1}{2} + \tfrac{1}{3} + \tfrac{1}{4} + \ldots\right)$$
$$= 0.$$

'Therefore' $0 > \frac{1}{2}$.

It is not very hard to find the flaw in this argument. Notice that in line 2 both brackets contain the divergent (and therefore meaningless) series $\sum \frac{1}{i}$. If you write out the argument in terms of partial sums, it takes the form

$$1 - \frac{1}{2} + \frac{1}{3} - \frac{1}{4} + \frac{1}{5} - \frac{1}{6} + \frac{1}{7} - \frac{1}{8} + \dots + \frac{1}{2n-1} - \frac{1}{2n}$$

$$= \left(1 + \frac{1}{2} + \frac{1}{3} + \frac{1}{4} + \frac{1}{5} + \frac{1}{6} + \frac{1}{7} + \frac{1}{8} + \dots + \frac{1}{2n} \right) - 2 \times \left(\frac{1}{2} + \frac{1}{4} + \frac{1}{6} + \frac{1}{8} + \dots + \frac{1}{2n} \right)$$

$$= \left(1 + \frac{1}{2} + \frac{1}{3} + \frac{1}{4} + \dots + \frac{1}{2n} \right) - \left(1 + \frac{1}{2} + \frac{1}{3} + \frac{1}{4} + \dots + \frac{1}{n} \right)$$

$$= \frac{1}{n+1} + \frac{1}{n+2} + \dots + \frac{1}{2n}.$$

This is quite an interesting result in itself. It was stated in Section 6.1 that the sum to infinity of $\sum \frac{(-1)^{i-1}}{i}$ is $\ln 2$; this can now be proved, since you showed in Exercise 4B Question 6 that

$$\lim_{n \to \infty} \left(\frac{1}{n+1} + \frac{1}{n+2} + \dots + \frac{1}{2n} \right) = \ln 2.$$

But what is more surprising is that if you carry out the 'illegal' algebra in Example 6.3.1 with the series $\sum 10 \times (-0.9)^{i-1}$ (which is absolutely convergent), you *don't* arrive at an absurd conclusion. (See Exercise 6 Question 5.) You can carry out algebraic operations much more freely when the series are absolutely convergent than when they are conditionally convergent.

Example 6.3.2
The multiplication paradox: the product of two convergent series may not be convergent.

If you square the conditionally convergent series $\sum \frac{(-1)^{i-1}}{\sqrt{i}}$, multiplying out the brackets in the same way as you do with polynomials, you get

$$\left(\frac{1}{\sqrt{1}} - \frac{1}{\sqrt{2}} + \frac{1}{\sqrt{3}} - \dots \right)\left(\frac{1}{\sqrt{1}} - \frac{1}{\sqrt{2}} + \frac{1}{\sqrt{3}} - \dots \right)$$

$$= \left(\frac{1}{\sqrt{1}} \times \frac{1}{\sqrt{1}} \right) - \left(\frac{1}{\sqrt{1}} \times \frac{1}{\sqrt{2}} + \frac{1}{\sqrt{2}} \times \frac{1}{\sqrt{1}} \right) + \left(\frac{1}{\sqrt{1}} \times \frac{1}{\sqrt{3}} + \frac{1}{\sqrt{2}} \times \frac{1}{\sqrt{2}} + \frac{1}{\sqrt{3}} \times \frac{1}{\sqrt{1}} \right) - \dots \ .$$

You could write this as $\sum (-1)^{i-1} v_i$, where

$$v_i = \frac{1}{\sqrt{1}} \times \frac{1}{\sqrt{i}} + \frac{1}{\sqrt{2}} \times \frac{1}{\sqrt{i-1}} + \dots + \frac{1}{\sqrt{i}} \times \frac{1}{\sqrt{1}}$$

$$= \frac{1}{\sqrt{1 \times i}} + \frac{1}{\sqrt{2 \times (i-1)}} + \dots + \frac{1}{\sqrt{i \times 1}}.$$

There are i terms in this sum, and it can be written as $\displaystyle\sum_{k=1}^{i} \frac{1}{\sqrt{k(i+1-k)}}$.

Now if you write the expression under the $\sqrt{}$ sign in completed square form, you get

$$k(i+1-k) = \left(\frac{i+1}{2} \right)^2 - \left(k - \frac{i+1}{2} \right)^2.$$

It follows that, for each value of k,

$$k(i+1-k) \le \left(\frac{i+1}{2}\right)^2, \quad \text{so} \quad \frac{1}{\sqrt{k(i+1-k)}} \ge \frac{2}{i+1}.$$

Therefore

$$v_i \ge i \times \frac{2}{i+1} = \frac{2}{1+\frac{1}{i}},$$

and $\lim\limits_{i \to \infty} v_i = 2$.

But it was shown in Section 2.3 that for the series $\sum (-1)^{i-1} v_i$ to converge it is necessary that $\lim\limits_{i \to \infty} v_i = 0$. So the product series $\sum (-1)^{i-1} v_i$ is not convergent.

Again, this could not happen when you square an absolutely convergent series. If you square an absolutely convergent series using the method in Example 6.3.2, the result is another absolutely convergent series. (See Exercise 6 Question 6.)

You can use the comparison test in Section 2.3 to find some properties of absolutely and conditionally convergent series which help to explain the differences in their behaviour.

Suppose that u_i is a series with some positive and some negative terms, with a sum sequence $S_n = \sum\limits_{i=1}^{n} u_i$.

From this you can obtain three other series:

- the absolute term series, with terms $v_i = |u_i|$ and sum sequence $A_n = \sum\limits_{i=1}^{n} v_i$

- the positive term series, with terms $y_i = u_i$ when u_i is positive or zero and 0 when u_i is negative, and sum sequence $P_n = \sum\limits_{i=1}^{n} y_i$

- the negative term series, with terms $z_i = u_i$ when u_i is negative or zero and 0 when u_i is positive, and sum sequence $Q_n = \sum\limits_{i=1}^{n} z_i$.

For example, if u_i is the sequence $1, \ -\frac{1}{2}, \ \frac{1}{3}, \ \frac{1}{4}, \ -\frac{1}{5}, \ \frac{1}{6}, \ \dots$, then

$$S_6 = 1 - \frac{1}{2} + \frac{1}{3} + \frac{1}{4} - \frac{1}{5} + \frac{1}{6}, \qquad A_6 = 1 + \frac{1}{2} + \frac{1}{3} + \frac{1}{4} + \frac{1}{5} + \frac{1}{6},$$

$$P_6 = 1 + 0 + \frac{1}{3} + \frac{1}{4} + 0 + \frac{1}{6}, \qquad Q_6 = 0 - \frac{1}{2} + 0 + 0 - \frac{1}{5} + 0.$$

These are of course not independent. You can easily check that

$$u_i = y_i + z_i \qquad \text{and} \qquad v_i = y_i - z_i,$$

so $\quad S_n = P_n + Q_n \qquad \text{and} \qquad A_n = P_n - Q_n.$

Begin by supposing that $\sum v_i = \sum |u_i|$ is convergent. What can you deduce about $\sum y_i$ and $\sum z_i$?

Clearly $y_i \geq 0$, and $y_i \leq v_i$ for all i. So by the comparison test, since $\sum v_i$ is convergent, $\sum y_i$ is convergent. Call its sum P_∞.

Also $-z_i \geq 0$, and $-z_i \leq v_i$ for all i. So by the comparison test, since $\sum v_i$ is convergent, $\sum -z_i$ is convergent, and therefore $\sum z_i$ is convergent. Call its sum Q_∞.

Then $\lim_{n \to \infty} (P_n + Q_n) = P_\infty + Q_\infty$, so that $S_n = P_n + Q_n$ tends to a limit. That is, $\sum u_i$ is convergent.

Here is a summary of what has been proved so far.

> If $\sum |u_i|$ is a convergent series, then
>
> - the positive sum series $\sum y_i$ is convergent,
> - the negative sum series $\sum z_i$ is convergent,
> - the series $\sum u_i$ is convergent.
>
> That is, an absolutely convergent series is convergent.

You may think that the last statement is obvious. Perhaps it is, but it still needs proving!

Now suppose that $\sum u_i$ is convergent but not absolutely convergent. Then, because $A_n = P_n - Q_n$ is divergent, $\sum y_i$ and $\sum z_i$ can't both be convergent. But it is impossible for one of them to be convergent but not the other. For example, if $\sum y_i$ is convergent with sum to infinity P_∞, then $Q_n = S_n - P_n$ tends to $S_\infty - P_\infty$ as $n \to \infty$; that is, $\sum z_i$ is convergent. So, since $\sum u_i$ is not absolutely convergent, both $\sum y_i$ and $\sum z_i$ are divergent.

> If $\sum u_i$ is a conditionally convergent series, then the series of positive terms diverges to $+\infty$ and the series of negative terms diverges to $-\infty$.

A remarkable consequence of this is that, by rearranging the order of the terms, you can convert a conditionally convergent series $\sum u_i$ into another series $\sum w_i$ which converges to any sum L that you like. The process is described by the following algorithm.

Let $T_n = \sum_{i=1}^{n} w_i$, and define $T_0 = 0$. Start with $n = 0$.

Step 1   If $T_n \geq L$, define w_{n+1} as the next negative (or zero) term of $\sum u_i$.

If $T_n < L$, define w_{n+1} as the next positive (or zero) term of $\sum u_i$.

Step 2   Increase n by 1, and go back to Step 1.

So you need to be very careful when you work with conditionally convergent series!

<hr>

Exercise 6

1   For the following alternating series, find a value of n for which you can be sure that the partial sum S_n approximates to the sum to infinity with an error less than 0.0001. Hence find bounds between which you can be sure that the sum to infinity lies. Give these bounds to 6 decimal places, rounding the lower bound down and the upper bound up.

(a) $\sum \dfrac{(-1)^{i-1}}{i^3}$　　　　(b) $\sum \dfrac{(-1)^{i-1}}{i^i}$　　　　(c) $\sum \dfrac{(-1)^{i-1}}{i!}$　(d) $\sum \dfrac{(-1)^{i-1}2^i}{i!}$

2   For the following infinite series, state if they are absolutely convergent or conditionally convergent. If they are neither, describe their limiting behaviour as the number of terms tends to infinity.

(a) $\sum \dfrac{(-1)^{i-1}}{i^2}$　　　　(b) $\sum \dfrac{(-1)^{i-1}}{i+10}$　　　　(c) $\sum \sin(\tfrac{1}{2}\pi i)$　(d) $\sum \dfrac{\sin(\tfrac{1}{2}\pi i)}{i}$

(e) $\sum (-1)^{i-1} i$　　　　(f) $\sum (-1)^{i-1} i^2$　　　　(g) $\sum (-2)^{i-1}$　(h) $\sum \dfrac{(-1)^{i-1} i}{(i+1)(i+2)}$

(i) $\sum \dfrac{(-1)^{i-1} i}{(i+1)(i+2)(i+3)}$　(j) $\sum \dfrac{1+3\times(-1)^{i-1}}{i}$　(k) $\sum (-1)^{\frac{1}{2}i(i+1)}$　(l) $\sum (-1)^{\frac{1}{2}i(i+1)} i$

3   You are given that $\displaystyle\sum_{i=1}^{\infty} \dfrac{1}{i^4} = \dfrac{1}{90}\pi^4$. For the infinite series $\sum \dfrac{(-1)^{i-1}}{i^4}$, find (with the notation of Section 6.3)

(a) Q_∞,　　　　　　(b) P_∞,　　　　　　(c) S_∞.

4   Use the algorithm at the end of Section 6.3 to find the first 10 terms of a rearrangement of the series $1 - \tfrac{1}{2} + \tfrac{1}{3} - \tfrac{1}{4} + \tfrac{1}{5} - \tfrac{1}{6} + \dots$ which converges to

(a) 0.4,　　　　　　(b) 1.1,　　　　　　(c) −0.2.

What property of conditionally convergent series makes such rearrangements possible?

5   Show that if you carry out steps on the absolutely convergent series $\sum \left(-\tfrac{1}{2}\right)^{i-1}$ similar to those carried out on $\sum \dfrac{(-1)^{i-1}}{i}$ in Example 6.3.1, you can arrive at the conclusion

$$1 - \tfrac{1}{2} + \tfrac{1}{4} - \tfrac{1}{8} + \tfrac{1}{16} - \dots = \tfrac{1}{2} + \tfrac{1}{8} + \tfrac{1}{32} + \tfrac{1}{128} + \dots .$$

Use the formula for the sum to infinity of a geometric series to show that this equation is in fact true.

6* (a) Find the series $\sum u_i$ which results when the series $\sum \left(-\tfrac{1}{2}\right)^{i-1}$ is squared using the method of Example 6.3.2.

(b) Use the result in Example 2.4.1 to show that $\sum u_i$ is absolutely convergent, and state the value of $\sum |u_i|$.

(c) Use the result of Exercise 2C Question 2(b) to calculate the sum of the series of negative terms in the series $\sum u_i$.

(d) Hence calculate $\displaystyle\sum_{i=1}^{\infty} u_i$, and show that it is equal to the square of $\displaystyle\sum_{i=1}^{\infty} \left(-\tfrac{1}{2}\right)^{i-1}$.

7 The theory of limits

This chapter develops and shows how to apply a definition of the limit of a sequence. When you have completed it, you should

- know how to define the limit of a sequence as $n \to \infty$
- be able to use the definition to give proofs of the limits of particular sequences
- understand how the definition can be used to prove general theorems about limits of sequences.

7.1 The definition of a limit

You have been using limits for a long time: as $\delta x \to 0$ for differentiation, as $x \to a$ for asymptotes, as $n \to \infty$ for convergence of sequences. Sometimes various properties of limits have been assumed, for example that the limit of the product of two functions is equal to the product of the limits. But to justify these properties you need to have a definition of what is meant by a limit.

This chapter gives a definition for the limit of a sequence u_n as $n \to \infty$. Definitions of other limits, such as $\lim_{x \to a} f(x)$, are very similar, and proofs of the various properties are almost identical to those for $\lim_{n \to \infty} u_n$.

The basic idea of what is meant by $\lim_{n \to \infty} u_n = L$ is illustrated by the graph in Fig. 7.1. This shows a set of points with coordinates (n, u_n) approaching the line $y = L$ as n increases, and two lines $y = p$ and $y = q$ with $p < L < q$, so that $y = L$ lies inside the shaded strip between them. The numbers p and q are not fixed: p can be any number less than L, and q can be any number greater than L. But whatever numbers you take for p and q, there is a number m such that, beyond $n = m$, all the points (n, u_n) are inside the shaded strip.

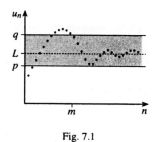

Fig. 7.1

Example 7.1.1

Show that, if $u_n = \dfrac{3n+1}{n}$, then $\lim_{n \to \infty} u_n = 3$.

Suppose that you take $p = 2.9$ and $q = 3.2$. Since $\dfrac{3n+1}{n} = 3 + \dfrac{1}{n}$, clearly u_n is less than 3.2 when n is greater than 5. Also u_n is always greater than 3, so it is certainly greater than 2.9. That is, $2.9 < u_n < 3.2$ if $n > 5$. To the right of $n = 5$, all the points (n, u_n) are inside the strip between the lines $y = 2.9$ and $y = 3.2$.

This doesn't of course prove that $u_n \to 3$. If you were to take a larger value of p and a smaller value of q, you would need a larger value of m so that $p < u_n < q$ for $n > m$. For example, if $p = 2.99$ and $q = 3.02$, you need to take n greater than 50 to get $p < u_n < q$.

For a proof you have to show that you can find such an inequality whatever numbers p and q you take such that $p < 3 < q$. In this example, the value of p doesn't affect the choice of m; since $\frac{1}{n} > 0$, $u_n > 3 > p$ for all n. So you merely have to find the values of n for which $u_n < q$, that is $3 + \frac{1}{n} < q$.

$$3 + \frac{1}{n} < q \iff q - 3 > \frac{1}{n} \iff n > \frac{1}{q - 3} \qquad \text{(since } q - 3 \text{ is positive).}$$

Therefore, if $n > \frac{1}{q-3}$, $p < u_n < q$. Since this works for any numbers p and q with $p < 3$ and $q > 3$, this proves that $\lim_{n \to \infty} u_n = 3$.

Example 7.1.2

Show that, if $u_n = \frac{3n + (-1)^n}{n}$, then $\lim_{n \to \infty} u_n = 3$.

Since $\frac{3n + (-1)^n}{n} = 3 + \frac{(-1)^n}{n}$, u_n is greater than 3 when n is even and less than 3 when n is odd. So you must consider even and odd values of n separately.

If n is even, then $u_n = 3 + \frac{1}{n}$, and you have the same situation as in Example 7.1.1. That is, if n is even and greater than $\frac{1}{q-3}$, then $p < u_n < q$.

If n is odd, then $u_n = 3 - \frac{1}{n}$. This is certainly less than q, since $q > 3$. Also

$$3 - \frac{1}{n} > p \iff 3 - p > \frac{1}{n} \iff n > \frac{1}{3 - p} \qquad \text{(since } 3 - p \text{ is positive).}$$

Therefore, if n is odd and greater than $\frac{1}{3-p}$, then $p < u_n < q$.

So to be certain of getting $p < u_n < q$, you need to have $n > \frac{1}{q-3}$ if n is even, and $n > \frac{1}{3-p}$ if n is odd. The safe way of ensuring that both inequalities are satisfied is to define m as the greater of $\frac{1}{q-3}$ and $\frac{1}{3-p}$. This is sometimes written as $\max\left(\frac{1}{q-3}, \frac{1}{3-p}\right)$. Then, when $n > m$, $p < u_n < q$, whether n is odd or even.

What these examples illustrate is how the proof depends on the definition. This can now be stated formally.

> **Limit of a sequence**   If, for any numbers p and q such that $p < L < q$, there is a positive number m such that, for all $n > m$, $p < u_n < q$, then $\lim\limits_{n \to \infty} u_n = L$.

There are several points to notice about this definition.

- Once the value of m has been settled, the inequality $p < u_n < q$ has to hold for *all* n greater than m, without exception.
- The value of m usually depends on p and q. Generally, the closer that p and q are to L, the larger the value of m.
- Although $n \in \mathbb{Z}^+$, there is no requirement for m to be an integer.
- There may also be some values of n less than m for which $p < u_n < q$, but they are not relevant. This is shown in Fig. 7.1, where you can see that there are some points to the left of m inside the shaded strip. In Example 7.1.2, if you take $p = 2.99$ and $q = 3.02$, then u_n is between p and q for $n = 52, 54, 56, \ldots$, but not for $n = 53, 55, 57, \ldots , 99$. The conditions are not satisfied for all $n > m$ until $n = 100$.
- You aren't allowed to place restrictions on the values chosen for p and q such as that 'they may not be too close to L'. But you will find in later examples that it is sometimes convenient to specify that 'they may not be too far from L'. There is no objection to that.
- There is no special merit in trying to find the smallest possible value of m which satisfies the conditions. All that is required is to be able to find *some* number m. It can be as large as you like. This is illustrated in Example 7.1.3.

In Examples 7.1.1 and 7.1.2 you may have wondered why p and q were not taken at equal distances from L above and below. The answer is that they could have been, and indeed the definition is often given by writing p as $L - \varepsilon$ and q as $L + \varepsilon$. (The Greek letter ε, 'epsilon', is like the English short 'e'.) The condition $p < u_n < q$ then becomes $L - \varepsilon < u_n < L + \varepsilon$, which can be written more neatly as $|u_n - L| < \varepsilon$. You can then write the definition of a limit in a different way:

> **Limit of a sequence (alternative definition)**   If, for any positive number ε there is a positive number m such that, for all $n > m$, $|u_n - L| < \varepsilon$, then $\lim\limits_{n \to \infty} u_n = L$.

You might think that this is a less demanding requirement than the previous definition, since it restricts the number of shaded strips you can use. But this isn't so. The two definitions are in fact logically equivalent to each other. If a sequence u_n tends to L according to one definition, then it does so according to the other definition, so you can use whichever definition you prefer. In practice, proofs are sometimes a little shorter if you use one definition rather than the other. Some of the proofs in this chapter use the p, q definition, while others use ε.

Example 7.1.3

Prove that $\lim\limits_{n \to \infty} \dfrac{\cos n}{n} = 0$.

Before reading on, display the graph of $u_n = \dfrac{\cos n}{n}$ on your calculator. Remember to put it into radian mode first.

The proof is given using the ε definition.

One difference between this and the examples earlier in this chapter is that you can't solve the inequalities $\dfrac{\cos n}{n} < \varepsilon$ and $\dfrac{\cos n}{n} > -\varepsilon$. But you know that, for all $n \in \mathbb{Z}^+$, $|\cos n| < 1$, so that

$$\left| \frac{\cos n}{n} \right| < \frac{1}{n}.$$

You can also solve the inequality $\dfrac{1}{n} < \varepsilon$, as

$$\frac{1}{n} < \varepsilon \quad \Leftrightarrow \quad n > \frac{1}{\varepsilon}.$$

(Recall that, in the definition, ε has to be a positive number.) So it is certainly true that, if $n > \dfrac{1}{\varepsilon}$,

$$\left| \frac{\cos n}{n} \right| < \frac{1}{n} < \varepsilon.$$

This is all you need. You have found a number $m = \dfrac{1}{\varepsilon}$ such that, for all $n > m$, $\left| \dfrac{\cos n}{n} - 0 \right| < \varepsilon$.

Therefore, from the definition, $\displaystyle\lim_{n \to \infty} \dfrac{\cos n}{n} = 0$.

This is an example of a sequence for which it is very likely that there will also be values of n less than m for which the inequality is satisfied. And for some values of ε, m will not be the smallest number such that the inequality is satisfied 'for all $n > m$'. For example, if you take $\varepsilon = 0.01$, you will find that $\left| \dfrac{\cos n}{n} \right| < 0.01$ when n is equal to 95, 96, 97, 98, 99 and 100 as well as for all $n > 100$; that is, the inequality holds for all $n > 94$. But, as stated above, this is of no importance. Once you have found that $m = 100$ satisfies the conditions, it is a waste of time to look any further.

Exercise 7A

1   Prove that

(a) $\displaystyle\lim_{n \to \infty} \dfrac{2n+3}{n+2} = 2$,

(b) $\displaystyle\lim_{n \to \infty} \dfrac{n}{2n-1} = \tfrac{1}{2}$.

2   If $u_n = \dfrac{2 + (-1)^n}{n}$, find a number m such that

(a) $u_n < 0.01$ for all $n > m$,

(b) $u_n < 0.001$ for all $n > m$,

(c) $u_n < q$ for all $n > m$, where $q > 0$.

3   If $u_n = \dfrac{1 + 2 \times (-1)^n}{n}$, find a number m such that

(a) $-0.05 < u_n < 0.1$ for all $n > m$,

(b) $p < u_n < q$ for all $n > m$, where $p < 0$ and $q > 0$.

4   Find

(a) $\displaystyle\lim_{n \to \infty} \dfrac{3n-4}{2n+1}$,

(b) $\displaystyle\lim_{n \to \infty} \dfrac{n + 2 \times (-1)^n}{n+1}$.

Use the definition to prove your answers.

5   (a) Prove that $\lim\limits_{n\to\infty}\dfrac{1}{\sqrt{n}}=0$.

(b) Use the identity $(\sqrt{n+1}-\sqrt{n})(\sqrt{n+1}+\sqrt{n})\equiv 1$ to prove that $\lim\limits_{n\to\infty}(\sqrt{n+1}-\sqrt{n})=0$.

6   By comparing the area under $y=\dfrac{1}{x}$ with the area of two rectangles, prove that (for $n>0$)

$$\frac{1}{n+1}<\ln\left(1+\frac{1}{n}\right)<\frac{1}{n}.$$

Hence find $\lim\limits_{n\to\infty} n\ln\left(1+\dfrac{1}{n}\right)$, and prove that your answer is correct.

7   Prove that, if $x>0$, $(1+x)^n>nx$. Hence show that, if $\sqrt[n]{2}=1+x$, then $nx<2$. Use this inequality to prove that $\lim\limits_{n\to\infty}\sqrt[n]{2}=1$.

8   Prove that, if $\sqrt[n]{n}=1+y$, then $(n-1)y^2<2$. Use this inequality to find $\lim\limits_{n\to\infty}\sqrt[n]{n}$.

7.2 Theorems about limits

You would probably think it obvious that, if $\lim\limits_{n\to\infty} u_n=L$, then $\lim\limits_{n\to\infty}(-u_n)=-L$, $\lim\limits_{n\to\infty}(5u_n)=5L$ and $\lim\limits_{n\to\infty} u_n^{\,2}=L^2$, These conclusions are in fact correct, and now that you have a definition of $\lim\limits_{n\to\infty} u_n$ you can prove them.

To show the logical structure these proofs are set out as a sequence of theorems. The paragraphs in italic are not part of the proofs, but remarks to help you understand how such proofs are constructed.

The first theorem is very simple, since the results follow directly from the definition.

Theorem 1   If $\lim\limits_{n\to\infty} u_n=L$ and b is constant, then

(a) $\lim\limits_{n\to\infty}(u_n+b)=L+b$,   (b) $\lim\limits_{n\to\infty}(-u_n)=-L$.

Proof
You are given that $\lim\limits_{n\to\infty} u_n=L$. So, if you are given any positive number ε, there is a number m such that, for all $n>m$, $|u_n-L|<\varepsilon$.

Now (a) $|(u_n+b)-(L+b)|=|u_n-L|$ and (b) $|(-u_n)-(-L)|=|-(u_n-L)|=|u_n-L|$.

It follows that, for the given number ε, there is a number m such that, for all $n>m$,

(a) $|(u_n+b)-(L+b)|<\varepsilon$ and (b) $|(-u_n)-(-L)|<\varepsilon$.

And these are just the properties you need to prove that

(a) $\lim\limits_{n\to\infty}(u_n+b)=L+b$ and (b) $\lim\limits_{n\to\infty}(-u_n)=-L$.

Before proving the next theorem it may be useful to illustrate it with a trivial example.

Example 7.2.1

Find numbers m such that, for all $n > m$,   (a) $\dfrac{1}{n^2} < 0.01$,   (b) $\dfrac{4}{n^2} < 0.01$.

(a) $\dfrac{1}{n^2} < 0.01 \iff n^2 > 100 \iff n > 10$ (since $n \in \mathbb{Z}^+$).

So $m = 10$ satisfies the condition.

(b) $\dfrac{4}{n^2} < 0.01 \iff \dfrac{1}{n^2} < 0.0025 \iff n > 20$.

So $m = 20$ satisfies the condition.

The point of this example is that, since $\dfrac{4}{n^2}$ is $4 \times \dfrac{1}{n^2}$, you have to solve the inequality $\dfrac{1}{n^2} < \tfrac{1}{4} \times 0.01$.

Because $\lim\limits_{n \to \infty} \dfrac{1}{n^2} = 0$, this is certainly possible, but you are using a different value for ' ε ', so you need a different value of m.

Theorem 2   If $\lim\limits_{n \to \infty} u_n = L$ and a is a positive constant, then $\lim\limits_{n \to \infty} (au_n) = aL$.

This is slightly more complicated, since if you know that $|u_n - L| < \varepsilon$ you can only deduce that $|au_n - aL| < a\varepsilon$. But to prove that $\lim\limits_{n \to \infty} (au_n) = aL$ you have to show that, if you are given any positive number ε, $|au_n - aL| < \varepsilon$ for all $n > m$. To do this you need to begin with the inequality $|u_n - L| < \dfrac{\varepsilon}{a}$.

What you are given is that $\lim\limits_{n \to \infty} u_n = L$. This means that, for any positive number whatever, you can make $|u_n - L|$ less than this number. So begin the proof by applying this, not with the number ε, but with $\dfrac{\varepsilon}{a}$.

Proof
Let ε be any positive number. Since $\lim\limits_{n \to \infty} u_n = L$, there is a number m such that, for all $n > m$,

$|u_n - L| < \dfrac{\varepsilon}{a}$. Therefore, for all $n > m$,

$$|au_n - aL| = |a(u_n - L)| = a \times |u_n - L| < a \times \dfrac{\varepsilon}{a} = \varepsilon.$$

That is, $\lim\limits_{n \to \infty} (au_n) = aL$.

By putting Theorems 1 and 2 together you can establish the limit of any linear function of u_n. For example, if $\lim\limits_{n \to \infty} u_n = L$, then

$$\lim\limits_{n \to \infty} (-5u_n + 2) = \lim\limits_{n \to \infty} (-5u_n) + 2 \quad \text{(by Theorem 1(a))}$$
$$= -\lim\limits_{n \to \infty} (5u_n) + 2 \quad \text{(by Theorem 1(b))}$$
$$= -5 \lim\limits_{n \to \infty} u_n + 2 \quad \text{(by Theorem 2)}$$
$$= -5L + 2.$$

What about other functions of u_n? Is it generally true that, if $\lim_{n \to \infty} u_n = L$, then $\lim_{n \to \infty} f(u_n) = f(L)$?

The answer is yes, provided that the function f is continuous. To prove this, you need to define what you mean by a continuous function, and that would go beyond the scope of this book. However, it is possible to give proofs for particular functions. The next theorem does this for the reciprocal function. In this case it is simpler to use the p, q definition.

Theorem 3   If $\lim_{n \to \infty} u_n = L$, then $\lim_{n \to \infty} \dfrac{1}{u_n} = \dfrac{1}{L}$ (a) if $L > 0$,   (b) if $L < 0$.

The logic is similar to that in Theorem 2. You start with given numbers p and q such that $p < \dfrac{1}{L}$ and

$q > \dfrac{1}{L}$, and have to prove that, beyond a certain number m, $\dfrac{1}{u_n}$ lies between p and q. The proof has to

be constructed by using the given fact that $\lim_{n \to \infty} u_n = L$.

In part (a) it is helpful to restrict p to be a positive number. Since $\dfrac{1}{L} > 0$, there is no problem with this. As

mentioned in Section 7.1, it is quite acceptable to specify that p should be 'not too far from $\dfrac{1}{L}$'.

Proof
(a)   Let p, q be any numbers such that $0 < p < \dfrac{1}{L} < q$. Then $L > \dfrac{1}{q}$ and $L < \dfrac{1}{p}$. This is illustrated in

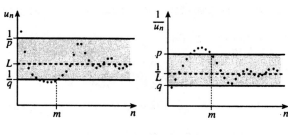

Fig. 7.2, where the graph on the left shows values of u_n and the graph on the right shows values of $\dfrac{1}{u_n}$.

Fig. 7.2

You are given that $\lim_{n \to \infty} u_n = L$. This means that, from the definition, there is a number m such that, for all $n > m$,

$$\frac{1}{q} < u_n < \frac{1}{p}.$$

It follows that $\dfrac{1}{u_n} < q$ and $\dfrac{1}{u_n} > p$, that is

$$p < \frac{1}{u_n} < q \qquad \text{for all } n > m.$$

And since p and q are any numbers such that $p < \dfrac{1}{L} < q$, it follows from the definition that

$$\lim_{n \to \infty} \frac{1}{u_n} = \frac{1}{L}.$$

(b)   If L is negative, you can combine Theorem 1(b) with the result of part (a). Since $\lim_{n\to\infty} u_n = L < 0$, $\lim_{n\to\infty}(-u_n) = -L > 0$ by Theorem 1(b). So you can apply part (a) to the sequence $-u_n$, and deduce that

$$\lim_{n\to\infty}\frac{1}{-u_n} = \frac{1}{-L} = -\frac{1}{L}.$$

But $\lim_{n\to\infty}\dfrac{1}{-u_n} = \lim_{n\to\infty}\left(-\dfrac{1}{u_n}\right)$

$$= -\lim_{n\to\infty}\frac{1}{u_n},$$

using Theorem 1(b) a second time. Therefore

$$-\lim_{n\to\infty}\frac{1}{u_n} = -\frac{1}{L}, \quad \text{that is} \quad \lim_{n\to\infty}\frac{1}{u_n} = \frac{1}{L}.$$

Theorem 3 is clearly meaningless if $L = 0$. In fact, if $\lim_{n\to\infty} u_n = 0$, the sequence $\dfrac{1}{u_n}$ may diverge either to $-\infty$ or to ∞, or it may oscillate infinitely. But it cannot tend to a finite limit.

Exercise 7B

1   If $\lim_{n\to\infty} u_n = 3$, find

(a) $\lim_{n\to\infty}(2u_n - 5)$,   (b) $\lim_{n\to\infty}\dfrac{1}{1-2u_n}$,   (c) $\lim_{n\to\infty}\left(1 - \dfrac{2}{u_n}\right)$.

State at each step which of Theorems 1–3 you are using.

2   Use the result of Exercise 7A Question 7 to find

(a) $\lim_{n\to\infty}\left(\sqrt[n]{2} - 1\right)$,   (b) $\lim_{n\to\infty}\dfrac{1}{1+\sqrt[n]{2}}$,   (c) $\lim_{n\to\infty}\dfrac{\sqrt[n]{2}}{1+\sqrt[n]{2}}$,   (d) $\lim_{n\to\infty}\sqrt[n]{0.5}$.

State at each step which of Theorems 1–3 you are using.

3   Give examples of sequences u_n such that $\lim_{n\to\infty} u_n = 0$ for which $\lim_{n\to\infty}\dfrac{1}{u_n}$

(a)   diverges to $+\infty$,   (b)   diverges to $-\infty$,   (c)   oscillates infinitely.

7.3   Combinations of two sequences

The theorems in Section 7.2 were concerned with functions of one sequence u_n whose limit L was known. This section considers a pair of sequences u_n and v_n whose limits L_1 and L_2 are known and investigates the limits of combinations of these sequences such as $u_n + v_n$, $u_n \times v_n$ and $\dfrac{u_n}{v_n}$.

The next example illustrates what is involved.

Example 7.3.1

(a) Find a number m such that $\sqrt[n]{2}+\sqrt[n]{3}<2.01$ for all $n>m$.   (b) Prove that $\lim_{n\to\infty}\left(\sqrt[n]{2}+\sqrt[n]{3}\right)=2$.

(a)   Both $\sqrt[n]{2}$ and $\sqrt[n]{3}$ are greater than 1 for all $n\in\mathbb{Z}^+$, so for their sum to be less than 2.01 each must certainly be less than 1.01. It would be simplest to find n such that each is less than 1.005, though there are of course other possibilities; for example, you could if you prefer make $\sqrt[n]{2}$ less than 1.004 and $\sqrt[n]{3}$ less than 1.006. This might produce a smaller value for m, but that is not required.

In Exercise 7A Question 7 you proved that, if $\sqrt[n]{2}=1+x$, then $nx<2$. So if n is a number greater than $\dfrac{2}{0.005}=400$,

$$\sqrt[n]{2}=1+x<1+\frac{2}{n}<1+\frac{2}{400}=1.005.$$

In just the same way, if $\sqrt[n]{3}=1+y$, then $ny<3$. So if n is a number greater than $\dfrac{3}{0.005}=600$,

$$\sqrt[n]{3}=1+y<1+\frac{3}{n}<1+\frac{3}{600}=1.005.$$

You want both of these inequalities to hold simultaneously, and this will happen if n is greater than both 400 and 600; that is, if $n>\max(400,600)=600$. So,

if $n>600$, $\sqrt[n]{2}+\sqrt[n]{3}<1.005+1.005=2.01$.

That is, $m=600$ satisfies the requirement.

In fact, you can check with a calculator that the inequality is satisfied by $n=180$ but not by $n=179$, so $m=179$ would do. But there is no way of finding this by an algebraic method.

(b)   If you are given a positive number ε, you have to find a number m such that, for all $n>m$, $\left|\sqrt[n]{2}+\sqrt[n]{3}-2\right|<\varepsilon$. Since $\sqrt[n]{2}+\sqrt[n]{3}$ is always greater than 2, it is certainly greater than the lower bound $2-\varepsilon$. So all that is needed is to find values of n such that $\sqrt[n]{2}+\sqrt[n]{3}<2+\varepsilon$.

This is the problem in part (a) with ε in place of 0.01. So it can be solved by finding values of n such that both $\sqrt[n]{2}<1+\frac{1}{2}\varepsilon$ and $\sqrt[n]{3}<1+\frac{1}{2}\varepsilon$. This will certainly be true if n is greater than both $\dfrac{2}{\frac{1}{2}\varepsilon}=\dfrac{4}{\varepsilon}$ and $\dfrac{3}{\frac{1}{2}\varepsilon}=\dfrac{6}{\varepsilon}$.

So take $m=\max\left(\dfrac{4}{\varepsilon},\dfrac{6}{\varepsilon}\right)=\dfrac{6}{\varepsilon}$. Then, for all $n>m$,

$$\sqrt[n]{2}+\sqrt[n]{3}<\left(1+\frac{2}{n}\right)+\left(1+\frac{3}{n}\right)<2+\frac{2}{\left(\frac{6}{\varepsilon}\right)}+\frac{3}{\left(\frac{6}{\varepsilon}\right)}=2+\tfrac{5}{6}\varepsilon<2+\varepsilon.$$

Since also $\sqrt[n]{2}+\sqrt[n]{3}>2>2-\varepsilon$, it follows that $\lim_{n\to\infty}\left(\sqrt[n]{2}+\sqrt[n]{3}\right)=2$.

To prove that the limit of the sum of two sequences is equal to the sum of the limits, you can use the method in Example 7.3.1 in a general form. The essential idea is to split the number ε into two parts of $\frac{1}{2}\varepsilon$, and to use one of these parts with each of the separate sequences.

Theorem 4   If $\lim\limits_{n\to\infty} u_n = L_1$ and $\lim\limits_{n\to\infty} v_n = L_2$, then $\lim\limits_{n\to\infty}(u_n + v_n) = L_1 + L_2$.

Proof

Let ε be any positive number. Then, since $\lim\limits_{n\to\infty} u_n = L_1$, there is a number m_1 such that, for all $n > m_1$,

$$L_1 - \tfrac{1}{2}\varepsilon < u_n < L_1 + \tfrac{1}{2}\varepsilon.$$

Similarly, since $\lim\limits_{n\to\infty} v_n = L_2$, there is a number m_2 such that, for all $n > m_2$,

$$L_2 - \tfrac{1}{2}\varepsilon < v_n < L_2 + \tfrac{1}{2}\varepsilon.$$

Let $m = \max(m_1, m_2)$. Then, for all $n > m$, both sets of inequalities hold. So

$$\left(L_1 - \tfrac{1}{2}\varepsilon\right) + \left(L_2 - \tfrac{1}{2}\varepsilon\right) < u_n + v_n < \left(L_1 + \tfrac{1}{2}\varepsilon\right) + \left(L_2 + \tfrac{1}{2}\varepsilon\right).$$

That is, $(L_1 + L_2) - \varepsilon < u_n + v_n < (L_1 + L_2) + \varepsilon$.

Since this is true for any positive number ε, it follows that $\lim\limits_{n\to\infty}(u_n + v_n) = L_1 + L_2$.

There is an exactly similar theorem for the product of two sequences. It is simplest to begin with the special case in which L_1 and L_2 are both 0. Then what you have to do is to write ε as the product of two numbers, rather than (as in Theorem 4) as the sum of two numbers. The most obvious choice is to split it as $\varepsilon = \sqrt{\varepsilon} \times \sqrt{\varepsilon}$. The proof is then very similar to that of Theorem 4, with multiplication in place of addition.

Theorem 5   If $\lim\limits_{n\to\infty} u_n = 0$ and $\lim\limits_{n\to\infty} v_n = 0$, then $\lim\limits_{n\to\infty}(u_n v_n) = 0$.

Proof

Let ε be any positive number. Then, since $\lim\limits_{n\to\infty} u_n = 0$, there is a number m_1 such that, for all $n > m_1$,

$$|u_n - 0| < \sqrt{\varepsilon}, \quad \text{that is} \quad |u_n| < \sqrt{\varepsilon}.$$

Similarly, since $\lim\limits_{n\to\infty} v_n = 0$, there is a number m_2 such that, for all $n > m_2$,

$$|v_n| < \sqrt{\varepsilon}.$$

Let $m = \max(m_1, m_2)$. Then, for all $n > m$, both inequalities hold. So

$$|u_n v_n| = |u_n| \times |v_n| < \sqrt{\varepsilon} \times \sqrt{\varepsilon} = \varepsilon.$$

Since this is true for any positive number ε, it follows that $\lim\limits_{n\to\infty}(u_n v_n) = 0$.

You need just two more theorems, about multiplication in general and division, but these can be easily deduced from what has already been proved. No more 'ε' or 'p,q' type proofs are needed.

Theorem 6   If $\lim_{n\to\infty} u_n = L_1$ and $\lim_{n\to\infty} v_n = L_2$, then $\lim_{n\to\infty}(u_n v_n) = L_1 L_2$.

Proof
Define two new sequences, a_n and b_n, by

$$a_n = u_n - L_1 \qquad \text{and} \qquad b_n = v_n - L_2.$$

Then, by Theorem 1(a),

$$\lim_{n\to\infty} a_n = \lim_{n\to\infty} u_n - L_1 = L_1 - L_1 = 0 \qquad \text{and} \qquad \lim_{n\to\infty} b_n = \lim_{n\to\infty} v_n - L_2 = L_2 - L_2 = 0.$$

So

$$
\begin{aligned}
\lim_{n\to\infty} u_n v_n &= \lim_{n\to\infty}(a_n + L_1)(b_n + L_2) \\
&= \lim_{n\to\infty}(a_n b_n) + \lim_{n\to\infty}(L_1 b_n) + \lim_{n\to\infty}(a_n L_2) + L_1 L_2 \quad \text{(by Theorems 1(a) and 4)} \\
&= 0 + L_1 \times \lim_{n\to\infty} b_n + L_2 \times \lim_{n\to\infty} a_n + L_1 L_2 \qquad \text{(by Theorems 2 and 5)} \\
&= 0 + L_1 \times 0 + L_2 \times 0 + L_1 L_2 \\
&= L_1 L_2.
\end{aligned}
$$

Theorem 7   If $\lim_{n\to\infty} u_n = L_1$ and $\lim_{n\to\infty} v_n = L_2$, where $L_2 \neq 0$, then $\lim_{n\to\infty} \dfrac{u_n}{v_n} = \dfrac{L_1}{L_2}$.

Proof
By Theorem 3, since $L_2 \neq 0$, $\lim_{n\to\infty} \dfrac{1}{v_n} = \dfrac{1}{L_2}$.

Therefore, by Theorem 6,

$$
\begin{aligned}
\lim_{n\to\infty} \frac{u_n}{v_n} &= \lim_{n\to\infty}\left(u_n \times \frac{1}{v_n}\right) \\
&= \lim_{n\to\infty} u_n \times \lim_{n\to\infty} \frac{1}{v_n} \\
&= L_1 \times \frac{1}{L_2} = \frac{L_1}{L_2}.
\end{aligned}
$$

7.4   The squeeze theorem

A method of finding limits that is sometimes useful is to show that a sequence can be squeezed between two other sequences, each of which tends to the same limit.

You have already met special cases of this process. In Higher Level Book 2 Section 21.1 the inequality $\cos\theta < \dfrac{\sin\theta}{\theta} < 1$ was used to prove that $\lim_{\theta\to 0} \dfrac{\sin\theta}{\theta} = 1$. The graph of $y = \dfrac{\sin\theta}{\theta}$ was squeezed between the graph of $y = \cos\theta$ and the line $y = 1$, its tangent where $\theta = 0$. There is another example in Section 4.1 of this book, where the area under a curve was shown to be squeezed between lower and upper sums, both having the same limits.

In these examples one of the three elements is constant: the line $y = 1$ in the first case, and the actual value of the area under the curve in the second. But in general applications all three may vary.

Theorem 8   (the squeeze theorem)   If two sequences u_n and v_n have the same limit L as $n \to \infty$, and if w_n is between u_n and v_n for all n, then $\lim\limits_{n \to \infty} w_n = L$.

This theorem is perhaps the most 'obvious' of all. The proof follows directly from the definition of a limit.

Let p and q be any two numbers such that $p < L < q$.

Since $\lim\limits_{n \to \infty} u_n = L$, there is a number m_1 such that $p < u_n < q$ for all $n > m_1$.

Since $\lim\limits_{n \to \infty} v_n = L$, there is a number m_2 such that $p < v_n < q$ for all $n > m_2$.

Therefore, if $m = \max(m_1, m_2)$, both $p < u_n < q$ and $p < v_n < q$ for all $n > m$.

Suppose that $u_n \leq v_n$, so that $u_n \leq w_n \leq v_n$, Then, if $n > m$,

$$w_n \leq v_n < q \qquad \text{and} \qquad w_n \geq u_n > p,$$

so $p < w_n < q$. This conclusion follows similarly if $u_n > v_n$.

Therefore, for all $n > m$, $p < w_n < q$. And since p and q are any numbers such that $p < L < q$, it follows from the definition that $\lim\limits_{n \to \infty} w_n = L$.

Example 7.4.1

Prove that $\lim\limits_{n \to \infty} \dfrac{\cos n}{n} = 0$.   (See Example 7.1.3.)

Let $w_n = \dfrac{\cos n}{n}$. Since, for all $n \in \mathbb{Z}^+$, $-1 < \cos n < 1$,

$$-\frac{1}{n} < \frac{\cos n}{n} < \frac{1}{n}.$$

But $\lim\limits_{n \to \infty} \dfrac{1}{n} = 0$ and $\lim\limits_{n \to \infty}\left(-\dfrac{1}{n}\right) = -\lim\limits_{n \to \infty} \dfrac{1}{n} = 0$ (Theorem 1(b)).

Therefore, by the squeeze theorem, $\lim\limits_{n \to \infty} w_n = 0$.

Example 7.4.2

If $s_n = \dfrac{1}{n^2} + \dfrac{1}{(n+1)^2} + \dfrac{1}{(n+2)^2} + \ldots + \dfrac{1}{(2n)^2}$, find $\lim\limits_{n \to \infty}(n s_n)$.

In Fig. 7.3 s_n is represented as the sum of the areas of rectangles of width 1 and heights $\dfrac{1}{n^2}, \dfrac{1}{(n+1)^2}, \dfrac{1}{(n+2)^2}, \ldots, \dfrac{1}{(2n)^2}$. The graph on the left shows this sum as a lower sum for the area under $y = \dfrac{1}{x^2}$ from $x = n-1$ to $x = 2n$. The graph on the right shows it as an upper sum for the area under the same curve from $x = n$ to $x = 2n+1$.

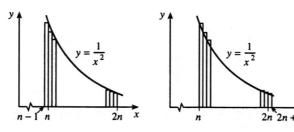

Fig. 7.3

Therefore

$$\int_n^{2n+1} \frac{1}{x^2}\,dx < s_n < \int_{n-1}^{2n} \frac{1}{x^2}\,dx,$$

and

$$\int_n^{2n+1} \frac{1}{x^2}\,dx = \left[-\frac{1}{x}\right]_n^{2n+1} \qquad \int_{n-1}^{2n} \frac{1}{x^2}\,dx = \left[-\frac{1}{x}\right]_{n-1}^{2n}$$

$$= -\frac{1}{2n+1} + \frac{1}{n} \qquad\qquad = -\frac{1}{2n} + \frac{1}{n-1}$$

$$\text{and}$$

$$= \frac{-n+(2n+1)}{n(2n+1)} \qquad\qquad = \frac{-(n-1)+2n}{2n(n-1)}$$

$$= \frac{n+1}{n(2n+1)}, \qquad\qquad\quad = \frac{n+1}{2n(n-1)}.$$

So $\quad \dfrac{n+1}{n(2n+1)} < s_n < \dfrac{n+1}{2n(n-1)}.$

Multiplying by n,

$$\frac{n+1}{2n+1} < ns_n < \frac{n+1}{2n-2}.$$

Now, using Theorem 7,

$$\lim_{n\to\infty} \frac{n+1}{2n+1} = \lim_{n\to\infty} \frac{1+\dfrac{1}{n}}{2+\dfrac{1}{n}} \qquad\qquad \lim_{n\to\infty} \frac{n+1}{2n-2} = \lim_{n\to\infty} \frac{1+\dfrac{1}{n}}{2-\dfrac{2}{n}}$$

$$\text{and}$$

$$= \frac{\displaystyle\lim_{n\to\infty}\left(1+\frac{1}{n}\right)}{\displaystyle\lim_{n\to\infty}\left(2+\frac{1}{n}\right)} = \frac{1}{2} \qquad\qquad = \frac{\displaystyle\lim_{n\to\infty}\left(1+\frac{1}{n}\right)}{\displaystyle\lim_{n\to\infty}\left(2-\frac{2}{n}\right)} = \frac{1}{2}.$$

Therefore, by the squeeze theorem,

$$\lim_{n\to\infty}\left(ns_n\right) = \tfrac{1}{2}.$$

Exercise 7C

1 If $\lim_{n\to\infty} u_n = 4$ and $\lim_{n\to\infty} v_n = -1$, find

    (a) $\lim_{n\to\infty} \dfrac{u_n + v_n}{u_n - v_n}$,   (b) $\lim_{n\to\infty} (u_n + 2v_n)^2$.

    State at each step which theorem you are using.

2 Find

    (a) $\lim_{n\to\infty} \dfrac{n^2 + 2n}{3n^2 - 4}$,   (b) $\lim_{n\to\infty} \sqrt[n]{n^2}$,   (c) $\lim_{n\to\infty} \left(\sqrt[n]{10} - \sqrt[n]{0.1}\right)$,   (d) $\lim_{n\to\infty} \dfrac{e^n - n^2}{e^n + n^2}$.

3 By comparing the area under the graph of $y = \dfrac{1}{x}$ with the area of two rectangles, prove that, if $a > 0$ and $n > 0$,

$$\frac{a}{n+a} < \ln\left(1 + \frac{a}{n}\right) < \frac{a}{n}.$$

    Hence find $\lim_{n\to\infty} \ln\left(1 + \dfrac{a}{n}\right)^n$, and deduce $\lim_{n\to\infty} \left(1 + \dfrac{a}{n}\right)^n$.

    In the last step, what assumption are you making that you have not proved?

4 Find the limits, as $n \to \infty$, of

    (a) $n \times \sum_{i=n}^{3n} \dfrac{1}{i^2}$,   (b) $n^2 \times \sum_{i=n}^{3n} \dfrac{1}{i^3}$,   (c) $\sum_{i=n}^{3n} \dfrac{1}{i}$.

    Check your answers with a calculator.

5* (a)   Use the fact that $\lim_{n\to\infty} \sqrt[n]{n} = 1$ (see Exercise 7A Question 8) to find $\lim_{n\to\infty} \dfrac{\ln n}{n}$.

    (b)   By writing $\dfrac{\ln(n+1)}{n}$ as $\dfrac{n+1}{n} \times \dfrac{\ln(n+1)}{n+1}$, find $\lim_{n\to\infty} \dfrac{\ln(n+1)}{n}$.

    (c)   Draw a diagram to show that $\displaystyle\int_1^n \ln x \, dx < \ln n! < \int_1^{n+1} \ln x \, dx$.

    (d)   Deduce from part (c) that $-1 + \dfrac{1}{n} < \ln \dfrac{\sqrt[n]{n!}}{n} < \ln\left(1 + \dfrac{1}{n}\right) + \dfrac{\ln(n+1)}{n} - 1$.

    (e)   Hence show that $\lim_{n\to\infty} \dfrac{\sqrt[n]{n!}}{n} = \dfrac{1}{e}$.

    (f)   Use a calculator to check that, when n is large, $\dfrac{\sqrt[n]{n!}}{n} \approx \dfrac{1}{e}$.

8 Power series

In this chapter the terms of the series include powers of a variable x. When you have completed it, you should

- know what is meant by a power series
- understand that a power series defines a function whose natural domain is the interval of convergence
- be able to use the ratio test and understand other methods to find the interval of convergence.

8.1 Definitions

So far the terms of almost all series have been functions simply of a positive integer variable i, and for convergent series the sum has been a number.

The series in this chapter are different, since each term also includes a power of a real (or possibly complex) variable x, so that

$$u_i = a_i x^i,$$

where a_i is a sequence of numbers.

One example which you will recognise is the infinite geometric series

$$1 + x + x^2 + x^3 + \ldots,$$

for which $a_i = 1$ for all i. This is convergent if $|x| < 1$. If you replace x by $-2x$ or $\frac{1}{3}x$ you get other infinite geometric series,

$$1 - 2x + 4x^2 - 8x^3 + \ldots \quad \text{or} \quad 1 + \tfrac{1}{3}x + \tfrac{1}{9}x^2 + \tfrac{1}{27}x^3 + \ldots ,$$

with $a_i = (-2)^i$ and $a_i = \left(\tfrac{1}{3}\right)^i$ respectively. These are convergent if $|-2x| < 1$ and $\left|\tfrac{1}{3}x\right| < 1$, that is if $-\tfrac{1}{2} < x < \tfrac{1}{2}$ and $-3 < x < 3$.

You will notice one difference between these examples and the series in earlier chapters. As well as terms with powers of x, there is also a 'constant term', $u_0 = a_0 x^0$. When you use sigma notation to describe the series, the values of i will start at 0 rather than 1. You could think of the series as 'infinite polynomials', and the partial sum

$$S_n = \sum_{i=0}^{n} a_i x^i$$

is a polynomial of degree n, written with ascending powers of x.

> A **power series** is an infinite series $\sum u_i$ where $u_i = a_i x^i$ for $i = 0, 1, 2, \ldots$.

Obviously all power series are convergent when $x = 0$, since there is then only one non-zero term a_0. There are some power series which are convergent for all $x \in \mathbb{R}$. But many power series are convergent for some values of x but not for others. In that case there is an **interval of convergence**, denoted by I.

For the geometric series above you can use the formula for S_n to write down algebraic expressions for the sum over the interval of convergence. Thus

$$\sum_{i=0}^{\infty} x^i = \frac{1}{1-x} \text{ for } -1 < x < 1, \qquad \sum_{i=0}^{\infty} (-2)^i x^i = \frac{1}{1+2x} \text{ for } -\tfrac{1}{2} < x < \tfrac{1}{2}$$

and

$$\sum_{i=0}^{\infty} \left(\tfrac{1}{3}\right)^i x^i = \frac{1}{1-\tfrac{1}{3}x} \text{ for } -3 < x < 3.$$

Notice that the expressions for the sum also have a meaning when x is outside the interval of convergence (except at $x = 1$, $-\tfrac{1}{2}$ and 3 respectively), but the function is not then represented by the series.

In the same way, any power series defines a function of x. But unlike the geometric series, it is unusual to be able to give an algebraic expression for the sum. In that case the power series itself serves as the definition of the function.

> A power series $\sum a_i x^i$ is convergent within an interval of convergence I. It then defines a function
>
> $$S(x) = \sum_{i=0}^{\infty} a_i x^i$$
>
> whose natural domain is I.

8.2 The interval of convergence

For the geometric series in Section 8.1 it was possible to write down the intervals of convergence because you know formulae for the partial sums S_n. Usually you don't, and then you have to use another method. One way of finding the interval of convergence which often works is to use the ratio test in Section 3.2:

If $\sum u_i$ is a series of positive terms such that $\lim_{i \to \infty} \dfrac{u_i}{u_{i-1}} < 1$, then the series is convergent.

You might object that in a power series the coefficients a_i may not all be positive, and also x might be negative. To get round this, begin by asking for what values of x the series is *absolutely* convergent. The ratio test then becomes:

If $\lim_{i \to \infty} \dfrac{|u_i|}{|u_{i-1}|} < 1$, then the series $\sum u_i$ is absolutely convergent.

To apply this to a power series, write $u_i = a_i x^i$ and remember the rules for the modulus, that

$$|s \times t| = |s| \times |t| \text{ and } \left|\frac{s}{t}\right| = \frac{|s|}{|t|}.$$

Then

$$\frac{|u_i|}{|u_{i-1}|} = \frac{|a_i x^i|}{|a_{i-1} x^{i-1}|} = \left|\frac{a_i}{a_{i-1}}\right| \times |x|.$$

The condition $\lim\limits_{i \to \infty} \dfrac{|u_i|}{|u_{i-1}|} < 1$ then becomes $\lim\limits_{i \to \infty}\left(\left|\dfrac{a_i}{a_{i-1}}\right| \times |x|\right) < 1$. You can use the results of Theorems 2 and 3 in Section 7.2 to write this as

$$|x| < \lim_{i \to \infty}\left|\frac{a_{i-1}}{a_i}\right|.$$

You can also reverse the argument to find what happens if $|x| > \lim\limits_{i \to \infty}\left|\dfrac{a_{i-1}}{a_i}\right|$. Working backwards, you

reach the conclusion that $\lim\limits_{i \to \infty} \dfrac{|u_i|}{|u_{i-1}|} > 1$. This means that, for values of i beyond a certain point,

$|u_i| > |u_{i-1}|$. That is, the terms of the series increase in absolute value, and therefore can't tend to 0, so the series is not convergent.

These results can be summarised as follows.

> If $\lim\limits_{i \to \infty}\left|\dfrac{a_{i-1}}{a_i}\right| = R$, then the power series $\sum a_i x^i$ is convergent for $|x| < R$ and
>
> divergent for $|x| > R$.

This is illustrated in Fig. 8.1. The interval of convergence certainly includes the whole of the open interval $]-R, R[$ and doesn't extend outside the closed interval $[-R, R]$. But there are question marks over what happens when $x = -R$ and $x = R$. The ratio test doesn't help here, and you need to consider each case individually.

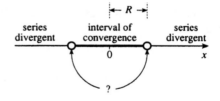

Fig. 8.1

Example 8.2.1

Find the intervals of convergence for the power series   (a) $\sum \dfrac{x^i}{(i+1)^2}$,   (b) $\sum \dfrac{x^i}{i+1}$,   (c) $\sum i x^i$.

(a)   Since $a_i = \dfrac{1}{(i+1)^2}$, $R = \lim\limits_{i \to \infty}\left|\dfrac{\frac{1}{(i)^2}}{\frac{1}{(i+1)^2}}\right| = \lim\limits_{i \to \infty}\dfrac{(i+1)^2}{i^2} = \lim\limits_{i \to \infty}\left(1 + \dfrac{1}{i}\right)^2 = 1.$

The series is therefore convergent for $|x| < 1$ and divergent for $|x| > 1$. When $x = 1$ and $x = -1$ the series becomes

$$\frac{1}{1^2} + \frac{1}{2^2} + \frac{1}{3^2} + \dots \quad \text{and} \quad \frac{1}{1^2} - \frac{1}{2^2} + \frac{1}{3^2} - \dots ,$$

and you know from Sections 2.2 and 6.1 that these are convergent. The interval of convergence is therefore the closed interval $[-1,1]$.

(b)   Since $a_i = \dfrac{1}{i+1}$, $R = \lim\limits_{i \to \infty} \left| \dfrac{\frac{1}{i}}{\frac{1}{i+1}} \right| = \lim\limits_{i \to \infty} \left| \dfrac{i+1}{i} \right| = \lim\limits_{i \to \infty} \left| 1 + \dfrac{1}{i} \right| = 1$.

When $x = 1$ the series becomes

$$\tfrac{1}{1} + \tfrac{1}{2} + \tfrac{1}{3} + \ldots,$$

which is not convergent. But when $x = -1$ the series is

$$\tfrac{1}{1} - \tfrac{1}{2} + \tfrac{1}{3} - \ldots,$$

which was shown to be convergent in Section 6.1. So the interval of convergence is $[-1,1[$.

(c)   Since $a_i = i$, $R = \lim\limits_{i \to \infty} \left| \dfrac{i-1}{i} \right| = \lim\limits_{i \to \infty} \left| 1 - \dfrac{1}{i} \right| = 1$.

But this series cannot converge when $x = 1$ or $x = -1$, because then $|u_i| = |a_i x^i| = i$, which does not tend to 0 as $i \to \infty$. So the interval of convergence is the open interval $]-1,1[$.

You will see from Example 8.2.1 that the ratio test can be very effective when $\lim\limits_{i \to \infty} \left| \dfrac{a_{i-1}}{a_i} \right|$ exists. But sometimes it doesn't, as in the next two examples. You then need to find the interval of convergence by another method.

Example 8.2.2
Find the interval of convergence of the power series $\sum \left(2 - (-1)^i \right) x^i$.

The series begins

$$1 + 3x + x^2 + 3x^3 + x^4 + 3x^5 + \ldots,$$

with $a_i = 1$ when i is even and $a_i = 3$ when i is odd. So the ratio $\dfrac{a_{i-1}}{a_i}$ takes alternately the values $\tfrac{1}{3}, 3, \tfrac{1}{3}, 3, \tfrac{1}{3}, \ldots$. This clearly does not tend to a limit.

The series consists of two interleaved geometric series,

$$1 + x^2 + x^4 + \ldots \quad \text{and} \quad 3x + 3x^3 + 3x^5 + \ldots,$$

each with common ratio x^2. These are convergent when $x^2 < 1$, that is when $-1 < x < 1$. The interval of convergence is therefore $]-1,1[$.

Example 8.2.3
Find the interval of convergence of the power series $\sum (\cos i)x^i$.

A glance at the graph of the sequence $a_i = \cos i$ (see Section 6.2, Fig. 6.7) will convince you that $\left| \dfrac{\cos(i-1)}{\cos i} \right|$ doesn't tend to a limit as $i \to \infty$. So you can't use the ratio test.

But since $|\cos i| \le 1$ for all $i \in \mathbb{N}$, you know that, for any value of x, $\left| (\cos i)x^i \right| \le |x|^i$. And since the geometric series $\sum |x|^i$ is convergent for $|x| < 1$, you can use the comparison test in Section 2.3 to deduce that $\sum \left| (\cos i)x^i \right|$ is convergent for $|x| < 1$.

When $x = 1$ and $x = -1$ the series becomes $\sum \cos i$ and $\sum (-1)^i \cos i$ respectively. Neither of these can converge, since $\cos i$ doesn't tend to a limit as $i \to \infty$ (see Example 6.2.3). So the interval of convergence is $]-1,1[$.

What these examples illustrate is that, even when $\lim\limits_{i\to\infty} \left| \dfrac{a_{i-1}}{a_i} \right|$ does not exist, there is still a number R which separates the values of $|x|$ for which the series is absolutely convergent from those for which it is divergent. This is in fact true for almost any power series, but it is not so easy to prove.

There are just two exceptions. If $\lim\limits_{i\to\infty} \left| \dfrac{a_{i-1}}{a_i} \right| = 0$, then the ratio

$$\frac{|u_i|}{|u_{i-1}|} = \left| \frac{a_i}{a_{i-1}} \right| \times |x|$$

tends to infinity for every value of x except 0. In that case the power series converges only when $x = 0$. And if $\left| \dfrac{a_{i-1}}{a_i} \right|$ tends to infinity as $i \to \infty$, then the ratio $\dfrac{|u_i|}{|u_{i-1}|}$ tends to 0 whatever the value of x, so the power series converges for all values of x.

Example 8.2.4
For what values of x are the following infinite series convergent?

(a) $\sum \dfrac{x^i}{(i+1)^i}$ (b) $\sum (i+1)^i x^i$

(a)   If $a_i = \dfrac{1}{(i+1)^i}$, then $\left| \dfrac{a_{i-1}}{a_i} \right| = \dfrac{(i+1)^i}{i^{i-1}} = \left(\dfrac{i+1}{i} \right)^i \times i$. The first factor of this expression is greater than 1 and the second tends to infinity, so $\left| \dfrac{a_{i-1}}{a_i} \right|$ tends to infinity as $i \to \infty$. The series therefore converges for all values of x.

(b) If $a_i = (i+1)^i$, then $\left|\dfrac{a_{i-1}}{a_i}\right| = \dfrac{i^{i-1}}{(i+1)^i} = \left(\dfrac{i}{i+1}\right)^i \times \dfrac{1}{i}$. The first factor of this expression is less

than 1 and the second tends to 0, so $\displaystyle\lim_{i\to\infty}\left|\dfrac{a_{i-1}}{a_i}\right| = 0$. The series converges only if $x = 0$, and

its value is then the constant term $(0+1)^0 = 1^0 = 1$.

To summarise:

> For any power series $\sum a_i x^i$,
>
> *either*   the series converges only when $x = 0$,
>
> *or*   the series converges for all values of x,
>
> *or*   there is a number R such that the series is convergent for $|x| < R$ and
>   divergent for $|x| > R$.
>
> The number R is called the **radius of convergence** of the series.

You may be surprised at the use of the word 'radius'. The reason is that the theory of power series can be extended to allow x to be a complex number (see Higher Level Book 2 Section 36.5), and sometimes also to series where the coefficients a_i may be complex. The number R is then the radius of a circle in the complex plane which separates the points for which the series converges from those for which it diverges. The corresponding property when x is real is that the points on the number line which separate the interval of convergence from the intervals of divergence are at a distance R from the origin.

Exercise 8

1   Find the interval of convergence for the following power series.

(a) $\displaystyle\sum\frac{x^i}{(i+1)(i+2)}$ (b) $\displaystyle\sum\frac{x^i}{\sqrt{i+1}}$ (c) $\displaystyle\sum\frac{x^i}{i!}$

(d) $\displaystyle\sum\frac{2^i}{i+1}x^i$ (e) $\displaystyle\sum i!\,x^i$ (f) $\displaystyle\sum\frac{i+1}{2i+1}x^i$

(g) $\displaystyle\sum\frac{x^i}{1+2\times(-1)^i}$ (h) $\displaystyle\sum\binom{n+i}{i}x^i$ for $n\in\mathbb{Z}^+$ (i) $\displaystyle\sum\binom{2i}{i}x^i$

[To decide about the end points in part (i), you may find it helpful to use *Stirling's approximation*, that $n! \approx \sqrt{2\pi}\,n^{n+\frac{1}{2}}\,e^{-n}$ when n is large.]

2   Find the radius of convergence for the following power series.

(a) $\displaystyle\sum\frac{x^i}{3i+1}$ (b) $\displaystyle\sum\frac{x^i}{2+(-1)^i}$ (c) $\displaystyle\sum\frac{x^i}{1+(-2)^i}$ (d) $\displaystyle\sum\frac{x^{2i}}{2^i}$

9 Maclaurin series

In this chapter functions are associated with power series. When you have completed it, you should

- be able to find Maclaurin polynomials, and understand why they give good approximations to functions
- know the Maclaurin series for a number of functions, and be able to extend these by using substitutions
- understand what is meant by the interval of validity of a series
- know how to find series using integration
- be able to use series to find limits.

9.1 Agreement between functions

Suppose that $n \in \mathbb{Z}^+$, and that you want to expand $(1+x)^n$ in ascending powers of x as

$$1 + a_1 x + a_2 x^2 + \dots + a_i x^i + \dots + a_n x^n.$$

It was shown in Higher Level Book 1 Section 4.4 that the terms can be generated inductively, each coefficient being found from the one before:

$$1 \xrightarrow{\times \frac{n}{1}} a_1 \xrightarrow{\times \frac{n-1}{2}} a_2 \xrightarrow{\times \frac{n-2}{3}} a_3 \to \dots \to a_{i-1} \xrightarrow{\times \frac{n-i+1}{i}} a_i \to \dots \xrightarrow{\times \frac{1}{n}} a_n.$$

In the sequence of multipliers $\frac{n}{1}, \frac{n-1}{2}, \frac{n-2}{3}, \ \dots \ , \frac{1}{n}$ the denominators go up by 1 at each step, and the numerators go down by 1. The sequence of coefficients stops at a_n, because the next multiplier would be $\frac{1-1}{n+1}$, which is 0.

But if you generate a series by the same rule with a value of n which is not a positive integer, the sequence of coefficients will never end, and the expression would be an infinite power series. For example, if $n = \frac{1}{2}$, the multipliers would be

$$\frac{\frac{1}{2}}{1}, \frac{-\frac{1}{2}}{2}, \frac{-\frac{3}{2}}{3}, \frac{-\frac{5}{2}}{4}, \ \dots$$

which would produce coefficients

$$1 \xrightarrow{\times \frac{1}{2}} \frac{1}{2} \xrightarrow{\times (-\frac{1}{4})} -\frac{1}{8} \xrightarrow{\times (-\frac{1}{2})} \frac{1}{16} \xrightarrow{\times (-\frac{5}{8})} -\frac{5}{128} \to \dots$$

and an infinite series $S(x)$ whose first few terms are

$$S(x) = 1 + \frac{1}{2}x - \frac{1}{8}x^2 + \frac{1}{16}x^3 - \frac{5}{128}x^4 + \dots \ .$$

This is called a **binomial series**. But does it have any connection with $(1+x)^{\frac{1}{2}}$?

To investigate this, Fig. 9.1, Fig. 9.2 and Fig. 9.3 compare the graph of $f(x) = (1+x)^{\frac{1}{2}}$, or $\sqrt{1+x}$, with the graphs of the partial sums of degrees 1, 2 and 3 of $S(x)$. These are

$$S_1(x) = 1 + \tfrac{1}{2}x,$$

$$S_2(x) = 1 + \tfrac{1}{2}x - \tfrac{1}{8}x^2,$$

$$S_3(x) = 1 + \tfrac{1}{2}x - \tfrac{1}{8}x^2 + \tfrac{1}{16}x^3.$$

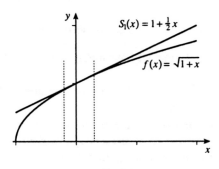

Fig. 9.1

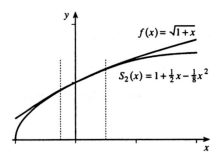

Fig. 9.2

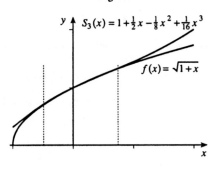

Fig. 9.3

The dotted lines indicate the intervals of values of x for which you can't distinguish the pairs of graphs by eye. You can see that the more terms you take, the wider the interval over which the polynomial gives a good approximation to $\sqrt{1+x}$.

The polynomial $S_1(x)$ has the same value as $f(x)$ when $x = 0$, and also the same gradient. Thus $f(0) = \sqrt{1+0} = 1$ and $S_1(0) = 1$. Also, since

$$f'(x) = \tfrac{1}{2}(1+x)^{-\frac{1}{2}} \quad \text{and} \quad S_1'(x) = \tfrac{1}{2},$$

you find that $f'(0) = S_1'(0) = \tfrac{1}{2}$.

The reason why $S_2(x)$ fits $f(x)$ better than $S_1(x)$ is that, by adding a term in x^2, the graph can be made to bend into a curve. The coefficient of x^2 ensures that the two graphs bend at the same rate when $x = 0$; that is, their second derivatives are the same. Thus

$$f''(x) = -\tfrac{1}{4}(1+x)^{-\frac{3}{2}} \quad \text{and} \quad S_2''(x) = -\tfrac{1}{4},$$

so that $f''(0) = S_2''(0) = -\tfrac{1}{4}$.

The functions $S_3(x)$ and $f(x)$ agree even better, since they not only bend at the same rate at $x = 0$, but also their rates of bending are changing at the same rate. You can check for yourself that $f'''(0) = S_3'''(0) = \tfrac{3}{8}$.

The ideas above can be summarised with the help of a definition:

> **Definition**   The functions f and g **agree to the nth degree** at $x = 0$ if
>
> $$f(0) = g(0), \quad f'(0) = g'(0), \quad f''(0) = g''(0), \quad \dots, \quad f^{(n)}(0) = g^{(n)}(0);$$
>
> that is, if $f^{(i)}(0) = g^{(i)}(0)$ where i is an integer and $0 \le i \le n$.

Thus $f(x)$ and $S_1(x)$ agree to the first degree, $f(x)$ and $S_2(x)$ agree to the second degree, and $f(x)$ and $S_3(x)$ agree to the third degree.

You can extend this idea to other functions.

Example 9.1.1
Find a cubic polynomial which agrees with $\tan x$ to the third degree.

Writing $\tan x$ as $f(x)$, use the chain rule and the product rule to find

$$f'(x) = \sec^2 x,$$
$$f''(x) = \sec x \tan x \times 2 \sec x$$
$$= 2 \sec^2 x \tan x,$$
$$f'''(x) = \sec x \tan x \times 4 \sec x \times \tan x + 2 \sec^2 x \times \sec^2 x$$
$$= 2 \sec^2 x \left(2 \tan^2 x + \sec^2 x \right).$$

Since $\tan 0 = 0$ and $\sec 0 = 1$,

$$f(0) = 0, \quad f'(0) = 1, \quad f''(0) = 0, \quad f'''(0) = 2.$$

If the required cubic polynomial is $p(x) = a + bx + cx^2 + dx^3$, then

$$p'(x) = b + 2cx + 3dx^2, \qquad p''(x) = 2c + 6dx, \qquad p'''(x) = 6d.$$

So

$$p(0) = a, \quad p'(0) = b, \quad p''(0) = 2c, \quad p'''(0) = 6d.$$

For $p(x)$ and $f(x)$ to agree at $x = 0$, you need

$$a = 0, \quad b = 1, \quad 2c = 0, \quad 6d = 2.$$

Therefore $p(x) = x + \frac{1}{3}x^3$.

It is interesting to plot the graphs of $\tan x$ and $p(x) = x + \frac{1}{3}x^3$ on a calculator, and to suggest an interval over which you would consider that $p(x)$ is a good approximation to $\tan x$.

9.2 Maclaurin polynomials

You can generalise the argument in the last section to give polynomial approximations to any function $f(x)$ around $x = 0$, provided that all the derivatives of the function are defined.

The polynomial of degree n which agrees with $f(x)$ to the nth degree at $x = 0$ is

$$p_n(x) = f(0) + \frac{f'(0)}{1!}x + \frac{f''(0)}{2!}x^2 + \ldots + \frac{f^{(i)}(0)}{i!}x^i + \ldots + \frac{f^{(n)}(0)}{n!}x^n.$$

This is called the **Maclaurin polynomial for $f(x)$ of degree n**.

In sigma notation it can be written as $p_n(x) = \displaystyle\sum_{i=0}^{n} \frac{f^{(i)}(0)}{i!}x^i.$

It is named after Colin Maclaurin, a Scottish mathematician who lived in the first half of the 18th century.

A proof of this result is given below. First, here is an example to show how it can be used.

Example 9.2.1
Find the Maclaurin polynomial of degree 4 for the function $f(x) = (1+x)^{-3}$.

The first four derivatives are

$$f'(x) = -3(1+x)^{-4}, \quad f''(x) = 12(1+x)^{-5},$$

$$f'''(x) = -60(1+x)^{-6}, \quad f^{(4)}(x) = 360(1+x)^{-7}.$$

Therefore

$$f(0) = 1, \quad f'(0) = -3, \quad f''(0) = 12, \quad f'''(0) = -60, \quad f^{(4)}(0) = 360.$$

This gives

$$p_4(x) = 1 + \frac{(-3)}{1!}x + \frac{12}{2!}x^2 + \frac{(-60)}{3!}x^3 + \frac{360}{4!}x^4$$
$$= 1 - 3x + 6x^2 - 10x^3 + 15x^4.$$

You can check that this is the same as the partial sum of degree 4 of the binomial series for $(1+x)^{-3}$ up to and including the term in x^4.

To prove the result in the shaded box, what you have to show is that if the polynomial

$$p_n(x) \equiv a_0 + a_1x + a_2x^2 + \ldots + a_ix^i + \ldots + a_nx^n$$

agrees with $f(x)$ to the nth degree at $x = 0$, then the coefficient a_i is equal to $\dfrac{f^{(i)}(0)}{i!}$ for $i = 0, 1, 2, \ldots, n$. To do this, bracket off the terms as

$$p_n(x) \equiv \left(a_0 + a_1x + a_2x^2 + \ldots + a_{i-1}x^{i-1}\right) + \left(a_ix^i\right) + \left(a_{i+1}x^{i+1} + \ldots + a_nx^n\right)$$

and consider what happens to each bracket when you differentiate the identity i times.

Each time that you differentiate a term a_rx^r the index goes down by 1. After r differentiations the index is 0 so that the term is reduced to a constant, and after $r+1$ differentiations the term vanishes.

- In the first bracket all the terms have $r \leq i - 1$, so $r + 1 \leq i$. Therefore after i differentiations all the terms in this bracket have vanished.
- In the last bracket all the terms have $r \geq i + 1$, so after i differentiations the index is $r - i \geq 1$. So x is a factor of all the terms in this bracket.
- After i differentiations the index in the term $a_i x^i$ becomes $i - i = 0$, so that this term becomes a constant. Successive derivatives of x^i are

$$i x^{i-1}, \quad i(i-1)x^{i-2}, \quad i(i-1)(i-2)x^{i-3}, \dots, \quad i(i-1)(i-2)\dots 1 x^0,$$

so $\dfrac{\mathrm{d}^i}{\mathrm{d}x^i}\left(a_i x^i\right) = a_i \times i!.$

Combining these, you find that

$$p_n^{(i)}(x) \equiv (0) + \left(a_i \times i!\right) + \left(\text{terms having a factor } x\right).$$

So, putting x equal to 0,

$$p_n^{(i)}(0) = 0 + a_i \times i! + 0 = a_i \times i!.$$

Now the aim is to make $p_n(x)$ agree with $f(x)$ to the nth degree at $x = 0$, that is

$$p_n^{(i)}(0) = f^{(i)}(0) \quad \text{for } i = 0,1,2,\dots,n.$$

So you must choose a_i so that

$$a_i \times i! = f^{(i)}(0).$$

That is, $a_i = \dfrac{f^{(i)}(0)}{i!}$, which is what you set out to prove.

Example 9.2.2
Find the Maclaurin polynomial of degree 4 for $f(x) = \cos x$.

Differentiating four times in succession,

$$f'(x) = -\sin x, \quad f''(x) = -\cos x, \quad f'''(x) = \sin x, \quad f^{(4)}(x) = \cos x.$$

So

$$f(0) = 1, \quad f'(0) = 0, \quad f''(0) = -1, \quad f'''(0) = 0, \quad f^{(4)}(0) = 1.$$

Using the equation in the shaded box with $n = 4$, the Maclaurin polynomial is

$$p_4(x) = 1 + \frac{0}{1!}x + \frac{-1}{2!}x^2 + \frac{0}{3!}x^3 + \frac{1}{4!}x^4$$
$$= 1 - \frac{1}{2}x^2 + \frac{1}{24}x^4.$$

Use a calculator to display the graphs of $y = \cos x$ and $y = p_4(x)$ with the same axes. Over what interval would you say that $p_4(x)$ is a good approximation to $\cos x$?

<hr>

Exercise 9A

1   For the following expressions $f(x)$ write down the partial sums $S_3(x)$ of the binomial series. Verify that $f(x)$ and $S_3(x)$ agree to the third degree at $x = 0$. Display graphs of $f(x)$ and $S_3(x)$ on a calculator, and estimate the interval over which you cannot distinguish between the graphs.

    (a) $(1+x)^{\frac{2}{3}}$ (b) $(1-x)^{-\frac{3}{2}}$

2   For the following expressions $f(x)$ find the Maclaurin polynomial $p_n(x)$ of the given degree n. Illustrate your answers by comparing the graphs of $f(x)$ and $p_n(x)$.

    (a) $\sin x, \quad n = 5$ (b) $\sin 2x, \quad n = 5$ (c) $e^x, \quad n = 4$

    (d) $e^{-3x}, \quad n = 4$ (e) $\sin^2 x, \quad n = 3$ (f) $\cos^2 x, \quad n = 3$

    (g) $\ln(1-x), \quad n = 4$ (h) $\dfrac{1}{\sqrt{1-2x}}, \quad n = 3$ (i) $e^{-\frac{1}{2}x^2}, \quad n = 4$

    (j) $\ln\!\left(1+x^2\right), \quad n = 4$

3   For the binomial series with $n = \frac{1}{2}$ in Section 9.1, use the multiplier from a_{i-1} to a_i to show that the radius of convergence is 1.

4   Show that it is possible to find numbers a and b such that $a + bx^2$ and $\sec x$ agree to degree 3 at $x = 0$.

5   Find the Maclaurin polynomial of degree 4 for $(1+x)^p$, where p is not a positive integer. Verify that this agrees with the first five terms of the binomial series for $(1+x)^p$.

<hr>

9.3 Maclaurin series and intervals of validity

The power series

$$f(0) + \frac{f'(0)}{1!}x + \frac{f''(0)}{2!}x^2 + \ldots + \frac{f^{(i)}(0)}{i!}x^i + \ldots,$$

continued indefinitely, is called the **Maclaurin series** of $f(x)$. The partial sums obtained by cutting off the series after the second, third, fourth, ... terms produce a sequence of Maclaurin polynomials $p_1(x)$, $p_2(x)$, $p_3(x)$, ...

Fig. 9.1, Fig. 9.2 and Fig. 9.3 showed how such a sequence of polynomials can give better and better approximations to $f(x)$ for certain values of x. In such cases you can say that $f(x)$ is the limit of the sequence of polynomial values as n tends to infinity. Thus

$$f(x) = \lim_{n \to \infty} p_n(x) = \lim_{n \to \infty} \sum_{i=0}^{n} \frac{f^{(i)}(0)}{i!} x^i, \quad \text{or} \quad \sum_{i=0}^{\infty} \frac{f^{(i)}(0)}{i!} x^i.$$

This means that, by taking n large enough, you can (for a particular value of x) make $p_n(x)$ as close as you like to $f(x)$.

For many functions this is true for some but not all values of x. For example, if $f(x) = \ln(1+x)$, then

$$f'(x) = (1+x)^{-1}, \quad f''(x) = -(1+x)^{-2}, \quad f'''(x) = 2(1+x)^{-3}, \quad \ldots,$$

so that

$$f'(0) = 1, \quad f''(0) = -1, \quad f'''(0) = 2, \quad \ldots \ .$$

The general term is positive when i is odd and negative when i is even. It is not difficult to check that

$$f^{(i)}(x) = (-1)^{i-1}(i-1)!(1+x)^{-i},$$

so that

$$\frac{f^{(i)}(0)}{i!} = \frac{(-1)^{i-1}(i-1)!}{i!} = (-1)^{i-1}\frac{1}{i}.$$

The Maclaurin series is therefore

$$\ln(1+x) = x - \tfrac{1}{2}x^2 + \tfrac{1}{3}x^3 - \tfrac{1}{4}x^4 + \ldots \ .$$

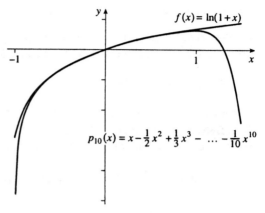

Fig. 9.4

Fig. 9.4 shows a comparison of the graphs of $\ln(1+x)$ and the 10th Maclaurin polynomial, ending with the term $-\tfrac{1}{10}x^{10}$. It is striking how closely the Maclaurin polynomial follows the function from just above -1 to just below 1, but that beyond 1 the two functions separate very sharply. However many terms you take, you can never get $p_n(x)$ to come close to $\ln(1+x)$ for $x > 1$.

Contrast this with the function $f(x) = \sin x$. Since the derivatives are successively

$$\cos x, \ -\sin x, \ -\cos x, \ \sin x, \ldots$$

and then repeat through the same cycle, the values of $f^{(i)}(0)$ are successively

$$1, \ 0, \ -1, \ 0, \ 1, \ 0, \ \ldots \ .$$

Also $f(0) = 0$. The Maclaurin series is therefore

$$\sin x = \frac{x}{1!} - \frac{x^3}{3!} + \frac{x^5}{5!} - \frac{x^7}{7!} + \ldots \ .$$

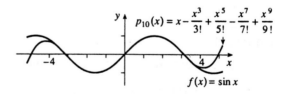

Fig. 9.5

Fig. 9.5 shows a comparison of the graphs of $\sin x$ and the 10th Maclaurin polynomial. (The last non-zero term of $p_{10}(x)$ is $\frac{x^9}{9!}$, because $f^{(10)}(0) = 0$.) You can see that already the graphs cannot be distinguished from each other by eye between about -4 and $+4$. And in fact, by taking enough terms, you can get a Maclaurin polynomial which fits the $\sin x$ graph over as wide an interval as you like.

The set of values of x for which the Maclaurin series can be made to fit a function, provided that enough terms are taken, is called the **interval of validity** of the series. For the function $\ln(1+x)$ the interval of validity is $-1 < x \le 1$; the series for $\sin x$ is valid for all real values of x, so its interval of validity is $\mathbb{R}$.

Obviously the interval of validity for a Maclaurin series can't be larger than the interval of convergence of the power series. In fact, the two intervals are generally the same, though this is not easy to prove. For example, the Maclaurin series for $\ln(1+x)$ has $|a_{i-1}| = \frac{1}{i-1}$ and $|a_i| = \frac{1}{i}$, so the radius of convergence is

$\lim\limits_{i\to\infty} \left| \frac{a_{i-1}}{a_i} \right| = \lim\limits_{i\to\infty} \frac{i}{i-1} = 1$. You know that the series is convergent when $x = 1$ but not when $x = -1$, so the interval of convergence is $-1 < x \leq 1$. This is the same as the interval of validity.

The only condition for a function to have a Maclaurin series is that $f(0)$ and all the derivatives $f^{(i)}(0)$ must be defined. So $\csc x$ and $\ln x$ do not have Maclaurin series, because they are not defined when $x = 0$; and $|x|$ does not have one, since $\frac{d}{dx}(|x|)$ is not defined when $x = 0$.

But many of the standard functions do have Maclaurin series, and the most important ones are listed below. Before reading on, you should check these for yourself; it is worth remembering the first few terms of each series, but not the expression for the general term.

Maclaurin series for some standard functions

$$e^x = 1 + \frac{x}{1!} + \frac{x^2}{2!} + \frac{x^3}{3!} + \ldots + \frac{x^i}{i!} + \ldots, \quad \text{for } x \in \mathbb{R}.$$

$$\sin x = \frac{x}{1!} - \frac{x^3}{3!} + \frac{x^5}{5!} - \frac{x^7}{7!} + \ldots + (-1)^i \frac{x^{2i+1}}{(2i+1)!} + \ldots, \quad \text{for } x \in \mathbb{R}.$$

$$\cos x = 1 - \frac{x^2}{2!} + \frac{x^4}{4!} - \frac{x^6}{6!} + \ldots + (-1)^i \frac{x^{2i}}{(2i)!} + \ldots, \quad \text{for } x \in \mathbb{R}.$$

$$\ln(1+x) = x - \tfrac{1}{2}x^2 + \tfrac{1}{3}x^3 - \tfrac{1}{4}x^4 + \ldots + (-1)^{i-1}\tfrac{1}{i}x^i + \ldots, \quad \text{for } -1 < x \leq 1.$$

$$(1+x)^p = 1 + px + \frac{p(p-1)}{2!}x^2 + \frac{p(p-1)(p-2)}{3!}x^3 + \ldots$$

$$+ \frac{p(p-1)(p-2)\ldots(p-(i-1))}{i!}x^i + \ldots, \quad \text{for } x \in \mathbb{R} \text{ if } p \in \mathbb{N},$$

otherwise for $-1 < x < 1$ (and, in some cases, also for $x = -1$ or $x = 1$).

Example 9.3.1

Use Maclaurin series to find e and $\frac{1}{e}$, correct to 4 decimal places.

You can evaluate these by substituting $x = 1$ and $x = -1$ in the series for e^x:

$$e = 1 + \frac{1}{1!} + \frac{1}{2!} + \frac{1}{3!} + \frac{1}{4!} + \ldots,$$

$$\frac{1}{e} = 1 - \frac{1}{1!} + \frac{1}{2!} - \frac{1}{3!} + \frac{1}{4!} - \ldots.$$

The calculation is very simple, since $(i+1)! = (i+1) \times i!$, so that you can find $\frac{1}{(i+1)!}$ by dividing $\frac{1}{i!}$ by $i+1$.

Table 9.6 lists values of $\frac{1}{i!}$ up to $r = 9$.

$1 = 1$	$\frac{1}{1!} = 1$
$\frac{1}{2!} = 0.5$	$\frac{1}{3!} = 0.166\,667$
$\frac{1}{4!} = 0.041\,667$	$\frac{1}{5!} = 0.008\,333$
$\frac{1}{6!} = 0.001\,389$	$\frac{1}{7!} = 0.000\,198$
$\frac{1}{8!} = 0.000\,025$	$\frac{1}{9!} = 0.000\,003$
1.543\,081	1.175\,201

Table 9.6

So $e \approx 1.543\,081 + 1.175\,201 \approx 2.7183,$

$\dfrac{1}{e} \approx 1.543\,081 - 1.175\,201 \approx 0.3679$, both correct to 4 decimal places.

Exercise 9B

1 Use Maclaurin series to find, correct to 4 decimal places, the values of
   (a) $\sqrt{e}$,   (b) $\sin 1$,   (c) $\sqrt[3]{0.9}$,   (d) $\cos 20°$,
   (e) $\ln 0.95$,   (f) $\ln 2.25$,   (g) $\cos 3$.

2 Find the Maclaurin series for $\ln\dfrac{1+x}{1-x}$, and state its interval of validity. By choosing a suitable value for x, calculate the value of $\ln 3$, correct to 3 decimal places.

   Why can't you find $\ln 3$ directly from the Maclaurin series for $\ln(1+x)$?

3 Find, as far as the term in x^4, Maclaurin series for
   (a) $\sec x$ (b) $\arctan x$.

   For each function, find the percentage error in using the Maclaurin series as an approximation when $x = 0.1$, correct to 2 significant figures.

4 An approximate value for π can be found by putting $x = \frac{1}{2}\pi$ in the Maclaurin series of $\cos x$ and neglecting all the terms of degree greater than 4, and then solving a quartic polynomial equation for π. How accurate is the approximation?

   An alternative method is to use the substitution $x = \frac{1}{3}\pi$. How accurate is the resulting approximation?

   Which method gives the better approximation? Suggest a reason why.

9.4 Modifying Maclaurin series

If you want to find the Maclaurin series for a function such as $\sin 5x$ or $\ln(1+x^2)$, you could use the general expression at the beginning of Section 9.3 with $f(x) = \sin 5x$ or $f(x) = \ln(1+x^2)$. This is quite easy for $\sin 5x$, since the derivatives are successively $5\cos 5x$, $-5^2 \sin 5x$, $-5^3 \cos 5x$, ... , whose values for $x = 0$ are 5, 0, -5^3, ... It is easy to see how this continues. The Maclaurin series then begins

$$\frac{5}{1!}x - \frac{5^3}{3!}x^3 + \frac{5^5}{5!}x^5 - \dots .$$

You can write this as

$$\frac{(5x)}{1!} - \frac{(5x)^3}{3!} + \frac{(5x)^5}{5!} - \dots ,$$

which is (as you would probably expect) what you would get by simply replacing x by $5x$ in the Maclaurin expansion for $\sin x$.

Differentiating $\ln(1+x^2)$ several times is a lot more difficult, and you might not recognise the general pattern. But, just as with $\sin 5x$, you can find the Maclaurin series by substitution, in this case by simply replacing x by x^2 in the Maclaurin series of $\ln(1+x)$. This gives

$$\ln(1+x^2) = (x^2) - \tfrac{1}{2}(x^2)^2 + \tfrac{1}{3}(x^2)^3 - \tfrac{1}{4}(x^2)^4 + \dots$$
$$= x^2 - \tfrac{1}{2}x^4 + \tfrac{1}{3}x^6 - \tfrac{1}{4}x^8 + \dots \ .$$

Since the series for $\ln(1+x)$ is valid when $-1 < x \leq 1$, this series is valid when $-1 < x^2 \leq 1$, that is when $-1 \leq x \leq 1$.

Sometimes it is worth using some special property of the function before finding the Maclaurin series, as in the following example.

Example 9.4.1
Find Maclaurin series for   (a) $\sin\left(x + \tfrac{1}{4}\pi\right)$,   (b) $\ln(2-4x)$.

(a)   By the addition formula, $\sin\left(x + \tfrac{1}{4}\pi\right) = \sin x \cos\tfrac{1}{4}\pi + \cos x \sin\tfrac{1}{4}\pi$.

Since $\sin\tfrac{1}{4}\pi = \cos\tfrac{1}{4}\pi = \dfrac{1}{\sqrt{2}}$,

$$\sin\left(x + \tfrac{1}{4}\pi\right) = \frac{1}{\sqrt{2}}(\sin x + \cos x)$$

$$= \frac{1}{\sqrt{2}}\left(\left(\frac{x}{1!} - \frac{x^3}{3!} + \frac{x^5}{5!} - \dots\right) + \left(1 - \frac{x^2}{2!} + \frac{x^4}{4!} - \dots\right)\right)$$

$$= \frac{1}{\sqrt{2}}\left(1 + \frac{x}{1!} - \frac{x^2}{2!} - \frac{x^3}{3!} + \frac{x^4}{4!} + \frac{x^5}{5!} - \dots\right).$$

(b)   Use the multiplication rule of logarithms to write

$$\ln(2-4x) = \ln 2 + \ln(1-2x).$$

Then use the Maclaurin series for $\ln(1+x)$, replacing x by $-2x$, to get

$$\ln(2-4x) = \ln 2 + (-2x) - \tfrac{1}{2}(-2x)^2 + \tfrac{1}{3}(-2x)^3 - \tfrac{1}{4}(-2x)^4 - \dots$$
$$= \ln 2 - 2x - 2x^2 - \tfrac{8}{3}x^3 - 4x^4 - \dots \ .$$

This is valid if $-1 < -2x \leq 1$, that is if $\dfrac{(-1)}{(-2)} > x \geq \dfrac{1}{(-2)}$, or $-\tfrac{1}{2} \leq x < \tfrac{1}{2}$.

Sometimes you want to find a Maclaurin series for a function which is the product of two simpler functions. Although you could do this by the usual Maclaurin method, finding the derivatives by the rule for differentiating a product, it is often simpler to expand the two functions separately as far as is needed and then to multiply the two polynomials together.

The next example compares the two methods.

Example 9.4.2

Find the Maclaurin series, as far as the term in x^4, for $f(x) = e^{2x} \cos 3x$

(a) by direct application of the Maclaurin series formula,

(b) by multiplying together the series for the separate factors.

(a)   Differentiating four times in succession, using the product rule,

$$f'(x) = 2e^{2x} \cos 3x + e^{2x}(-3 \sin 3x)$$
$$= e^{2x}(2 \cos 3x - 3 \sin 3x);$$

$$f''(x) = 2e^{2x}(2 \cos 3x - 3 \sin 3x) + e^{2x}(-6 \sin 3x - 9 \cos 3x)$$
$$= e^{2x}(-5 \cos 3x - 12 \sin 3x);$$

$$f'''(x) = 2e^{2x}(-5 \cos 3x - 12 \sin 3x) + e^{2x}(15 \sin 3x - 36 \cos 3x)$$
$$= e^{2x}(-46 \cos 3x - 9 \sin 3x);$$

$$f^{(4)}(x) = 2e^{2x}(-46 \cos 3x - 9 \sin 3x) + e^{2x}(138 \sin 3x - 27 \cos 3x)$$
$$= e^{2x}(-119 \cos 3x + 120 \sin 3x).$$

So $f(0) = 1, \quad f'(0) = 2, \quad f''(0) = -5, \quad f'''(0) = -46, \quad f^{(4)}(0) = -119.$

Using the formula in Section 9.3, the Maclaurin series as far as the term in x^4 is

$$e^{2x} \cos 3x = 1 + \frac{2}{1!}x + \frac{-5}{2!}x^2 + \frac{-46}{3!}x^3 + \frac{-119}{4!}x^4$$
$$= 1 + 2x - \frac{5}{2}x^2 - \frac{23}{3}x^3 - \frac{119}{24}x^4.$$

(b)   Using the standard series for e^x and $\cos x$, with x replaced by $2x$ and $3x$ respectively, gives

$$e^{2x} = 1 + \frac{(2x)}{1!} + \frac{(2x)^2}{2!} + \frac{(2x)^3}{3!} + \frac{(2x)^4}{4!} + \dots$$
$$= 1 + 2x + 2x^2 + \frac{4}{3}x^3 + \frac{2}{3}x^4 + \dots,$$

and

$$\cos 3x = 1 - \frac{(3x)^2}{2!} + \frac{(3x)^4}{4!} - \dots$$
$$= 1 - \frac{9}{2}x^2 + \frac{27}{8}x^4 - \dots .$$

So

$$e^{2x} \cos 3x = \left(1 + 2x + 2x^2 + \frac{4}{3}x^3 + \frac{2}{3}x^4 + \dots\right)\left(1 - \frac{9}{2}x^2 + \frac{27}{8}x^4 - \dots\right)$$
$$= 1 + 2x + \left(2 - \frac{9}{2}\right)x^2 + \left(\frac{4}{3} - 2 \times \frac{9}{2}\right)x^3 + \left(\frac{27}{8} - 2 \times \frac{9}{2} + \frac{2}{3}\right)x^4 + \dots$$
$$= 1 + 2x - \frac{5}{2}x^2 - \frac{23}{3}x^3 - \frac{119}{24}x^4,$$

as far as the term in x^4.

Example 9.4.3
Find the Maclaurin polynomial of degree 4 for $\ln\cos x$.

The function in this example involves two expansions. The work can be eased by discarding powers of x higher than x^4 as you go along.

$$\ln\cos x = \ln\left(1 - \frac{x^2}{2!} + \frac{x^4}{4!} - \dots\right)$$

$$= \ln\left(1 + \left(-\tfrac{1}{2}x^2 + \tfrac{1}{24}x^4 - \dots\right)\right)$$

$$= \left(-\tfrac{1}{2}x^2 + \tfrac{1}{24}x^4 - \dots\right) - \tfrac{1}{2}\left(-\tfrac{1}{2}x^2 + \tfrac{1}{24}x^4 - \dots\right)^2 + \dots$$

$$= \left(-\tfrac{1}{2}x^2 + \tfrac{1}{24}x^4\right) - \tfrac{1}{2}\left(\tfrac{1}{4}x^4\right) \text{ to degree 4}$$

$$= -\tfrac{1}{2}x^2 + \left(\tfrac{1}{24} - \tfrac{1}{8}\right)x^4 = -\tfrac{1}{2}x^2 - \tfrac{1}{12}x^4.$$

9.5   Differentiating and integrating series

Another way of obtaining series is to use differentiation and integration. Suppose for example that you want to find the function represented by the infinite series

$$S(x) = \frac{x}{1^2} + \frac{x^2}{2^2} + \frac{x^3}{3^2} + \dots + \frac{x^i}{i^2} + \dots \ .$$

If the series were a finite series, you could find the derivative by differentiating each term separately. Assuming that you can still do this with an infinite series, you would get

$$S'(x) = \frac{1}{1^2} + \frac{2x}{2^2} + \frac{3x^2}{3^2} + \dots + \frac{ix^{i-1}}{i^2} + \dots$$

$$= 1 + \frac{x}{2} + \frac{x^2}{3} + \dots + \frac{x^{i-1}}{i} + \dots \ .$$

You know the sum of this last series. If you substitute $-x$ for x in the series for $\ln(1+x)$, you get

$$\ln(1-x) = -x - \frac{x^2}{2} - \frac{x^3}{3} - \dots - \frac{x^i}{i} - \dots$$

$$= -x\left(1 + \frac{x}{2} + \frac{x^2}{3} + \dots + \frac{x^{i-1}}{i} + \dots\right),$$

which is $-xS'(x)$. So

$$S'(x) = -\frac{1}{x}\ln(1-x).$$

There are two ways you might continue from here. You could write $S(x)$ as an indefinite integral,

$$S(x) = \int -\frac{1}{x}\ln(1-x)\,dx,$$

remembering that you need an arbitrary constant to ensure that $S(0) = 0$. This would be fine if you knew an expression for the indefinite integral, but unfortunately you don't in this case.

So a better method is to write $S(x)$ as a definite integral,

$$S(x) = \int_0^x -\frac{1}{t} \ln(1-t)\, dt.$$

Taking the lower limit of integration to be 0 ensures that $S(0) = 0$. Although you can't get any further by expressing the integral in terms of known functions, you do at least have a definite expression for $S(x)$. You could, for example, now use the integration program on your calculator to find the value of the sum for a particular numerical value of x.

See the note in Section 4.1 about the use of the letter t rather than x inside the integral.

But is the process valid? The answer is 'yes, but with reservations'. One point to notice is that the interval of convergence for the original series $S(x)$ is $-1 \leq x \leq 1$, but the interval of convergence for the $\ln(1-x)$ series is only $-1 \leq x < 1$. So although the radius of convergence of both series is 1, there is a value of x on the boundary for which the original series converges but the differentiated series does not converge.

These features are true in general for power series.

> If a power series $\sum a_i x^i$ converges to $S(x)$ with radius of convergence R, then its differentiated series $\sum i a_i x^{i-1}$ converges to $S'(x)$ with the same radius of convergence. There may, however, be values of x such that $|x| = R$ for which the original series converges but the differentiated series does not converge.

This process is known as **term-by-term differentiation**.

Example 9.5.1
Write Maclaurin series, $M_2(x)$ and $M_3(x)$, for $(1+x)^{-2}$ and $(1+x)^{-3}$. Show that $M_3(x)$ could be obtained from $M_2(x)$ using term-by-term differentiation.

Using the series for $(1+x)^p$ in Section 9.3 with $p = -2$ and -3,

$$M_2(x) = 1 + \frac{(-2)}{1!}x + \frac{(-2)\times(-3)}{2!}x^2 + \dots + \frac{(-2)\times(-3)\times\dots\times(-i-1)}{i!}x^i + \dots$$
$$= 1 - 2x + 3x^2 - 4x^3 + \dots + (-1)^i(i+1)x^i + \dots,$$

$$M_3(x) = 1 + \frac{(-3)}{1!}x + \frac{(-3)\times(-4)}{2!}x^2 + \dots + \frac{(-3)\times(-4)\times\dots\times(-i-2)}{i!}x^i + \dots$$
$$= 1 - 3x + 6x^2 - 10x^3 + \dots + (-1)^i\frac{(i+1)(i+2)}{2}x^i + \dots.$$

Term-by-term differentiation of $M_2(x)$ gives

$$\frac{d}{dx}M_2(x) = -2 + 6x - 12x^2 + \ldots + (-1)^i i(i+1)x^{i-1} + \ldots$$

$$= -2\left(1 - 3x + 6x^2 - \ldots + (-1)^{i-1}\frac{i(i+1)}{2}x^{i-1} + \ldots\right).$$

To compare the general terms, replace $i-1$ by i. Then this becomes

$$\frac{d}{dx}M_2(x) = -2\left(1 - 3x + 6x^2 - \ldots + (-1)^i\frac{(i+1)(i+2)}{2}x^i + \ldots\right)$$

$$= -2M_3(x).$$

This is what you would expect, since $\frac{d}{dx}(1+x)^{-2} = -2(1+x)^{-3}$.

But term-by-term differentiation does not work for all series. For example, it can be proved that the series

$$\sin x - \tfrac{1}{2}\sin 2x + \tfrac{1}{3}\sin 3x - \ldots$$

is convergent with sum $\tfrac{1}{2}x$ in the interval $-\pi < x < \pi$. But the series of differentiated terms,

$$\cos x - \cos 2x + \cos 3x - \ldots$$

is not convergent because $\lim_{i\to\infty}\cos ix$ is not equal to 0. So you should not think that the statement in the shaded box is obvious; it has to be proved, though the proof is too difficult to give here.

Example 9.5.2

Find the Maclaurin series for $\arctan x$.

Since $\int_0^x \frac{1}{1+t^2}\,dt = [\arctan t]_0^x = \arctan x - \arctan 0 = \arctan x$, you can find the series for $\arctan x$ by integrating the terms of the binomial series for $\left(1+t^2\right)^{-1} = 1 - t^2 + t^4 - t^6 + \ldots$ from 0 to x.

That is,

$$\arctan x = x - \tfrac{1}{3}x^3 + \tfrac{1}{5}x^5 - \tfrac{1}{7}x^7 + \ldots$$

$$= \sum_{i=0}^{\infty}(-1)^i\frac{1}{2i+1}x^{2i+1}.$$

When you integrate a power series term-by-term, the interval of validity of the result may include more values than the original series. In Example 9.5.2, the binomial series for $\left(1+x^2\right)^{-1}$ is valid for $-1 < x < 1$, but the $\arctan x$ series is also valid when $x = \pm 1$. The value $x = 1$ produces the delightful (but not very useful) result

$$\tfrac{1}{4}\pi = 1 - \tfrac{1}{3} + \tfrac{1}{5} - \tfrac{1}{7} + \ldots \; .$$

Example 9.5.3

Use term-by-term integration of a Maclaurin series to find the value of $\dfrac{1}{\sqrt{2\pi}}\displaystyle\int_{-1}^{1} e^{-\frac{1}{2}t^2}\,dt$.

This integral is important in probability. It gives the probability that a normal random variable takes a value within one standard deviation of the mean.

Using the Maclaurin series for e^x with $x = -\frac{1}{2}t^2$,

$$e^{-\frac{1}{2}t^2} = 1 - \frac{1}{1!}\frac{t^2}{2} + \frac{1}{2!}\left(\frac{t^2}{2}\right)^2 - \ldots .$$

So

$$\int_0^1 e^{-\frac{1}{2}t^2}\,dt = \left[t - \frac{1}{2}\frac{t^3}{3} + \frac{1}{8}\frac{t^5}{5} - \frac{1}{48}\frac{t^7}{7} + \frac{1}{384}\frac{t^9}{9} - \frac{1}{3840}\frac{t^{11}}{11} + \ldots\right]_0^1$$

$$= 1 - \frac{1}{6} + \frac{1}{40} - \frac{1}{336} + \frac{1}{3456} - \frac{1}{42240} + \ldots = 0.85562\ldots .$$

Since $e^{-\frac{1}{2}t^2}$ is an even function, the integral from -1 to 1 is double the integral from 0 to 1. The probability required is therefore

$$\frac{1}{\sqrt{2\pi}} \times 2 \times 0.85562\ldots \approx 0.683, \text{ correct to 3 decimal places.}$$

9.6 Using series to find limits

A useful application of Maclaurin series is to find limits as $x \to 0$ of expressions of the form $\dfrac{f(x)}{g(x)}$ where both $f(0)$ and $g(0)$ are equal to 0. Then both $f(x)$ and $g(x)$ have x (or a power of x) as a factor. This can be cancelled so as to replace the expression by a function whose value can be calculated at $x = 0$.

Example 9.6.1

Find   (a) $\displaystyle\lim_{x \to 0} \frac{\sqrt{1+2x} - \sqrt{1+x}}{x}$,   (b) $\displaystyle\lim_{x \to 0} \frac{x(1 - \cos x)}{x - \sin x}$.

(a)   Using the Maclaurin series for $(1+x)^p$ with $p = \frac{1}{2}$,

$$\sqrt{1+x} = 1 + \tfrac{1}{2}x - \tfrac{1}{8}x^2 + \ldots .$$

Also, substituting $2x$ for x,

$$\sqrt{1+2x} = 1 + \tfrac{1}{2}(2x) - \tfrac{1}{8}(2x)^2 + \ldots$$
$$= 1 + x - \tfrac{1}{2}x^2 + \ldots .$$

So $\sqrt{1+2x} - \sqrt{1+x} = \tfrac{1}{2}x - \tfrac{3}{8}x^2 + \ldots$,

and $\dfrac{\sqrt{1+2x} - \sqrt{1+x}}{x} = \tfrac{1}{2} - \tfrac{3}{8}x + \ldots .$

Therefore $\displaystyle\lim_{x \to 0} \frac{\sqrt{1+2x} - \sqrt{1+x}}{x} = \lim_{x \to 0}\left(\tfrac{1}{2} - \tfrac{3}{8}x + \ldots\right) = \tfrac{1}{2}.$

(b)   Using the Maclaurin series for $\cos x$ and $\sin x$,

$$\lim_{x \to 0} \frac{x(1 - \cos x)}{x - \sin x} = \lim_{x \to 0} \frac{x\left(1 - \left(1 - \frac{1}{2}x^2 + \frac{1}{24}x^4 - \ldots\right)\right)}{x - \left(x - \frac{1}{6}x^3 + \frac{1}{120}x^5 - \ldots\right)}$$

$$= \lim_{x \to 0} \frac{\frac{1}{2}x^3 - \frac{1}{24}x^5 + \ldots}{\frac{1}{6}x^3 - \frac{1}{120}x^5 + \ldots}$$

$$= \lim_{x \to 0} \frac{\frac{1}{2} - \frac{1}{24}x^2 + \ldots}{\frac{1}{6} - \frac{1}{120}x^2 + \ldots}$$

$$= \frac{\frac{1}{2}}{\frac{1}{6}} = 3.$$

Exercise 9C

1   Each of the following expressions $f(x)$ can be written as $g(h(x))$, where g is one of the functions whose Maclaurin series is listed in Section 9.3. Expand $f(x)$ as far as the term in x^4 by two methods: (i) by finding $f^{(r)}(x)$ for $r = 1, 2, 3, 4$ and using the general formula for a Maclaurin series, and (ii) by substituting $h(x)$ in place of x in the series for $g(x)$. Verify that both methods give the same answer.

(a) $f(x) = (1 + 2x)^{\frac{3}{2}}$ $\qquad$ (b) $f(x) = e^{-2x}$

(c) $f(x) = \ln(1 + x^3)$ $\qquad$ (d) $f(x) = \sin x^3$

2   Write the Maclaurin series for the following, in each case giving the first three non-zero terms, an expression for the general term and the interval of validity.

(a) e^{3x} $\qquad$ (b) $\cos \frac{1}{2}x$ $\qquad$ (c) $\sqrt{x} \sin \sqrt{x}$ $\qquad$ (d) $\ln(1 - x)$

(e) $\ln(1 + 2x)$ $\qquad$ (f) e^{1+x} $\qquad$ (g) $\cos^2 x$ $\qquad$ (h) $\ln(e + x)$

(i) $\cos(1 + x)$

3   Find the Maclaurin series for the following functions as far as the term in x^4.

(a) $e^{-x} \sin x$ $\qquad$ (b) $\sqrt{1 - x} \cos x$ $\qquad$ (c) $\dfrac{e^x}{1 + x}$

(d) $(1 + x)^2 \ln(1 + x)$ $\qquad$ (e) $e^{-2x} \ln(1 + 3x)$ $\qquad$ (f) $\ln(1 - 2x) \sin 3x$

4   Find the Maclaurin polynomials of degree 4 for the following.

(a) $\cos(\sin x)$ $\qquad$ (b) $\ln(1 + e^x)$

5   Use the property $\arcsin x = \displaystyle\int_0^x \frac{1}{\sqrt{1 - t^2}}\, dt$ to find the Maclaurin series for $\arcsin x$. Hence find the series for $\arccos x$. By taking $x = \frac{1}{2}$, use your Maclaurin series to find the value of π, correct to 4 decimal places.

6   A function called the *sine integral* is defined by $\mathrm{Si}\,(x) = \int_0^x \frac{\sin u}{u}\,du$. Find the Maclaurin series for $\mathrm{Si}\,(x)$, and use this to obtain the graph of $y = \mathrm{Si}\,(x)$ for $x > 0$.

7   Find the Maclaurin series for $\int_0^x \frac{e^t - 1}{t}\,dt$. Hence evaluate $\int_0^{\frac{1}{2}} \frac{e^t - 1}{t}\,dt$, correct to 3 decimal places.

8   Show that, if you assume that a function can be differentiated by differentiating each term of its Maclaurin series, you get correct results for

   (a) $\dfrac{d}{dx}e^x$,   (b) $\dfrac{d}{dx}\sin x$,   (c) $\dfrac{d}{dx}\ln(1+x)$,   (d) $\dfrac{d}{dx}\sqrt{1+x}$.

9   Use the standard Maclaurin series to find the first two non-zero terms in the series for $x\cos x - \sin x$. Hence find the limit, as $x \to 0$, of $\dfrac{x\cos x - \sin x}{x^3}$.

10   Find the limit, as $x \to 0$, of

   (a) $\dfrac{e^x - e^{-x}}{x}$,   (b) $\dfrac{1 - \cos x}{x^2}$,   (c) $\dfrac{\ln(1+x)}{x}$,   (d) $\dfrac{\ln(1+x) - x}{x^2}$.

11*   The following construction is suggested to trisect a given angle θ. Make a triangle ABC with angle BAC equal to θ and angle ABC a right angle. Divide the side [BC] into three equal parts at X and Y, so that $\mathrm{BX} = \mathrm{XY} = \mathrm{YC}$. Then angle XAY is approximately $\frac{1}{3}\theta$.

   Prove that angle XAY is exactly $\arctan\!\left(\frac{2}{3}\tan\theta\right) - \arctan\!\left(\frac{1}{3}\tan\theta\right)$. Find the Maclaurin polynomial of degree 3 for this function, and use this to estimate the greatest value of θ for which the construction is accurate to within 5%.

12   A power series $S(x) = \sum\limits_{i=0}^{\infty} a_i x^i$ has radius of convergence $R = \lim\limits_{i\to\infty}\left|\dfrac{a_{i-1}}{a_i}\right|$. Prove that the derivative series $S'(x) = \sum\limits_{i=1}^{\infty} i a_i x^{i-1}$ also has radius of convergence R.

10 The error term

This chapter gives two formulae for the truncation error when a Maclaurin polynomial is used to find an approximation to the value of a function. When you have completed it, you should

- be familiar with the integral and the Lagrange expressions for the error term
- understand how the error term can be used to determine the interval of validity of a Maclaurin series.

10.1 Approximation by a Maclaurin polynomial

In Chapter 9 you used Maclaurin polynomials to find approximations to the values of functions such as e^x and $\sin x$. But an approximation is not much use unless you have some idea of the size of the error, which is defined by the equation

$$\text{error} = \text{exact value} - \text{approximate value}.$$

You can't of course find the error exactly, because if you did you would know the exact value of the function, and there would be no point in calculating the approximation. So what is wanted is a statement like 'if you use the nth Maclaurin polynomial as an approximation to $f(x)$ for a particular value of x, the error is not greater than such-and-such'.

So you have a function $f(x)$ represented by a Maclaurin series

$$f(x) = \sum_{i=0}^{\infty} \frac{f^{(i)}(0)}{i!} x^i,$$

and you approximate to it by the nth Maclaurin polynomial, or partial sum,

$$p_n(x) = \sum_{i=0}^{n} \frac{f^{(i)}(0)}{i!} x^i.$$

These differ by an amount called the **error term**, or the **remainder**, denoted by $R_n(x)$, so that

$$f(x) = p_n(x) + R_n(x).$$

The problem is to find an expression for $R_n(x)$ in terms of the function f and the numbers x and n.

Up to now, when working with power series, you have treated x as a variable, but in this chapter it is helpful to think of x as a fixed number, and to introduce a new variable t. The function $y = f(t)$ will then be considered in the interval $0 \le t \le x$. Fig. 10.1 shows its graph passing through the points with coordinates $(0, f(0))$ and $(x, f(x))$.

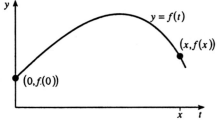

Fig. 10.1

It will be assumed that the function $f(t)$ is a 'well-behaved' function with no discontinuities in the interval $[0, x]$, for which it is possible to find as many higher derivatives $f^{(i)}(t)$ as you need.

The figure is drawn with $x > 0$, but the theory in this chapter also applies when $x < 0$.

10.2 The integral form

Begin with the very simplest case, with $n = 0$, so that $p_0(x)$ is just the constant term $f(0)$, and

$$f(x) = p_0(x) + R_0(x) = f(0) + R_0(x).$$

So $R_0(x) = f(x) - f(0).$

One way of writing the right side is as $[f(t)]_0^x$, which is the value of the definite integral $\int_0^x f'(t)\,dt$. You are going to find successive values of the error term $R_n(x)$ using integration by parts.

This may seem an odd suggestion, since the integrand $f'(t)$ is not the product of two functions. But you met a similar situation in Higher Level Book 2 Section 22.1, where $\int \ln x\,dx$ was found by writing the integrand $\ln x$ as $\ln x \times 1$. In just the same way you could write

$$R_0(x) = \int_0^x f'(t) \times 1\,dt,$$

and use integration by parts with $u = f'(t)$ and taking for v a function such that $\dfrac{dv}{dt} = 1$.

You now come to the ingenious part of the argument, which is to choose for v not the obvious function $v = t$, but to take $v = -(x - t)$. (Remember that x is being treated as a constant.) Then

$$R_0(x) = [f'(t) \times (-(x-t))]_0^x - \int_0^x f''(t) \times (-(x-t))\,dt$$

$$= f'(x) \times (-0) - f'(0) \times (-x) - \int_0^x -f''(t) \times (x-t)\,dt$$

$$= f'(0)x + \int_0^x f''(t) \times (x-t)\,dt.$$

Now recall that $R_0(x)$ is equal to $f(x) - f(0)$, so this equation can be written as

$$f(x) = \{f(0) + f'(0)x\} + \int_0^x f''(t) \times (x-t)\,dt.$$

You will recognise the expression in the curly brackets – it is just the Maclaurin polynomial $p_1(x)$. And since by definition $f(x) = p_1(x) + R_1(x)$, the integral on the right side must be the error term $R_1(x)$.

This looks promising, so try repeating the process with $R_1(x)$ rather than $R_0(x)$. If you integrate by parts again, with $u = f''(t)$ and $v = -\frac{1}{2}(x-t)^2$, so that $\dfrac{dv}{dt} = x - t$, you get

$$R_1(x) = \left[f''(t) \times \left(-\tfrac{1}{2}(x-t)^2\right)\right]_0^x - \int_0^x f'''(t) \times \left(-\tfrac{1}{2}(x-t)^2\right)dt$$

$$= \frac{f''(0)}{2}x^2 + \int_0^x \frac{f'''(t)}{2} \times (x-t)^2\,dt.$$

That is,

$$f(x) = \left\{ f(0) + f'(0)x + \frac{f''(0)}{2}x^2 \right\} + \int_0^x \frac{f'''(t)}{2} \times (x-t)^2 \, dt.$$

The expression in curly brackets is now the Maclaurin polynomial $p_2(x)$, so the integral is the error term $R_2(x)$.

If you go on like this you can reach a similar equation for any value of n.

The function $f(x)$ can be expressed as the sum of the nth Maclaurin polynomial

$$p_n(x) = f(0) + f'(0)x + \frac{f''(0)}{2!}x^2 + \ldots + \frac{f^{(n)}(0)}{n!}x^n$$

and an error term

$$R_n(x) = \int_0^x \frac{f^{(n+1)}(t)}{n!} \times (x-t)^n \, dt.$$

The way in which this was obtained by going from $n = 0$ to $n = 1$, and then from $n = 1$ to $n = 2$, suggests that the general result could be proved by mathematical induction. You would begin by assuming the expression for $p_n(x)$ and R_n with $n = k$, and then use integration by parts to show that

$$\int_0^x \frac{f^{(k+1)}(t)}{k!} \times (x-t)^k \, dt = \frac{f^{(k+1)}(0)}{(k+1)!}x^{k+1} + \int_0^x \frac{f^{(k+2)}(t)}{(k+1)!} \times (x-t)^{k+1} \, dt.$$

On the right the first term is the final term of $p_n(x)$ with $n = k+1$ and the integral is R_{k+1}. The details are left for you to verify.

10.3 The Lagrange form

There are drawbacks in using the integral form of the error term. For one thing, although the expression is exact its use is limited, since the integral can't be evaluated. It is not even obvious that its value is small, or that $p_n(x)$ is an increasingly good approximation to $f(x)$.

The form for the error term described in this section, known as Lagrange's form, is based directly on the idea of polynomial approximation. The idea is to try to find the polynomial of a given degree which agrees with $y = f(t)$ to the highest possible degree at $t = 0$ but whose graph also passes through the point $(x, f(x))$.

The proof depends on an idea which is very easy to understand (though not to prove!), illustrated in Fig. 10.2. This is that, if you have a function $\phi(t)$ for which $\phi(a)$ and $\phi(b)$ are both 0, then somewhere in the interval $a < x < b$ there is a number c for which $\phi'(c) = 0$. (There may of course be more than one such number.) This is known as Rolle's theorem.

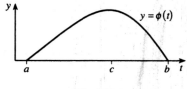

Fig. 10.2

Michel Rolle was a French mathematician at the end of the 17th century. His theorem appeared in a book on solving polynomial equations. Joseph-Louis Lagrange was probably the greatest French mathematician of the 18th century.

Turn back to Fig. 10.1 in Section 10.1. The simplest polynomial which approximates to $y = f(t)$ at $t = 0$ and also passes through $(x, f(x))$ is a linear polynomial $q_0(t) = a_0 + a_1 t$. There are two coefficients available, which can be chosen from two equations; you can make $q_0(0) = f(0)$ and $q_0(x) = f(x)$. So

$$f(0) = a_0 \quad \text{and} \quad f(x) = a_0 + a_1 x.$$

Fig. 10.3 shows the graphs of $y = f(t)$ and $y = q_0(t)$. The amount by which the first graph exceeds the second is denoted by $g_0(t)$. That is, $g_0(t) = f(t) - q_0(t)$.

The graph of $y = g_0(t)$ is shown in Fig. 10.4. You will see that it is similar to Fig. 10.2, with $g_0(t)$ in place of $\phi(t)$. Since $g_0(0) = 0$ and $g_0(x) = 0$, there is a number c_1 between 0 and x at which $g_0'(c_1) = 0$. That is,

$$f'(c_1) = q_0'(c_1) = a_1.$$

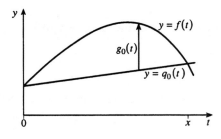

Fig. 10.3

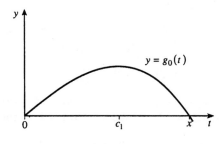

Fig. 10.4

Now combine this with the two equations for a_0 and a_1 above. Substituting $a_0 = f(0)$ and $a_1 = f'(c_1)$ in the equation $f(x) = a_0 + a_1 x$,

$$f(x) = f(0) + f'(c_1)x.$$

You may just recognise a slight resemblance to the Maclaurin series. You can get closer to it by taking a quadratic polynomial $q_1(t) = a_0 + a_1 t + a_2 t^2$ in place of $q_0(t)$.

You now have another coefficient at your disposal, so you can make the polynomial $q_1(t)$ satisfy another condition. To make it agree better with $y = f(t)$ at $t = 0$, you can choose the coefficients so that, as well as $q_1(0) = f(0)$ and $q_1(x) = f(x)$, the derivatives at 0 are equal, that is $q_1'(0) = f'(0)$. This is illustrated in Fig. 10.5.

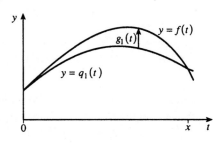

Fig. 10.5

You now have three equations for the coefficients of $q_1(t)$:

$$f(0) = a_0, \quad f'(0) = a_1 \quad \text{and} \quad f(x) = a_0 + a_1 x + a_2 x^2.$$

As before, define a function to represent the amount by which $f(t)$ exceeds $q_1(t)$, writing $g_1(t) = f(t) - q_1(t)$. Its graph is shown in Fig. 10.6. You will notice that it has the same two properties as $g_0(t)$, that $g_0(0) = 0$ and $g_0(x) = 0$. But, because $q_1'(0) = f'(0)$, it also has the additional property that $g_1'(0) = 0$.

This makes it possible to use Rolle's theorem twice. First, as before taking $\phi(t)$ to be $g_1(t)$, there is a number c_1 between 0 and x at which $g_1'(c_1) = 0$. (This isn't of course the same c_1 as before; compare Fig. 10.6 with Fig. 10.4.)

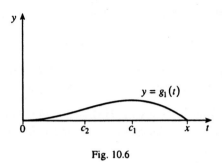

Then, since both $g_1'(0)$ and $g_1'(c_1) = 0$, you can use Rolle's theorem a second time taking $\phi(t)$ to be $g_1'(t)$. The conclusion is that there is a number c_2 between 0 and c_1 (and therefore between 0 and x) at which $g_1''(c_2) = 0$. That is,

Fig. 10.6

$$f''(c_2) = q_1''(c_2) = 2a_2.$$

Now combine this with the three equations for a_0, a_1 and a_2 above. Substituting $a_0 = f(0)$, $a_1 = f'(0)$ and $a_2 = \frac{1}{2} f''(c_2)$ in the equation for $f(x)$, you get

$$f(x) = f(0) + f'(0)x + \tfrac{1}{2} f''(c_2)x^2.$$

Now it is easy to see Maclaurin's series emerging. The first two terms on the right make up the Maclaurin polynomial $p_1(x)$, and the last term is the error term $R_1(x)$.

This is a special case with $n = 1$ of a general result.

> The function $f(x)$ can be expressed as the sum of the nth Maclaurin polynomial
>
> $$p_n(x) = f(0) + f'(0)x + \frac{f''(0)}{2!} x^2 + \ldots + \frac{f^{(n)}(0)}{n!} x^n$$
>
> and an error term
>
> $$R_n(x) = \frac{f^{(n+1)}(c)}{(n+1)!} x^{n+1}, \quad \text{where } c \text{ is a number between 0 and } x.$$
>
> This form of the error term is known as Lagrange's form.

To prove this, you would define a polynomial function $q_n(t) = a_0 + a_1 t + \ldots + a_{n+1} t^{n+1}$ which agrees with $f(t)$ to the nth degree at 0 and such that $q_n(x) = f(x)$. Then $g_n(t) = f(t) - q_n(t)$ would have $g_n(0) = g_n'(0) = g_n''(0) = \ldots = g_n^{(n)}(0) = 0$ and also $g_n(x) = 0$. Then apply Rolle's theorem $n + 1$ times and find a sequence of numbers $c_1, c_2, \ldots, c_{n+1}$ at which $g_n'(c_1) = 0, g_n''(c_2) = 0, g_n^{(n+1)}(c_{n+1}) = 0$, and this last equation would be shown to be $f^{(n+1)}(c_{n+1}) = (n+1)! a_{n+1}$. All of this is a direct extension of the proof given above with $n = 1$; the algebra looks more complicated, but the ideas are just the same. (In the shaded box the suffix has been dropped from c_{n+1}; it is useful in the proof to make the notation consistent, but there is no point in keeping it when you apply the result.)

Example 10.3.1
Give the error term if the nth Maclaurin polynomial is used as an approximation for $f(x) = e^x$ for $x > 0$,
(a) in the integral form,   (b) in the Lagrange form.
Use this to find an upper bound for the relative error in using the 4th Maclaurin polynomial to estimate the value of $e^{0.2}$.

Since $f'(x) = e^x$, it follows that $f^{(i)}(x) = e^x$ for all $i \in \mathbb{Z}^+$. So the error term $R_n(x)$ can be written as

$$(a) \quad \int_0^x \frac{e^t}{n!}(x-t)^n \, dt, \qquad \text{or as} \qquad (b) \quad \frac{e^c}{(n+1)!} x^{n+1}, \text{ where } 0 < c < x.$$

You might think that you could find the integral in part (a) by integrating by parts, but if you try you will just get back to the equation $e^x = e^x$!

To use the formula to estimate an error you need to find an inequality for $R_n(x)$. For $0 < t < x$, $(x-t)^n$ is positive and $e^t < e^x$, so

$$0 < e^t(x-t)^n < e^x(x-t)^n.$$

Therefore

$$0 < R_n(x) < \int_0^x \frac{e^x}{n!}(x-t)^n \, dt$$

$$= \frac{e^x}{n!} \times \int_0^x (x-t)^n \, dt$$

$$= \frac{e^x}{n!} \times \left[-\frac{1}{n+1}(x-t)^{n+1} \right]_0^x$$

$$= \frac{e^x}{(n+1)!} x^{n+1}.$$

You get just the same inequality if you use the Lagrange formula. The only thing you know about the number c is that it is between 0 and x, so that $e^c < e^x$ since $x > 0$. This again gives the inequality

$$0 < R_n(x) < \frac{e^x}{(n+1)!} x^{n+1}.$$

With $x = 0.2$ and $n = 4$,

$$0 < R_4(0.2) < \frac{e^{0.2}}{5!} \times 0.2^5$$

$$= e^{0.2} \times 2.67 \times 10^{-6}.$$

You might think that this is not much use, since the purpose of using the Maclaurin polynomial in the first place is to calculate the value of $e^{0.2}$. But what it does do is to give an upper bound for the *relative* error, that is the error as a proportion of the exact value. The equation shows that the relative error is less than 2.67×10^{-6}. (This is often given as a percentage, as $2.67 \times 10^{-4}\%$, or about 0.0003%.)

10.4 The interval of validity of Maclaurin series

The sum of an infinite series is defined as the limit of the sum of the first n terms (or the first $n+1$, if $i=0$ is included). That is, the difference between the sum of the infinite series and the finite sum is always smaller than any positive number ε when n is greater than some number m.

So when you say that $f(x)$ is the sum of an infinite Maclaurin series for a certain value of x, and write

$$f(x) = p_n(x) + R_n(x),$$

you are in effect stating that the limit as $n \to \infty$ of the error term $R_n(x)$ is 0.

Now that you have expressions for $R_n(x)$ you can use these to find the values of x for which the Maclaurin series is valid (the interval of validity). The examples in this section demonstrate the method for the two functions in Section 9.3 illustrated by the graphs in Fig. 9.5 and Fig. 9.4 respectively.

Example 10.4.1

Prove that the Maclaurin series for $\sin x$ is valid for all values of x.

If $f(x) = \sin x$, the derivatives are successively $\cos x, -\sin x, -\cos x, \sin x, \dots$. So for any value of r and any value of x you can be certain that $\left| f^{(r)}(x) \right| \le 1$.

The Lagrange formula for the error term is $R_n(x) = \dfrac{f^{(n+1)}(c)}{(n+1)!} x^{n+1}$. For any particular values of x and n you don't know the value of c, but you do know that $\left| f^{(n+1)}(c) \right| \le 1$, and therefore that

$$\left| R_n(x) \right| \le \frac{\left| x^{n+1} \right|}{(n+1)!} = \frac{|x|^{n+1}}{(n+1)!}.$$

If you can prove that this tends to 0 for all x, then it will follow that the Maclaurin series is valid for all x.

Before giving a general proof of this, it may help to consider a numerical example, such as $x = \pi$. Then you could write

$$\frac{\pi^{n+1}}{(n+1)!} \quad \text{as} \quad \frac{\pi \times \pi \times \pi \times \dots \times \pi}{1 \times 2 \times 3 \times \dots \times (n+1)} = \left(\frac{\pi \times \pi \times \pi}{1 \times 2 \times 3} \right) \times \left(\frac{\pi}{4} \times \frac{\pi}{5} \times \dots \times \frac{\pi}{n+1} \right).$$

The first bracket is the same whatever value you take for n, and all the $(n-2)$ factors in the second bracket except the first are less than $\frac{\pi}{4}$. So

$$\frac{\pi^{n+1}}{(n+1)!} < \frac{\pi^3}{3!} \times \left(\frac{\pi}{4} \right)^{n-2} = \frac{\pi^3}{3!} \div \left(\frac{\pi}{4} \right)^2 \times \left(\frac{\pi}{4} \right)^n,$$

which has the form, constant $\times a^n$, where $0 < a < 1$.

Then, for the general proof, you can do the same with any value of $\left| x \right|$. If K is the positive integer such that $K - 1 \le \left| x \right| < K$, you can write

$$\frac{|x|^{n+1}}{(n+1)!} \quad \text{as} \quad \left(\frac{|x| \times |x| \times |x| \times \dots \times |x|}{1 \times 2 \times \dots \times (K-1)}\right) \times \left(\frac{|x|}{K} \times \frac{|x|}{K+1} \times \dots \times \frac{|x|}{n+1}\right),$$

so

$$\frac{|x|^{n+1}}{(n+1)!} < \frac{|x|^{K-1}}{(K-1)!} \times \left(\frac{|x|}{K}\right)^{n-K+2} = \frac{|x|^{K-1}}{(K-1)!} \div \left(\frac{|x|}{K}\right)^{K-2} \times \left(\frac{|x|}{K}\right)^{n},$$

which again has the form, constant $\times a^n$, where $0 < a < 1$. And since $\lim_{n \to \infty} a^n = 0$ when $0 < a < 1$,

it follows that $\lim_{n \to \infty} \dfrac{|x|^{n+1}}{(n+1)!} = 0$, so that $\lim_{n \to \infty} R_n(x) = 0$.

That is, the Maclaurin series for $\sin x$ is valid for all values of x.

Example 10.4.2

Prove that the Maclaurin series for $\ln(1+x)$ is valid   (a) for $0 < x \le 1$,   (b) for $-1 < x < 0$.

(a)   If $f(x) = \ln(1+x)$, then

$$f'(x) = \frac{1}{1+x}, \quad f''(x) = \frac{-1}{(1+x)^2}, \quad f'''(x) = \frac{2}{(1+x)^3}, \quad \dots \quad , f^{(n+1)}(x) = \frac{(-1)^n \times n!}{(1+x)^{n+1}}.$$

So, in Lagrange's form,

$$R_n(x) = \frac{(-1)^n \times n!}{(1+c)^{n+1} \times (n+1)!} \times x^{n+1} = (-1)^n \times \frac{x^{n+1}}{(1+c)^{n+1} \times (n+1)}.$$

You want to prove that $\lim_{n \to \infty} |R_n(x)| = 0$ when $0 < x \le 1$.

Look first at the factor $(1+c)^{n+1}$. All that you know about the number c is that it is between 0 and x. Since $x > 0$, this means that $c > 0$, so that $1 + c > 1$.

Therefore $(1+c)^{n+1} > 1$ and, since $x \le 1$, $\left| x^{n+1} \right| \le 1$, so

$$|R_n(x)| < \frac{1}{n+1}.$$

And since $\lim_{n \to \infty} \dfrac{1}{n+1} = 0$, it follows that $\lim_{n \to \infty} R_n(x) = 0$. That is, the Maclaurin series for $\ln(1+x)$ is valid for $0 < x \le 1$.

(b)   The proof in part (a) cannot be used if x is negative, since then c is negative, so that $1 + c$ is not greater than 1.

It is easier to work with positive rather than negative numbers, so substitute $-x$ for x and consider the Maclaurin series for $f(x) = -\ln(1-x)$, which is

$$f(x) = x + \tfrac{1}{2}x^2 + \tfrac{1}{3}x^3 + \dots, \quad \text{where } 0 < x < 1.$$

For this function,

$$f'(x) = \frac{1}{1-x}, \quad f''(x) = \frac{1}{(1-x)^2}, \quad f'''(x) = \frac{2}{(1-x)^3}, \quad \dots, \quad f^{(n+1)}(x) = \frac{n!}{(1-x)^{n+1}}.$$

It is simpler to use the integral form for $R_n(x)$, which is

$$R_n(x) = \int_0^x \frac{n!}{(1-t)^{n+1} \times n!} (x-t)^n \, dt$$

$$= \int_0^x \frac{(x-t)^n}{(1-t)^{n+1}} \, dt$$

$$= \int_0^x \left(\frac{x-t}{1-t}\right)^n \times \frac{1}{1-t} \, dt.$$

Notice that, in the interval $0 < t < x$, $x - t > 0$ and $1 - t > 1 - x > 0$, so the integrand is positive. Therefore $R_n(x) > 0$.

To find an upper bound for $R_n(x)$, consider the function $g(t) = \dfrac{x-t}{1-t}$ whose graph is shown in Fig. 10.7. The important things to notice are that $g(0) = x$, $g(x) = 0$ and that the function is decreasing in the interval $0 < t < x$. Therefore, in this interval,

$$0 < \frac{x-t}{1-t} < x,$$

so the integrand is less than $x^n \times \dfrac{1}{1-t}$.

Therefore

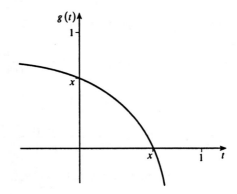

Fig. 10.7

$$0 < R_n(x) < \int_0^x x^n \times \frac{1}{1-t} \, dt$$

$$= x^n \times [-\ln(1-t)]_0^x$$

$$= -x^n \ln(1-x).$$

This is all you need. Since $0 < x < 1$, $\lim_{n \to \infty} x^n = 0$, and $-\ln(1-x)$ is a positive constant. So $\lim_{n \to \infty} R_n(x) = 0$, which means that the Maclaurin series is valid.

10.5   Other ways of finding errors

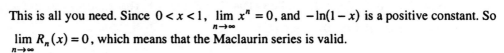

The advantage of the formulae for the error terms in Sections 10.2 and 10.3 is that they can be used with any function $f(x)$. But they are not the only way to find truncation errors. For some functions simpler methods are available.

Suppose, for example, that a power series has alternately positive and negative signs for some values of x, and that the terms are decreasing in absolute value. Then you can use the property of alternating series in Section 6.1, that the size of the error in taking the sum to n terms as an approximation to the sum to infinity is less than the absolute value of the next term.

Example 10.5.1
How many terms of the Maclaurin series for $\cos x$ would you need to take to find the value of $\cos 6$ with an error less than 10^{-4} in absolute value, using   (a) $x = 6$,   (b) $x = 2\pi - 6$?

(a)   With $x = 6$ the first few terms of the series increase in absolute value:

$$1 - \frac{6^2}{2!} + \frac{6^4}{4!} - \frac{6^6}{6!} + \ldots = 1 - 18 + 54 - 64.8 + \ldots .$$

But beyond the term $-\dfrac{6^6}{6!}$ they begin to decrease. And since $\dfrac{|x|^n}{n!}$ tends to 0 for any x (which was proved in Example 10.4.1) the alternating series property can then be used to find an upper bound for the error.

The nth term of the Maclaurin series for $\cos x$ is $(-1)^{n-1} \dfrac{x^{2n-2}}{(2n-2)!}$. So the error in using the first n terms as an approximation to $\cos x$ is less in magnitude than the $(n+1)$th term, which has absolute value $\dfrac{x^{2n}}{(2n)!}$. With $x = 6$, you want the smallest value of n for which $\dfrac{6^{2n}}{(2n)!} < 10^{-4}$, that is

$$(2n)! > 10\,000 \times 6^{2n}.$$

You can't solve this inequality algebraically, so n must be found by numerical experiment:

n	10	11	12
$(2n)!$	$2.43\ldots \times 10^{18}$	$1.12\ldots \times 10^{21}$	$6.20\ldots \times 10^{23}$
$10\,000 \times 6^{2n}$	$3.65\ldots \times 10^{19}$	$1.31\ldots \times 10^{21}$	$4.73\ldots \times 10^{22}$

You must take 12 terms of the series to be sure of finding $\cos 6$ with an error less than 10^{-4}.

(b)   With $x = 2\pi - 6 = 0.283\ldots$ the terms decrease in absolute value from the start. So you want the smallest value of n for which

$$(2n)! > 10\,000 \times (2\pi - 6)^{2n}.$$

By numerical experiment the smallest value of n is 3. You must take 3 terms of the series to be sure of finding $\cos 6$ with an error less than 10^{-4}.

Notice how much work can be saved by calculating $\cos 6$ with $x = 2\pi - 6$ rather than $x = 6$.

Another method that can sometimes be used is to integrate or differentiate a series for which an exact form for the error is known. For example, from the formula for the sum of a finite geometric series,

$$1 + x + x^2 + \ldots + x^{n-1} = \frac{1 - x^n}{1 - x},$$

you can deduce

$$\frac{1}{1 - x} = 1 + x + x^2 + \ldots + x^{n-1} + \frac{x^n}{1 - x}.$$

So if $f(x) = (1 - x)^{-1}$, the $(n-1)$th Maclaurin polynomial is $p_{n-1}(x) = 1 + x + x^2 + \ldots + x^{n-1}$, and the error term is $R_{n-1}(x) = f(x) - p_{n-1}(x) = \frac{x^n}{1 - x}$.

Example 10.5.2
Find bounds for the error term in the Maclaurin series for $-\ln(1 - x)$, where $0 < x < 1$.

Since $\displaystyle\int_0^x \frac{1}{1 - u}\, du = [-\ln(1 - u)]_0^x = -\ln(1 - x),$

$$-\ln(1 - x) = \int_0^x \left(1 + u + u^2 + \ldots + u^{n-1} + \frac{u^n}{1 - u} \right) du$$

$$= \left(x + \tfrac{1}{2} x^2 + \tfrac{1}{3} x^3 + \ldots + \tfrac{1}{n} x^n \right) + \int_0^x \frac{u^n}{1 - u}\, du.$$

The series in brackets is the Maclaurin polynomial $p_n(x)$ for $-\ln(1 - x)$, so the integral is the error term $R_n(x)$. You will notice that it is much simpler than the error term $\displaystyle\int_0^x \left(\frac{x - t}{1 - t} \right)^n \times \frac{1}{1 - t}\, dt$ found in Example 10.4.2(b).

To find bounds for the error term, note that if $0 < u < x$, then $1 > 1 - u > 1 - x$, so that $1 < \frac{1}{1 - u} < \frac{1}{1 - x}$ (since $x < 1$). Therefore

$$\int_0^x u^n\, du < \int_0^x \frac{u^n}{1 - u}\, du < \int_0^x \frac{u^n}{1 - x}\, du.$$

This gives both a lower and an upper bound for the error. A lower bound is

$$\int_0^x u^n\, du = \frac{1}{n + 1} x^{n+1}$$

and an upper bound is

$$\frac{1}{1 - x} \int_0^x u^n\, du.$$

Therefore the bounds for the error term are given by

$$\frac{1}{n+1}x^{n+1} < R_n(x) < \frac{1}{n+1} \times \frac{x^{n+1}}{1-x}.$$

Exercise 10

1   The Maclaurin polynomial of degree 4 is used to estimate the value of e^x for $x = -0.2$.

    (a) Find the value of $p_4(-0.2)$.

    (b) Use a calculator to find the error $R_4(-0.2)$.

    (c) Use the Lagrange form for $R_n(x)$ to write an expression for the error, and give an upper bound for its magnitude.

    (d) Use the alternating series property to find an upper bound for the magnitude of the error.

2   The Maclaurin polynomial of degree 5 is used to estimate the value of $\sin x$ for $x = 0.5$.

    (a) Find the value of $p_5(0.5)$.

    (b) Use a calculator to find the error $R_5(0.5)$.

    (c) Use the Lagrange form for $R_n(x)$ to write an expression for the error, and give an upper bound for its magnitude.

    (d) Use the alternating series property to find an upper bound for the magnitude of the error.

    (e) Compare your answers to parts (c) and (d) and comment on the difference.

3   Use the analysis in Examples 10.4.2 and 10.5.2 to find

    (a) an upper bound for the magnitude of the error when the Maclaurin polynomial of degree 5 is used to calculate $\ln 1.2$;

    (b) an upper bound for the value of the relative error when the Maclaurin polynomial of degree 5 is used to calculate $\ln 0.8$;

    (c) lower and upper bounds for the magnitude of the error when the Maclaurin polynomial of degree 5 is used to calculate $\ln 0.8$.

4   In Chapter 9, Fig. 9.5 and Fig. 9.4 respectively compare graphs of

    (a) $y = \sin x$,

    (b) $y = \ln(1 + x)$

with the corresponding Maclaurin polynomial approximations of degree 10. Use upper bounds for the remainders in Example 10.4.1 and Example 10.4.2 to find intervals of values of x within which you can be sure that the error in the approximation is less than 0.001 in absolute value.

5   How many terms of the Maclaurin series should you take to be sure of finding the value of e^x with an error of less than 0.0001 in absolute value

    (a) when $x = 2.5$,

    (b) when $x = -2.5$?

6 (a) Find an expression for the coefficient of x^i (where $i \geq 2$) in the Maclaurin series for $\sqrt{1-x}$.

   (b) Find the Lagrange form for the error $R_n(x)$ if the Maclaurin polynomial $p_n(x)$ of degree n is used as an approximation for $\sqrt{1-x}$.

   (c) Prove that, if $0 < x < 1$, then $|R_n(x)| < A_n(x)$, where $A_1(x) = \frac{1}{8} \frac{x^2}{(1-x)^{\frac{3}{2}}}$ and

   $$A_n(x) = \frac{2n-1}{2n+2} \times \frac{x}{1-x} A_{n-1}(x).$$

   (d) Find the smallest value of n for which you can be sure that the difference between $\sqrt{0.8}$ and $p_n(0.2)$ is less than 10^{-5}.

   (e) For the value of n you found in part (d) calculate the actual difference between $\sqrt{0.8}$ and $p_n(0.2)$.

7 (a) For the binomial series $(1+x)^{-3}$ use the Lagrange form of the remainder to find an upper bound for the magnitude of the error term. Hence prove that the series is valid for $0 < x < 1$.

   (b) For the binomial series $(1-x)^{-3}$ use the integral form of the remainder to find an upper bound for the error term. Hence prove that the series is valid for $0 < x < 1$.

8 By finding the second derivative of the expression for $(1-x)^{-1}$ as the sum of a polynomial of degree $n+2$ and a remainder term, obtain an expression for $(1-x)^{-3}$ in the form $p_n(x) + R_n(x)$. By using the result in Exercise 2C Question 1, deduce that the infinite binomial series for $(1-x)^{-3}$ is valid for $-1 < x < 1$.

9 For the function $-\ln(1-x)$, show that the form of the error term given in Example 10.4.2(b) can be found from the form given in Example 10.5.2 by substituting $u = \frac{x-t}{1-t}$.

10 What difficulty arises if you try to use the Maclaurin formula to find a series for $\arctan x$?

   In Example 9.5.2 a series for $\arctan x$ was found by integrating the series for $\frac{1}{1+x^2}$. Prove that the difference between $\arctan x$ and the first n non-zero terms of its Maclaurin series has absolute value $\int_0^{|x|} \frac{t^{2n}}{1+t^2} \, dt$, and show that this is less than $\frac{|x|^{2n+1}}{2n+1}$.

   Use this to estimate the smallest number of terms of the $\arctan x$ series that you might need to use to compute $\arctan 0.2$ with an error less than 10^{-10} in absolute magnitude.

11 Taylor series and l'Hôpital's rule

Maclaurin series can be modified to give approximations to a function around a general value of x. When you have completed this chapter, you should

- be able to find infinite series, polynomial approximations and error terms centred on a value of x other than 0
- understand how these approximations can be adapted to obtain a rule for finding limits.

11.1 Taylor series

An important use of Maclaurin series is to find approximations to values of a function in the neighbourhood of $x = 0$, when $|x|$ is small. Sometimes you want a similar approximation in the neighbourhood of some other value $x = a$, when $|x - a|$ is small.

Fig. 11.1 shows a graph $y = f(x)$ passing through a point $(a, f(a))$. The aim is to find a polynomial of degree n whose graph fits that of $y = f(x)$ as closely as possible around $x = a$. The figure shows another point on the curve close to $(a, f(a))$ with x-coordinate j and y-coordinate k, so that $k = f(j)$.

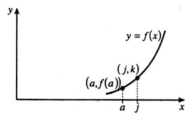

Fig. 11.1

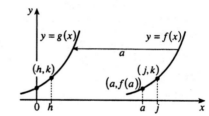

Fig. 11.2

In Fig. 11.2 the graph $y = f(x)$ has been translated by an amount a in the negative x-direction to produce another graph $y = g(x)$. The point (j, k) is then translated to (h, k), where $h = j - a$.

The two curves are identical in shape, so all the derivatives of $g(x)$ at $x = 0$ are equal to the corresponding derivatives of $f(x)$ at $x = a$.

Now you can find k in terms of h by a Maclaurin series, as

$$k = g(0) + \frac{g'(0)}{1!}h + \frac{g''(0)}{2!}h^2 + \dots .$$

Substituting $g(0) = f(a)$, $g'(0) = f'(a)$, $g''(0) = f''(a)$, ... and $h = j - a$, this becomes

$$k = f(a) + \frac{f'(a)}{1!}(j - a) + \frac{f''(a)}{2!}(j - a)^2 + \dots .$$

This last equation contains only quantities which appear in Fig. 11.1. And as j is the x-coordinate of any point on the curve around $(a, f(a))$, and $k = f(j)$, you can now change j to x and k to $f(x)$ and write

$$f(x) = f(a) + \frac{f'(a)}{1!}(x-a) + \frac{f''(a)}{2!}(x-a)^2 + \ldots = \sum_{i=0}^{\infty} \frac{f^{(i)}(a)}{i!}(x-a)^i.$$

This is known as a **Taylor series**.

Like Maclaurin, Brook Taylor belonged to the generation of mathematicians following Isaac Newton; but in fact the series attributed to them were known by an earlier Scottish mathematician, James Gregory.

Everything in the last three chapters about power series, Maclaurin series, Maclaurin polynomials and the error term can be generalised in this way. For example, if a power series $\sum c_i x^i$ is convergent for $|x| < R$, the power series $\sum c_i (x-a)^i$ is convergent for $|x-a| < R$, that is for $a - R < x < a + R$. The integral form for the error term has $\int_a^x$ in place of $\int_0^x$, and in the Lagrange form x^{n+1} is replaced by $(x-a)^{n+1}$ and c lies between a and x rather than between 0 and x. This is summarised below.

A function $f(x)$ can be expressed as a **Taylor series**

$$f(x) = \sum_{i=0}^{\infty} \frac{f^{(i)}(a)}{i!}(x-a)^i$$

within an interval of validity, or as the sum of a Taylor polynomial

$$f(x) = \sum_{i=0}^{n} \frac{f^{(i)}(a)}{i!}(x-a)^i$$

and an error term

$$R_n(x) = \int_a^x \frac{f^{(n+1)}(t)}{n!} \times (x-t)^n \, dt$$

or $R_n(x) = \dfrac{f^{(n+1)}(c)}{(n+1)!}(x-a)^{n+1}$ where c is a number between a and x.

Example 11.1.1
Find a Taylor series for $\ln x$ at $x = a$, where $a > 0$, and determine its interval of validity.

If $f(x) = \ln x$, then $f'(x) = \dfrac{1}{x}$, $f''(x) = -\dfrac{1}{x^2}$, $f'''(x) = \dfrac{2}{x^3}$, $\ldots$, $f^{(i)}(x) = (-1)^{i-1}\dfrac{(i-1)!}{x^i}$.

So $\ln x = \ln a + \dfrac{1}{a}(x-a) - \dfrac{1}{2a^2}(x-a)^2 + \dfrac{1}{3a^3}(x-a)^3 - \ldots + (-1)^{i-1} \times \dfrac{1}{ia^i}(x-a)^i + \ldots$.

The radius of convergence is given by

$$R = \lim_{i \to \infty} \left| \frac{(-1)^{i-2} \times \dfrac{1}{(i-1)a^{i-1}}}{(-1)^{i-1} \times \dfrac{1}{ia^i}} \right| = \lim_{i \to \infty} \frac{i}{i-1} \times a = 1 \times a = a \qquad \text{(see Section 8.2).}$$

So the series is convergent when $|x - a| < a$, that is if $0 < x < 2a$. It is also convergent when $x - a = a$, by the alternating series property (see Section 6.1). The complete interval of convergence, which is the same as the interval of validity, is $0 < x \leq 2a$.

Although the series in this example looks unfamiliar, it is not really new. Suppose for example that you put $x = 11$ and $a = 10$. Then you get

$$\ln 11 = \ln 10 + \tfrac{1}{10} \times 1 - \tfrac{1}{200} \times 1^2 + \tfrac{1}{3000} \times 1^3 - \dots,$$

or

$$\ln\left(\tfrac{11}{10}\right) = \tfrac{1}{10} - \tfrac{1}{2} \times \left(\tfrac{1}{10}\right)^2 + \tfrac{1}{3} \times \left(\tfrac{1}{10}\right)^3 - \dots.$$

This is just the Maclaurin series for $\ln\left(1 + \tfrac{1}{10}\right)$.

In general, you can write $\ln\left(\dfrac{x}{a}\right)$ as $\ln\left(1 + \dfrac{x - a}{a}\right)$, so the Maclaurin series is

$$\ln\left(\frac{x}{a}\right) = \frac{x - a}{a} - \frac{1}{2}\left(\frac{x - a}{a}\right)^2 + \frac{1}{3}\left(\frac{x - a}{a}\right)^3 - \dots.$$

And if you write $\ln\left(\dfrac{x}{a}\right)$ as $\ln x - \ln a$, this is the same as the series in Example 11.1.1. The Taylor series is a disguised version of the Maclaurin series.

11.2 Another form for Taylor series

Look back to the equations in Section 11.1 which begin '$k = \dots$'. Since $j - a = h$, and $k = f(j)$, you can write k as $f(a + h)$, and the equation for k then becomes

$$f(a + h) = f(a) + \frac{f'(a)}{1!} h + \frac{f''(a)}{2!} h^2 + \dots = \sum_{i=0}^{\infty} \frac{f^{(i)}(a)}{i!} h^i.$$

Sometimes this is a more convenient way of writing a Taylor series, and it is worth learning to recognize it in this form as well as the form given in Section 11.1.

The Lagrange form for the error term will then be

$$\frac{f^{(n+1)}(c)}{(n + 1)!} h^{n+1},$$

where c is a number between a and $a + h$. It is quite common to write c as $a + \theta h$, where θ is a number between 0 and 1. This has the advantage that it always stands for a number between a and $a + h$, whether h is positive or negative. You can therefore write the error term as

$$\frac{f^{(n)}(a + \theta h)}{(n + 1)!} h^{n+1}, \text{ where } 0 < \theta < 1.$$

11.3   l'Hôpital's rule

In Section 9.6 Maclaurin series were used to find limits as $x \to 0$ of expressions of the form $\dfrac{f(x)}{g(x)}$ when $f(0)$ and $g(0)$ are both 0. If you want limits as $x \to a$ when $f(a)$ and $g(a)$ are both 0 you would use Taylor series. Since $f(a) = 0$ and $g(a) = 0$ the first terms of the series are 0, so

$$\frac{f(x)}{g(x)} = \frac{f'(a)(x-a) + \frac{1}{2!}f''(a)(x-a)^2 + \frac{1}{3!}f'''(a)(x-a)^3 + \dots}{g'(a)(x-a) + \frac{1}{2!}g''(a)(x-a)^2 + \frac{1}{3!}g'''(a)(x-a)^3 + \dots}.$$

You can then cancel a factor $(x-a)$, so

$$\frac{f(x)}{g(x)} = \frac{f'(a) + \frac{1}{2!}f''(a)(x-a) + \frac{1}{3!}f'''(a)(x-a)^2 + \dots}{g'(a) + \frac{1}{2!}g''(a)(x-a) + \frac{1}{3!}g'''(a)(x-a)^2 + \dots}.$$

As $x \to a$ all the terms after the first in each series tend to 0, so provided that $g'(a)$ is not zero,

$$\lim_{x \to a} \frac{f(x)}{g(x)} = \frac{f'(a)}{g'(a)}.$$

> **l'Hôpital's rule**   If $f(a) = 0$ and $g(a) = 0$, and $g'(a) \neq 0$, then
>
> $$\lim_{x \to a} \frac{f(x)}{g(x)} = \frac{f'(a)}{g'(a)}.$$

The French mathematician Guillaume l'Hôpital published this rule in a textbook which appeared in 1696.

Example 11.3.1

Find $\lim\limits_{x \to 1} \dfrac{\sqrt[3]{x} - 1}{\sqrt{x} - 1}$.

If $f(x) = \sqrt[3]{x} - 1$ and $g(x) = \sqrt{x} - 1$, then both $f(1) = 0$ and $g(1) = 0$, and

$$f'(x) = \frac{1}{3\sqrt[3]{x^2}}, \quad g'(x) = \frac{1}{2\sqrt{x}}.$$

So $f'(1) = \frac{1}{3}$ and $g'(1) = \frac{1}{2}$. Therefore, by l'Hôpital's rule,

$$\lim_{x \to 1} \frac{\sqrt[3]{x} - 1}{\sqrt{x} - 1} = \frac{\frac{1}{3}}{\frac{1}{2}} = \frac{2}{3}.$$

What happens if in addition $f'(a)$ and $g'(a)$ are both 0?

In that case

$$\frac{f(x)}{g(x)} = \frac{\frac{1}{2!}f''(a)(x-a) + \frac{1}{3!}f'''(a)(x-a)^2 + \dots}{\frac{1}{2!}g''(a)(x-a) + \frac{1}{3!}g'''(a)(x-a)^2 + \dots}.$$

You can now cancel $\frac{1}{2}(x-a)$, which gives

$$\frac{f(x)}{g(x)} = \frac{f''(a) + \frac{1}{3}f'''(a)(x-a) + \dots}{g''(a) + \frac{1}{3}g'''(a)(x-a) + \dots}.$$

Then, if $g''(a) \neq 0$,

$$\lim_{x \to a} \frac{f(x)}{g(x)} = \frac{f''(a)}{g''(a)}.$$

But also, by using $f'(x)$ and $g'(x)$ in place of $f(x)$ and $g(x)$ in the previous shaded box,

$$\lim_{x \to a} \frac{f'(x)}{g'(x)} = \frac{f''(a)}{g''(a)}.$$

From this you can obtain a more general form of l'Hôpital's rule which includes the form given earlier as a special case.

> **l'Hôpital's rule (general form)**
>
> If $f(a) = 0$ and $g(a) = 0$, and if $\lim_{x \to a} \dfrac{f'(x)}{g'(x)} = L$, then $\lim_{x \to a} \dfrac{f(x)}{g(x)} = L$.

Example 11.3.2

Find (a) $\lim_{x \to \pi} \dfrac{(x-\pi)^2}{1 + \cos x}$,   (b) $\lim_{x \to 1} \dfrac{(\ln x)^2}{x^3 - x^2 - x + 1}$.

(a) If $f(x) = (x-\pi)^2$ and $g(x) = 1 + \cos x$, then $f'(x) = 2(x-\pi)$ and $g'(x) = -\sin x$, and $f''(x) = 2$ and $g''(x) = -\cos x$. So $f(\pi) = g(\pi) = 0$, $f'(\pi) = g'(\pi) = 0$ and $f''(\pi) = 2$, $g''(\pi) = -(-1) = 1$. Therefore, by l'Hôpital's rule,

$$\lim_{x \to \pi} \frac{f'(x)}{g'(x)} = \frac{f''(\pi)}{g''(\pi)} = 2, \quad \text{so} \quad \lim_{x \to \pi} \frac{f(x)}{g(x)} = 2.$$

(b) If $f(x) = (\ln x)^2$ and $g(x) = x^3 - x^2 - x + 1$, then $f'(x) = \dfrac{2\ln x}{x}$ and $g'(x) = 3x^2 - 2x - 1$. So $f(1) = g(1) = 0$, and $f'(1) = g'(1) = 0$.

You could go on to find $f''(x)$ and $g''(x)$ as in part (a), but it is slightly simpler to note that

$$\frac{f'(x)}{g'(x)} = \frac{2\ln x}{3x^3 - 2x^2 - x},$$

and to write $F(x) = 2 \ln x$ and $G(x) = 3x^3 - 2x^2 - x$, where $F(1) = G(1) = 0$. Then $F'(x) = \frac{2}{x}$ and $G'(x) = 9x^2 - 4x - 1$. So $F'(1) = 2$ and $G'(1) = 4$. Therefore, by l'Hôpital's rule,

$$\lim_{x \to 1} \frac{F(x)}{G(x)} = \frac{F'(1)}{G'(1)} = \tfrac{1}{2}.$$

And since $\dfrac{F(x)}{G(x)} = \dfrac{f'(x)}{g'(x)}$,

$$\lim_{x \to 1} \frac{f'(x)}{g'(x)} = \tfrac{1}{2}, \quad \text{so} \quad \lim_{x \to 1} \frac{f(x)}{g(x)} = \tfrac{1}{2}.$$

Exercise 11

1   Find a Taylor series for e^x around $x = a$. Show how your series is related to the Maclaurin series for e^x.

   If e^x is approximated by a Taylor approximation around $x = a$ of degree n, write expressions for the error term in both integral and Lagrange forms.

2   Write a Taylor polynomial of degree 6 for $\sin x$ around $x = \frac{1}{4}\pi$. Write an expression for the error term in the form of an integral. Use integration by parts to obtain the Taylor polynomial of degree 7 and the corresponding error term.

3   Expand $\sqrt[3]{1+h}$ as a series of powers of h as far as the term in h^3, and give an expression for the remainder. Use the series to find an approximation for $\sqrt[3]{1.15}$. State whether your answer is too large or too small, and find an upper bound for the error.

4   If $f(x) = x^3 - 5x + 2$ and $g(x) = x^3 - x^2 - 4$, show that $f(2) = g(2) = 0$. Hence factorise $f(x)$ and $g(x)$. Find $\lim\limits_{x \to 2} \dfrac{f(x)}{g(x)}$

   (a) by cancelling a common factor,   (b) by using l'Hôpital's rule.

5   Repeat Question 4 with $f(x) = x^3 - 3x^2 + 4$ and $g(x) = x^3 - 12x + 16$.

6   Find

   (a) $\lim\limits_{x \to 2} \dfrac{x^2 - 4}{\sin(x - 2)}$,

   (b) $\lim\limits_{x \to \pi} \dfrac{\tan x}{\cos \frac{1}{2} x}$,

   (c) $\lim\limits_{x \to e} \dfrac{1 - \ln x}{\sqrt{x} - \sqrt{e}}$,

   (d) $\lim\limits_{x \to 0} \dfrac{e^x - e^{-x}}{\sin x}$.

7   Find

   (a) $\lim\limits_{x \to 1} \dfrac{(x - 1)^2}{1 + \sin \frac{3}{2} \pi x}$,

   (b) $\lim\limits_{x \to \frac{1}{2}\pi} \dfrac{1 - \sin 5x}{1 + \cos 2x}$,

   (c) $\lim\limits_{x \to 1} \dfrac{\ln x + \ln(2 - x)}{1 - \cos(1 - x)}$,

   (d) $\lim\limits_{x \to 1} \dfrac{\sqrt{x} + \sqrt{2 - x} - 2}{(x - 1) \ln x}$.

12 Homogeneous differential equations

Higher Level Book 2, Chapters 23 and 27, showed how to solve certain types of differential equation. This chapter introduces another type. When you have completed it, you should

- know what is meant by a homogeneous differential equation, and that it can (if necessary) be solved by a substitution
- understand the geometrical significance of the differential equation, and that solution curves can be obtained from others by enlargement from the origin.

12.1 Some examples of homogeneous equations

You already know how to solve differential equations which have the forms $\dfrac{dy}{dx} = f(x)$ and $\dfrac{dy}{dx} = f(y)$ (Higher Level Book 2 Chapter 23), and $\dfrac{dy}{dx} = \dfrac{f(x)}{g(y)}$ (Higher Level Book 2 Section 27.3). Another type of differential equation for which there is a standard method of solution has the form $\dfrac{dy}{dx} = f\left(\dfrac{y}{x}\right)$. This is called a **homogeneous differential equation**.

The basic meaning of the word homogeneous is 'having the same degree'. In algebra, an equation such as $y^3 + 4x^2 y - 3x^3 = 0$ is homogeneous, as each term has degree 3 in x and/or y. But $y^3 + 4x^2 - 3 = 0$ is not homogeneous, because the first term has degree 3, the second has degree 2 and the third has degree 0.

Notice that the homogeneous equation $y^3 + 4x^2 y - 3x^3 = 0$ can be rewritten as $\left(\dfrac{y}{x}\right)^3 + 4\left(\dfrac{y}{x}\right) - 3 = 0$, that is as $f\left(\dfrac{y}{x}\right) = 0$. This is why the name 'homogeneous' is used to describe these differential equations.

Differential equations of this type are more common than you might at first think. Besides obvious examples such as $\dfrac{dy}{dx} = \left(\dfrac{y}{x}\right)^2$ (solved in Higher Level Book 2 Example 27.3.1) and $\dfrac{dy}{dx} = \sin\left(\dfrac{y}{x}\right)$ (for which no exact solution exists in terms of functions that you know), the description homogeneous includes differential equations such as

$$\frac{dy}{dx} = \ln x - \ln y, \qquad \frac{dy}{dx} = \frac{2x+y}{y} \qquad \text{and} \qquad \frac{dy}{dx} = \frac{xy}{x^2 - 3y^2},$$

because

$$\ln x - \ln y = -\ln\left(\frac{y}{x}\right), \qquad \frac{2x+y}{y} = \frac{2 + \dfrac{y}{x}}{\dfrac{y}{x}} \qquad \text{and} \qquad \frac{xy}{x^2 - 3y^2} = \frac{\dfrac{y}{x}}{1 - 3\left(\dfrac{y}{x}\right)^2}.$$

These all have the form $f\left(\dfrac{y}{x}\right)$ with $f(u) = -\ln u$, $\dfrac{2+u}{u}$ and $\dfrac{u}{1 - 3u^2}$ respectively.

You already know how to solve homogeneous equations of the special form $\frac{dy}{dx} = a\left(\frac{y}{x}\right)^m$, because this differential equation can be written with separable variables as $\frac{1}{y^m}\frac{dy}{dx} = \frac{a}{x^m}$.

Example 12.1.1

Find the solution curves of the differential equation $\frac{dy}{dx} = -\frac{y}{x}$ which pass through the points

(a) $(1,2)$,   (b) $(1,1)$,   (c) $(1,-1)$,   (d) $(1,0)$.

Note that the expression for $\frac{dy}{dx}$ is undefined when $x = 0$, so that the solution curves cannot cross from positive to negative values of x. So in solving the differential equation you need only consider $x > 0$.

The differential equation can be written as

$$\frac{1}{y}\frac{dy}{dx} = -\frac{1}{x}.$$

The left side is the derivative with respect to x of $\ln|y|$, so the equation can be integrated as

$$\ln|y| = -\ln x + k.$$

(Notice that, since $x > 0$, it is not necessary to write $\ln|x|$ on the right side.)

(a)   To pass through $(1,2)$ the constant k must satisfy

$$\ln|2| = -\ln 1 + k, \quad \text{so} \quad k = \ln 2.$$

Therefore

$$\ln|y| = -\ln x + \ln 2,$$

which gives

$$|y| = \frac{2}{x}, \quad \text{or} \quad y = \pm\frac{2}{x}.$$

Since the curve has to pass through $(1,2)$, the positive sign must be taken. The solution curve therefore has equation

$$y = \frac{2}{x}, \quad x > 0.$$

(b)   Using a similar method, to pass through $(1,1)$ the constant k must satisfy

$$\ln|1| = -\ln 1 + k,$$

so $k = 0$.

Therefore

$$\ln|y| = -\ln x,$$

which gives

$$y = \pm\frac{1}{x}.$$

As in part (a) the positive sign must be taken, so the equation of the solution curve is

$$y = \frac{1}{x}, \ x > 0.$$

(c)   To pass through $(1,-1)$, k must satisfy

$$\ln|-1| = \ln 1 + k,$$

which again gives $k = 0$, so $y = \pm\dfrac{1}{x}$. But to pass through $(1,-1)$ the negative sign must be taken, so the solution curve has equation

$$y = -\frac{1}{x}, \ x > 0.$$

(d)   The method used in parts (a) to (c) breaks down, because $\ln|0|$ has no meaning. The problem lies at the very first step of the solution, where the equation $\dfrac{dy}{dx} = -\dfrac{y}{x}$ is replaced by $\dfrac{1}{y}\dfrac{dy}{dx} = -\dfrac{1}{x}$, dividing both sides by y. This is not valid if $y = 0$, which occurs at the given point $(1,0)$. So you need a different approach.

Notice that in parts (a) to (c) the solution has the form $y = \dfrac{A}{x}$ for some constant A. So try an equation of this form satisfied by $x = 1$ and $y = 0$. This would require $A = 0$, giving the solution of the equation as

$$y = 0, \ x > 0.$$

The corresponding graph is the positive x-axis.

You can easily check that this satisfies the differential equation, since the axis has gradient 0, which is equal to $-\dfrac{y}{x}$ when $y = 0$, $x > 0$.

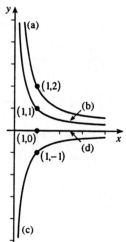

The four solution curves are shown in Fig. 12.1.

Fig. 12.1

12.2 Solution by substitution

The homogeneous differential equation in Example 12.1.1 is a very special case, because the variables are separable. If you try to use a similar method with an equation such as $\frac{dy}{dx} = 1 - \frac{y}{x}$, you will find that there is no way of expressing this in the form $g(y)\frac{dy}{dx} = f(x)$, so you need a different method.

A way of simplifying the equation would be to replace the $\frac{y}{x}$ in the expression $f\left(\frac{y}{x}\right)$ by a single letter. It could not of course be a constant, but you could write $\frac{y}{x}$ as a single variable z.

The question is then what happens to the other quantity in the equation, $\frac{dy}{dx}$. Since $y = xz$, you can use the product rule of differentiation to write this as

$$\frac{dy}{dx} = 1 \times z + x \times \frac{dz}{dx}$$
$$= z + x\frac{dz}{dx}.$$

The differential equation $\frac{dy}{dx} = f\left(\frac{y}{x}\right)$ then becomes

$$z + x\frac{dz}{dx} = f(z),$$

which can be rearranged as

$$x\frac{dz}{dx} = f(z) - z.$$

And now you have a differential equation in separable variables form, as

$$\frac{1}{f(z) - z}\frac{dz}{dx} = \frac{1}{x}.$$

So if you can find $\int \frac{1}{f(z) - z}dz$, you could integrate this differential equation as an equation connecting z and x. Finally, since $y = xz$, this can be written as an equation connecting $\frac{y}{x}$ and x; that is, as an equation connecting y and x.

Example 12.2.1

Find the solution curves of the differential equation $\frac{dy}{dx} = 1 - \frac{y}{x}$ which pass through the points
(a) $(1,2)$,   (b) $(1,1)$,   (c) $(1,-1)$,   (d) $(1,0)$.

If you write $\frac{y}{x} = z$, that is $y = xz$, you can differentiate with respect to x to get

$$\frac{dy}{dx} = z + x\frac{dz}{dx}.$$

The differential equation then becomes

$$z + x\frac{dz}{dx} = 1 - z,$$

which can be rearranged as

$$\frac{1}{2z-1}\frac{dz}{dx} = -\frac{1}{x}.$$

Notice that, as in Example 12.1.1, $\frac{dz}{dx}$ is undefined when $x = 0$, so the solution curves cannot pass from positive to negative values of x. You can therefore restrict the solution to $x > 0$, and the integral of $\frac{1}{x}$ can be taken as $\ln x$ rather than $\ln|x|$.

Integrating the differential equation for z,

$$\tfrac{1}{2}\ln|2z - 1| = -\ln x + k,$$

which you can write as

$$\ln|2z - 1| + 2\ln x = 2k.$$

This can be simplified by noting that

$$\ln|2z - 1| + 2\ln x = \ln\left(\left|2\frac{y}{x} - 1\right| \times x^2\right)$$
$$= \ln\left|2xy - x^2\right|.$$

So

$$\left|2xy - x^2\right| = e^{2k},$$

$$2xy - x^2 = \pm\, e^{2k}.$$

Write the constant on the right more simply as A. This can be found for the four solution curves by substituting the given values of x and y, as

(a) $A = 2\times 1\times 2 - 1^2 = 3,$ \qquad (b) $A = 2\times 1\times 1 - 1^2 = 1,$

(c) $A = 2\times 1\times(-1) - 1^2 = -3,$ \qquad (d) $A = 2\times 1\times 0 - 1^2 = -1.$

Then rearranging $2xy - x^2 = A$ as $y = \tfrac{1}{2}\left(x + \frac{A}{x}\right)$, the four solution curves have equations

(a) $y = \tfrac{1}{2}\left(x + \frac{3}{x}\right),$ \qquad (b) $y = \tfrac{1}{2}\left(x + \frac{1}{x}\right),$

(c) $y = \tfrac{1}{2}\left(x - \frac{3}{x}\right),$ \qquad (d) $y = \tfrac{1}{2}\left(x - \frac{1}{x}\right).$

It is a good idea to check these solutions, as it is easy to make a slip along the way.

If $\quad y = \frac{1}{2}\left(x + \frac{A}{x}\right)$,

then $\quad \dfrac{dy}{dx} = \frac{1}{2}\left(1 - \frac{A}{x^2}\right)$,

and $\quad 1 - \dfrac{y}{x} = 1 - \frac{1}{2}\left(1 + \frac{A}{x^2}\right) = \frac{1}{2}\left(1 - \frac{A}{x^2}\right)$,

so $\quad \dfrac{dy}{dx} = 1 - \dfrac{y}{x}$, as required.

The four solution curves are shown in Fig. 12.2.

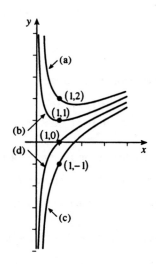

Fig. 12.2

Example 12.2.2

For the differential equation $\dfrac{dy}{dx} = \dfrac{y}{x + y}$, find the solution curve through $(1,1)$.

It is useful to note, for later reference, that $\dfrac{dy}{dx}$ is not defined when $x + y = 0$, so the solution curve cannot cross from positive to negative values of $x + y$. The whole solution curve must lie above the line with equation $x + y = 0$.

Writing $\dfrac{y}{x} = z$,

$$\frac{y}{x + y} = \frac{xz}{x + xz} = \frac{z}{1 + z}.$$

So, using $\dfrac{dy}{dx} = z + x\dfrac{dz}{dx}$, the differential equation becomes

$$z + x\frac{dz}{dx} = \frac{z}{1 + z},$$

$$x\frac{dz}{dx} = \frac{z}{1 + z} - z = \frac{z - z(1 + z)}{1 + z} = \frac{-z^2}{1 + z}.$$

This can be rearranged as

$$-\frac{1 + z}{z^2}\frac{dz}{dx} = \frac{1}{x},$$

or $\quad \left(-\dfrac{1}{z^2} - \dfrac{1}{z}\right)\dfrac{dz}{dx} = \dfrac{1}{x}.$

This is now in a form which you can integrate, as

$$\frac{1}{z} - \ln|z| = \ln|x| + k.$$

You can find the constant k by noting that, when $x = 1$ and $y = 1$, then $z = \frac{1}{1} = 1$, so

$$1 - \ln|1| = \ln|1| + k, \quad \text{which gives} \quad k = 1.$$

The solution is therefore

$$\frac{1}{z} - \ln|z| = \ln|x| + 1,$$

$$\frac{1}{z} = \ln|xz| + 1.$$

Writing $z = \frac{y}{x}$, the equation of the solution curve is

$$\frac{x}{y} = \ln|y| + 1, \quad \text{which is} \quad x = y(\ln|y| + 1).$$

When you solve differential equations it often happens that you can't write the solution in function form as $y = F(x)$, and this sometimes makes it difficult to draw the graph of the solution curve. But in this case the equation comes out in the form $x = F(y)$. So you could find its shape by drawing the graph of

$$y = x(\ln|x| + 1)$$

and then swopping the x- and y-axes by reflecting the graph in the line $y = x$. (Your calculator may have a program which does this for you.)

Fig. 12.3 shows the resulting graph. The part with $y > 0$ has equation $x = y(\ln y + 1)$, and the part with $y < 0$ has equation $x = y(\ln(-y) + 1)$. And since the graph of $y = x(\ln x + 1)$ has a minimum point at $(e^{-2}, -e^{-2})$, the graph of $x = y(\ln y + 1)$ has a tangent parallel to the y-axis at $(-e^{-2}, e^{-2})$.

This is where the remark at the beginning of the solution becomes relevant. You will notice that $(-e^{-2}, e^{-2})$ lies on the line $x + y = 0$, and it is only the part of the curve through $(1,1)$ for which $x + y > 0$ that forms the solution curve. This is the curve shown with the solid line in Fig. 12.3. The required solution is therefore given by

$$x = y(\ln y + 1), \quad y > e^{-2}.$$

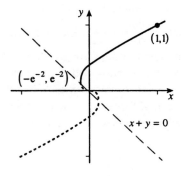

Fig. 12.3

Exercise 12A

Keep your answers to Questions 2(a), 4 and 6 for use in Exercise 12B Questions 2, 3 and 4.

1 Solve the differential equation $\dfrac{dy}{dx} = \dfrac{x}{y}$ for $y > 0$. Use a calculator to display the solution curves through $(0,1)$, $(0,2)$, $(1,1)$, $(-1,1)$, $(1,2)$, $(-1,2)$, $(2,1)$ and $(3,1)$.

2 Find equations of the solution curves in the first quadrant of the differential equations

(a) $\dfrac{dy}{dx} = \sqrt{\dfrac{y}{x}}$,
(b) $\dfrac{dy}{dx} = \sqrt{\dfrac{x}{y}}$

through the points $(1,9)$, $(1,4)$, $(1,1)$, $(4,1)$, $(9,1)$. State any restrictions on the values of x for which your solution is valid, and sketch the solution curves.

3 Find an equation for the general solution of the differential equation $\dfrac{dy}{dx} = \dfrac{x^2 + y^2}{xy}$ for $x > 0$, $y > 0$. Check your answer by substitution in the two sides of the differential equation.

4 Find the equations of the solution curves through $(1,2)$, $(2,4)$ and $(4,6)$ of the differential equations

(a) $\dfrac{dy}{dx} = \dfrac{x^2 + y^2}{2xy}$,
(b) $\dfrac{dy}{dx} = \dfrac{y^2 - x^2}{2xy}$.

5 Find the equation of the solution curve through $(1,1)$ of the differential equation $\dfrac{dy}{dx} = \dfrac{xy}{x^2 + y^2}$.

6 Solve the differential equation $\dfrac{dy}{dx} = \dfrac{xy - y^2}{x^2}$ for $x > 0$.

7 Find in the form of an implicit equation the solution of the differential equation $\dfrac{dy}{dx} = \dfrac{y - x}{y + x}$. Check the answer by differentiating your equation with respect to x.

12.3* Geometrical properties of the solution curves

Fig. 12.4 shows the solution curves of the differential equation $\dfrac{dy}{dx} = 1 - \dfrac{y}{x}$ which were found in Example 12.2.1.

A number of lines through the origin have been added to the figure, together with the tangents to the solution curves at the points of intersection. What this demonstrates is that, for each of these lines, the tangents to the solution curves which they intersect are parallel.

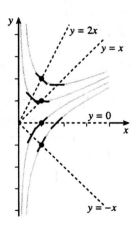

Fig. 12.4

It is easy to see why. Consider for example the line $y = 2x$, which intersects the solution curves $y = \frac{1}{2}\left(x + \frac{1}{x}\right)$ and $y = \frac{1}{2}\left(x + \frac{3}{x}\right)$. At each point of intersection $\frac{y}{x} = 2$, and from the differential equation $\frac{dy}{dx} = 1 - \frac{y}{x} = 1 - 2 = -1$. So the tangent to any solution curve at its intersection with $y = 2x$ has gradient -1.

Similarly for the other lines. At the intersection of a solution curve with $y = x$, $\frac{y}{x} = 1$ so that $\frac{dy}{dx} = 1 - 1 = 0$. You can see from Fig. 12.4 that the minimum points of each solution curve which intersects $y = x$ lie on this line.

The lines $y = 2x$ and $y = x$ don't intersect all the solution curves. But other solution curves have intersections with other lines through the origin. Fig. 12.4 shows the solution curves $y = \frac{1}{2}\left(x - \frac{1}{x}\right)$ and $y = \frac{1}{2}\left(x - \frac{3}{x}\right)$ intersected by $y = -x$ and $y = 0$. At these intersections the gradients of the tangents are respectively $1 - (-1) = 2$ and $1 - 0 = 1$.

You can use the same argument for any homogeneous differential equation and any line through the origin. If a solution curve of the differential equation $\frac{dy}{dx} = f\left(\frac{y}{x}\right)$ is intersected by a line $y = mx$ through the origin, then at the point of intersection $\frac{y}{x} = m$, so the gradient of the solution curve is $f(m)$. It follows that the tangents to all the solution curves which intersect $y = mx$ have the same gradient at the points of intersection, and are therefore parallel.

You can use this idea to draw sketches of solution curves for homogeneous differential equations when you can't find an exact equation for the solution. The method is described in the following example.

Example 12.3.1

For the differential equation $\frac{dy}{dx} = e^{\frac{y}{x}}$, sketch the solution curve through the point $(2, 0)$.

Begin by drawing at the point $(2, 0)$ a short line segment indicating the tangent to the solution curve, with gradient $e^{\frac{0}{2}} = e^0 = 1$.

Now draw a number of lines through the origin. In Fig. 12.5 these are $y = x$, $y = \frac{1}{2}x$, $y = \frac{1}{4}x$, $y = -\frac{1}{4}x$, $y = -\frac{1}{2}x$, $y = -x$ and $y = -2x$. On each of these lines draw several short line segments whose direction is that of the tangents to the solution curves which intersect the line; that is, with gradients e^1, $e^{\frac{1}{2}}$, $e^{\frac{1}{4}}$, $e^{-\frac{1}{4}}$, $e^{-\frac{1}{2}}$, e^{-1} and e^{-2}.

Finally, draw a curve so that the tangent at the intersection with each of the lines is parallel to the corresponding line segments. Although this can only be done approximately, the sketch gives a good idea of the shape of the solution curve.

Now suppose that in Example 12.3.1 you want to add a sketch of the solution curve through $(3,0)$. Using the same method, the tangent as the curve crosses each of the dotted lines in Fig. 12.5 would be parallel to that for the curve already drawn. You might guess that the new solution curve would have the same shape as the one already sketched, but enlarged in the ratio 3 to 2.

This is in fact correct. The property is illustrated by the exact solution curves in the next example.

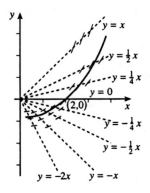

Fig. 12.5

Example 12.3.2

Find the general solution of the homogeneous differential equation $\dfrac{dy}{dx} = \dfrac{y}{x} - 2$ for $x > 0$.

Using the substitution $y = xz$, the equation becomes

$$z + x\frac{dz}{dx} = z - 2,$$

which reduces to

$$\frac{dz}{dx} = -\frac{2}{x}.$$

Integrating,

$$z = k - 2\ln x,$$

where k is an arbitrary constant. (No modulus sign is needed, since $x > 0$.) Finally, writing $z = \dfrac{y}{x}$ gives the general solution

$$y = x(k - 2\ln x).$$

Fig. 12.6 shows the solution curves for the equation in Example 12.3.2 with $k = 0, 1, 2$ and 3. The last three of these are enlargements of the first.

To show this, recall that replacing x by $\dfrac{x}{c}$ in an equation $y = f(x)$ stretches the graph by a factor c in the x-direction; and replacing y by $\dfrac{y}{c}$ stretches the graph by a factor c in the y-direction. So replacing both x and y by $\dfrac{x}{c}$ and $\dfrac{y}{c}$ produces stretches of factor c in both directions, that is an enlargement of factor c from the origin.

So the enlargement of the graph $y = -2x \ln x$ by a factor c produces the graph of $\frac{y}{c} = -2\frac{x}{c}\ln\left(\frac{x}{c}\right)$, which is $y = x(k - 2\ln x)$ with $k = 2\ln c$, that is $c = e^{\frac{1}{2}k}$.

So the graphs in Fig. 12.6 of

$$y = x(1 - 2\ln x),$$

$$y = x(2 - 2\ln x)$$

and $y = x(3 - 2\ln x)$

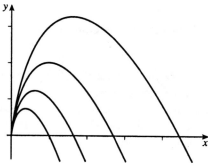

Fig. 12.6

are enlargements of $y = -2x \ln x$ with factors $e^{\frac{1}{2}}$, e and $e^{\frac{3}{2}}$ respectively.

What this illustrates is:

If S is a solution curve of a homogeneous differential equation, then any curve obtained from S by enlargement from the origin is also a solution curve.

You can prove this by using the chain rule. Suppose that (x, y) are the coordinates of a point on S, and that $X = cx$, $Y = cy$. Then you can find $\frac{dY}{dx}$ either as $\frac{dX}{dx} \times \frac{dY}{dX} = c \times \frac{dY}{dX}$ or as $\frac{dy}{dx} \times \frac{dY}{dy} = \frac{dy}{dx} \times c$. It follows that $\frac{dY}{dX} = \frac{dy}{dx}$. Also $\frac{Y}{X} = \frac{y}{x}$. So if (x, y) satisfies the homogeneous differential equation $\frac{dy}{dx} = f\left(\frac{y}{x}\right)$, (X, Y) satisfies $\frac{dY}{dX} = f\left(\frac{Y}{X}\right)$. That is, the curve obtained from S by enlargement of factor c from the origin is also a solution curve of the differential equation.

Exercise 12B *

1   In Example 12.2.1, find the enlargement factor which transforms the solution curve $y = \frac{1}{2}\left(x + \frac{1}{x}\right)$ to $y = \frac{1}{2}\left(x + \frac{3}{x}\right)$.

2   In Exercise 12A Question 2(a), show that there are two pairs of solution curves which are enlargements of each other.

3   In Exercise 12A Question 4 parts (a) and (b), show that the last two solution curves can be obtained from the first by enlargement from the origin, and find the enlargement factors.

4   In Exercise 12A Question 6, investigate whether all the solution curves can be obtained from the others by enlargement from the origin.

5   Use the method of Example 12.3.1 to sketch the solution curve of the differential equation
$\dfrac{dy}{dx} = \dfrac{\sqrt{x^2 + y^2}}{x}$ through the point $(5, 0)$.

6   Show that, if a solution curve of $\dfrac{dy}{dx} = \dfrac{y}{x} + \dfrac{y^2}{x^2}$ has any stationary points, then they lie on one of two lines, and state their equations.

Verify your answer by solving the equation and finding the coordinates of the stationary points on the solution curves.

13 Linear differential equations

This chapter describes another method which can be used to solve some differential equations. When you have completed it, you should

- be able to solve first order linear differential equations by using an integrating factor.

13.1 Solution using the product rule

Example 13.1.1

Find the general solution of the differential equation $3x^2y + x^3\dfrac{dy}{dx} = x^4$.

> When you have a differential equation to solve, you should begin by asking whether it is one of a type for which you already know a special method. For example, is $\dfrac{dy}{dx}$ a function of just x, or just y? Are the variables separable? Is the equation homogeneous?
>
> With the given differential equation, the answer to all these questions is 'no'. So where do you go next?
>
> Look at the left side of the equation. Does it remind you of anything? The factors involving x, that is $3x^2$ and x^3, should give you a clue, since $3x^2 = \dfrac{d}{dx}x^3$. So the left side could be written as
>
> $$\frac{d}{dx}x^3 \times y + x^3 \times \frac{dy}{dx}.$$
>
> This is just what you get when you differentiate x^3y using the product rule. So the differential equation is
>
> $$\frac{d}{dx}\left(x^3y\right) = x^4.$$
>
> It is now easy to complete the solution. Integrating with respect to x,
>
> $$x^3y = \tfrac{1}{5}x^5 + k.$$
>
> That is,
>
> $$y = \tfrac{1}{5}x^2 + \frac{k}{x^3}.$$

Check this answer for yourself by substitution into the original differential equation.

The trouble with this example is that it is most unlikely that you will be asked to solve

$$3x^2y + x^3\frac{dy}{dx} = x^4,$$

because all the terms of this equation have a common factor x^2. It is more likely that the equation will be presented as

$$3y + x\frac{dy}{dx} = x^2,$$

and then the left side is not the derivative of a product. How could you tell that the key to solving this equation is to multiply each term by x^2? Read on!

13.2 Integrating factors

This chapter is concerned with the general problem of solving differential equations of the form

$$f(x)\frac{dy}{dx} + g(x)y = h(x),$$

where f, g and h are given functions. Example 13.1.1 is such an equation with $f(x) = x^3$, $g(x) = 3x^2$ and $h(x) = x^4$. A differential equation like this is said to be **linear**, because $\frac{dy}{dx}$ and y appear only to the first degree; the equation has no terms involving $\left(\frac{dy}{dx}\right)^m$ or y^m with $m \neq 1$, nor are there any products like $y\frac{dy}{dx}$.

It isn't necessary to write this equation with three given functions, because you can divide through by $f(x)$ to get

$$\frac{dy}{dx} + \frac{g(x)}{f(x)}y = \frac{h(x)}{f(x)}$$

and then express $\frac{g(x)}{f(x)}$ as a single function $p(x)$, and $\frac{h(x)}{f(x)}$ as $q(x)$.

> The **standard form** of a first order linear differential equation is
>
> $$\frac{dy}{dx} + p(x)y = q(x),$$
>
> where $p(x)$ and $q(x)$ are given functions of x.

For example, the standard form of the equation discussed in Example 13.1.1 would be

$$\frac{dy}{dx} + \frac{3}{x} \times y = x.$$

You already know that this can be integrated by multiplying by x^3, which makes the left side $3x^2y + x^3\frac{dy}{dx}$. The question is, how can you find this multiplying factor x^3 from the knowledge that $p(x) = \frac{3}{x}$?

The answer comes in two steps. First, notice that

$$\int \frac{3}{x}\,dx = 3\ln x + k = \ln x^3 + k.$$

So you could say that the 'simplest' integral of $\dfrac{3}{x}$ is $\ln x^3$.

The second step is to get from $\ln x^3$ to the multiplying factor x^3, and to do this you simply have to take the exponential, since $e^{\ln x^3} = x^3$.

This works as a general rule. The multiplier x^3 is an example of an **integrating factor**. It is a function that you can use to convert a first order differential equation in standard form into a form which can be integrated.

> To find an integrating factor for the differential equation
>
> $$\frac{dy}{dx} + p(x)y = q(x)$$
>
> first find the simplest integral of $p(x)$, and call it $I(x)$; then $e^{I(x)}$ is an integrating factor.

Example 13.2.1

Find the general solution of the differential equation $\dfrac{dy}{dx} - \dfrac{y}{x} = x$.

This is already in standard form, with $p(x) = -\dfrac{1}{x}$. So find the simplest integral of $-\dfrac{1}{x}$, which is $-\ln x$, or $\ln\dfrac{1}{x}$. An integrating factor is therefore $e^{\ln\frac{1}{x}}$, which is simply $\dfrac{1}{x}$.

Multiplying the differential equation by $\dfrac{1}{x}$ gives

$$\frac{dy}{dx} \times \frac{1}{x} + y \times \left(-\frac{1}{x^2}\right) = 1.$$

The left side of this is $\dfrac{d}{dx}\left(y \times \dfrac{1}{x}\right)$, so the equation can be written as

$$\frac{d}{dx}\left(y \times \frac{1}{x}\right) = 1.$$

This can be integrated as

$$y \times \frac{1}{x} = x + k,$$

or more conveniently

$$y = x^2 + kx.$$

In an example like this, since the process is quite complicated, it is a good idea to check the answer by direct substitution. If $y = x^2 + kx$, then $\dfrac{dy}{dx} = 2x + k$ and $\dfrac{y}{x} = x + k$, so $\dfrac{dy}{dx} - \dfrac{y}{x} = (2x + k) - (x + k) = x$, as required.

In Example 13.2.1 all the solution curves are parabolas through the origin, including $y = x^2$ when $k = 0$. Fig. 13.1 shows a selection of these curves for various values of k.

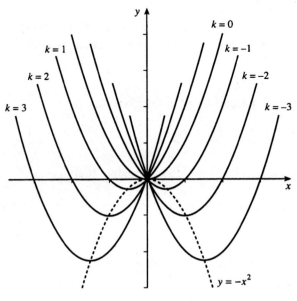

Fig. 13.1

It is interesting to notice that the minimum points on all the solution curves lie on the curve $y = -x^2$, shown dotted in Fig. 13.1. You can see the reason for this by going back to the differential equation and putting $\dfrac{dy}{dx} = 0$. This gives $-\dfrac{y}{x} = x$, which is $y = -x^2$.

The next example requires you to find the particular solution curve which passes through a given point.

Example 13.2.2

Find the curve through $(0,1)$ whose equation satisfies the differential equation $\dfrac{dy}{dx} + y = e^x$.

> For this differential equation $p(x)$ is simply 1, and the simplest integral of this is x. So an integrating factor is e^x.
>
> Multiplying the equation by e^x gives
>
> $$\frac{dy}{dx} \times e^x + y \times e^x = e^{2x}.$$

The left side is $\dfrac{d}{dx}\left(ye^x\right)$, so the equation can be written as $\dfrac{d}{dx}\left(ye^x\right)=e^{2x}$, and then integrated to give the general solution

$$ye^x = \tfrac{1}{2}e^{2x}+k.$$

The question asks for the solution for which $y=1$ when $x=0$, so substitute these values to obtain $1=\tfrac{1}{2}+k$, giving $k=\tfrac{1}{2}$.

The required solution is therefore

$$ye^x = \tfrac{1}{2}e^{2x}+\tfrac{1}{2},$$

which is best written as

$$y=\tfrac{1}{2}e^x+\tfrac{1}{2}e^{-x}.$$

Fig. 13.2 shows a number of solution curves for the differential equation in Example 13.2.2, with the curve through $(0,1)$ emphasised as a heavier line. In this case not all the curves have stationary points; for those which do, these points lie on $y=e^x$ (shown dotted in Fig. 13.2), which you get by putting $\dfrac{dy}{dx}=0$ in the differential equation.

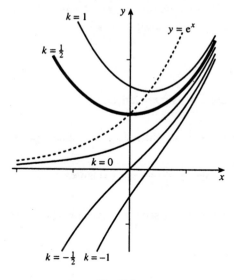

Fig. 13.2

It is important to remember that, to use the integrating factor rule, you have to begin with the differential equation in standard form. But it is always worth checking first that the equation isn't already in a form which can be integrated directly, as was the case with the example in Section 13.1. This is the point of the first step in the following algorithm, which summarises the method of using an integrating factor to solve first order linear differential equations..

To find the general solution of the differential equation $\frac{dy}{dx}f(x) + yg(x) = h(x)$ using an integrating factor:

Step 1   If $g(x) = f'(x)$, write the equation as $\frac{d}{dx}(y\,f(x)) = h(x)$ and go to Step 6.

Step 2   Divide the equation by $f(x)$ to obtain the standard form
$$\frac{dy}{dx} + y\,p(x) = q(x).$$

Step 3   Find the simplest integral of $p(x)$; denote it by $I(x)$.

Step 4   Write $u(x) = e^{I(x)}$, and simplify this if possible. This is the integrating factor.

Step 5   Multiply the equation (in its form after Step 2) by $u(x)$, and write the equation as $\frac{dy}{dx}(yu(x)) = q(x)u(x)$.

Step 6   Integrate the equation with respect to x, including an arbitrary constant.

Step 7   Put the solution into the form $y = \ldots$ by dividing by the function which multiplies y (that is $u(x)$ or $f(x)$).

Example 13.2.3

Find the general solution of $\frac{dy}{dx}\cos x + y\sin x = \tan x$.

Step 1 $f'(x)$ is $\frac{d}{dx}\cos x = -\sin x$, which does not equal $g(x) = \sin x$.

Step 2   Divide by $\cos x$ to obtain $\frac{dy}{dx} + y\tan x = \tan x \sec x$.

Step 3 $p(x) = \tan x$; $\displaystyle\int \tan x\, dx = \ln\sec x + k$, so take $I(x) = \ln\sec x$.

Step 4   The integrating factor is $u(x) = e^{\ln\sec x} = \sec x$.

Step 5   Multiply by $\sec x$: $\frac{dy}{dx}\sec x + y\sec x\tan x = \tan x \sec^2 x$, which is

$$\frac{d}{dx}(y\sec x) = \tan x \sec^2 x.$$

Step 6   Integrating, $y\sec x = \frac{1}{2}\tan^2 x + k$.

Step 7   Dividing by $\sec x$, $y = \dfrac{\sin^2 x}{2\cos x} + k\cos x$.

This is a perfectly acceptable answer to the question. However, it is worth noticing that it can be written as

$$y = \frac{1 - \cos^2 x}{2 \cos x} + k \cos x,$$

which is

$$y = \tfrac{1}{2}(\sec x - \cos x) + k \cos x = \tfrac{1}{2}\sec x + \left(k - \tfrac{1}{2}\right)\cos x.$$

Since k is an arbitrary constant, $k - \tfrac{1}{2}$ can be replaced by a single arbitrary constant c, giving the simplest form of the solution as

$$y = \tfrac{1}{2}\sec x + c \cos x.$$

After such a complicated calculation it is worth checking the answer to make sure you have not made a mistake. If $y = \tfrac{1}{2}\sec x + c \cos x$, then $\dfrac{dy}{dx} = \tfrac{1}{2}\sec x \tan x - c \sin x$, so that the left side of the original equation is

$$\left(\tfrac{1}{2}\sec x \tan x - c \sin x\right)\cos x + \left(\tfrac{1}{2}\sec x + c \cos x\right)\sin x$$

$$= \tfrac{1}{2}\tan x - c \sin x \cos x + \tfrac{1}{2}\tan x + c \cos x \sin x$$

$$= \tan x, \quad \text{as required.}$$

One small point to notice at Step 3 is that strictly the integral of $\tan x$ is $\ln|\sec x|$; that is, it is $\ln \sec x$ or $\ln(-\sec x)$ depending on whether $\sec x$ is positive or negative. If you use the minus sign, then at Step 4 you get $u(x) = -\sec x$ rather than $\sec x$. But this is not important, since it clearly makes no difference at Step 5 whether you multiply the equation by $\sec x$ or $-\sec x$.

13.3 Why the method works

It is quite easy to see why the rule for finding the integrating factor works. Since $I(x)$ is an integral of $p(x)$, it follows that $p(x) = I'(x)$. The left side of the differential equation, in standard form, is therefore

$$\frac{dy}{dx} + yI'(x).$$

After multiplying by $e^{I(x)}$, this becomes

$$\frac{dy}{dx}e^{I(x)} + ye^{I(x)}I'(x).$$

Now if $u(x) = e^{I(x)}$, then differentiation by the chain rule gives $u'(x) = I'(x) \times e^{I(x)}$.

So

$$\frac{dy}{dx}e^{I(x)} + yI'(x) \times e^{I(x)} = \frac{dy}{dx}u(x) + yu'(x), \text{ which is } \frac{d}{dx}(y\,u(x)).$$

You may also question why the algorithm in Section 13.2 specifies that you should choose $I(x)$ to be the *simplest* integral of $p(x)$. The answer is that you needn't. But if you chose some other integral of $p(x)$, this would have the form $I(x)+c$, for some constant c. The integrating factor would then be $e^{I(x)+c}$, which is $e^{I(x)} \times e^c$. So the only effect of taking one of the other integrals of $p(x)$ for $I(x)$ is to multiply the equation through by an additional numerical constant e^c, which is pointless.

Exercise 13

1   For each of the following differential equations, show that the left side is the derivative of a product. Hence find the general solution of the differential equation.

(a) $y + x\dfrac{dy}{dx} = x^2$

(b) $x\cos t + \dfrac{dx}{dt}\sin t = 1$

(c) $\dfrac{1}{x}\dfrac{dy}{dx} - \dfrac{1}{x^2}y = \dfrac{1}{x^3}$

(d) $e^{x^2}\dfrac{du}{dx} + 2xe^{x^2}u = 2$

2   Find the equation of the solution curve through the given point for each of the following differential equations.

(a) $2xy + x^2\dfrac{dy}{dx} = 1$ through $(1,0)$

(b) $2y\sin x\cos x + \dfrac{dy}{dx}\sin^2 x = \cos x$ through $\left(\tfrac{1}{2}\pi, 1\right)$

(c) $\dfrac{y}{\sqrt{x}} + 2\sqrt{x}\dfrac{dy}{dx} = x$ through $(1,1)$

3   Use integrating factors to find the general solutions of the following differential equations. Check your answers by substituting back into the original equations.

(a) $\dfrac{du}{dx} + \dfrac{2u}{x} = 1$

(b) $\dfrac{dy}{dx} - y\tan x = 2\sin x$

(c) $\dfrac{dx}{dt} - 4x = e^{2t}$

(d) $\dfrac{dy}{dx} - \dfrac{3y}{x} = x$

(e) $\dfrac{dy}{dt} + y\tan t = \cos t$

(f)* $\dfrac{dy}{dx}\sin x + y\sec x = \cos^2 x$

4   For the following differential equations, find the equations of the solution curves which pass through the given points. Use a calculator to display them on a single diagram.

(a) $\dfrac{dy}{dx} + 3y = 9x$ through $(0,-2), (0,-1), (0,0), (0,1), (0,2)$

(b) $x\dfrac{dy}{dx} + 2y = x^2$, for $x>0$, through $(1,0), (1,1), (1,2), (2,0), (2,1), (2,2)$

(c) $y\sin x + \dfrac{dy}{dx}\cos x = 2\tan x$, for $-\tfrac{1}{2}\pi < x < \tfrac{1}{2}\pi$, through $(0,-2),(0,-1),(0,0),(0,1),(0,2)$

(d) $x\dfrac{dy}{dx} = 3y + 2x$, for $x \neq 0$, through $(-1,-1), (-1,0), (-1,1), (1,-1), (1,0), (1,1)$

5   A curve passing through the point $(1,1)$ has the property that, at each point P of the curve, the gradient of the curve is 1 less than the gradient of (OP), where O is the origin. Find the equation of the curve, and illustrate your answer with a graph.

6 A sack containing a liquid chemical is placed in an empty tank. The chemical seeps out of the sack at a rate of $0.1x$ litres per hour, where x is the number of litres of the chemical remaining in the sack after t hours. The chemical in the tank evaporates at a rate $0.2y$ litres per hour, where y is the number of litres of the chemical in the tank after t hours. If the sack originally contained 50 litres of the chemical, find differential equations for x and for y, and solve them. Find the greatest amount of chemical in the tank, and when this occurs.

7 A will-o'-the-wisp is oscillating in a straight line so that its displacement from the origin at time t is $a + b\sin ct$, where a, b and c are positive constants. It is chased by a kitten which moves so that its velocity at any time is equal to cy, where y is the displacement of the will-o'-the-wisp from the kitten. If x denotes the displacement of the kitten from the origin at time t, find a differential equation connecting x and t. Show that, after some time, x is approximately equal to $a + \dfrac{1}{\sqrt{2}} b \sin\left(ct - \tfrac{1}{4}\pi\right)$. Draw graphs to illustrate the positions of the kitten and the will-o'-the-wisp during the chase.

8 A rope hangs over a rough circular peg of radius r. It is just about to slip with a vertical length p on one side and a vertical length q on the other, where $q > p$. It can be shown that, if the coefficient of friction is 1, the quantity $u = \dfrac{T}{\gamma g}$ satisfies the differential equation

$\dfrac{du}{d\theta} - u = r(\cos\theta - \sin\theta)$. ($\gamma$ is the mass of the rope per unit length, g is the acceleration due to gravity, θ is the angle that the radius to a point on the peg makes with the vertical and T is the tension in the rope at that point.) Given that $u = p$ when $\theta = -\tfrac{1}{2}\pi$, and $u = q$ when $\theta = \tfrac{1}{2}\pi$, prove that $q = pe^{\pi} + r\left(1 + e^{\pi}\right)$.

9 Find the general solution of the differential equation $x\dfrac{dy}{dx} = 2(y - x)$ for $x \neq 0$. Investigate the regions in which the gradient of the solution curve is positive, and those in which it is negative,
   (a) from the equation of the solution,
   (b) from the differential equation.
   Illustrate your answers with sketches of some solution curves.

10 Find the general solution of the differential equation $x\dfrac{dy}{dx} + y = \dfrac{1}{x^2}$ for $x > 0$. Use the differential equation to show that the stationary points on the solution curves all lie on $y = \dfrac{1}{x^2}$, and verify this from your equation for the general solution. Draw graphs to illustrate this property.

   By differentiating the differential equation, show that $\dfrac{d^2y}{dx^2} = \dfrac{2}{x^2}\left(y - \dfrac{2}{x^2}\right)$. Hence identify the regions in which the solution curves are concave up, and those in which they are concave down. Check your answer from your graphs.

14 Approximate methods

This chapter develops techniques for numerical and graphical solutions of differential equations. When you have completed it, you should

- be able to use Euler's method to find numerical approximations to the solutions of differential equations
- understand that the errors can be reduced by shortening the step length, the amount of reduction that can be expected, and why
- understand what is meant by a slope field, and how it can be used to sketch approximate solution curves.

14.1 Euler's method

You now know how to solve many differential equations, but there are some whose solutions can't be written as exact algebraic equations. However, you can still solve particular equations as accurately as you want by numerical methods. The first example illustrates the idea with an application in kinematics.

Example 14.1.1
A rocket is launched vertically into space. Table 14.1 gives the speed at 10-second intervals after lift-off for 50 seconds. Estimate the height of the rocket at these times.

Time, t (seconds)	0	10	20	30	40	50
Speed, v (km s^{-1})	0	0.63	1.42	2.47	3.99	6.67

Table 14.1

The speed is the rate at which the height of the rocket is increasing. So if the rocket is at height z km after t seconds, its speed is given by $v = \dfrac{dz}{dt}$. But as only numerical values of $\dfrac{dz}{dt}$ are available, you can't solve this algebraically to find z in terms of t. As a first approximation you can split the period into 5 time-steps of 10 seconds each, and suppose that over each step the rocket travels with the speed given in the table for the beginning of the step. The calculation can then be set out as in Table 14.2.

Time, t	0	10	20	30	40	50
Height, z	0	0	6.3	20.5		85.1
Speed, $v = \dfrac{dz}{dt}$	0	0.63	1.42	2.47		
Time interval, δt	10	10	10			
Increase in height, δz	0	6.3	14.2			

Table 14.2

You construct this table one column at a time. In column 1 the initial time (0 seconds) and height (0 km) are entered in rows 1 and 2. Copy the entry in row 3 (0 km s^{-1}) from Table 14.1, and enter the time-step (10 seconds) in row 4. Then find the number in row 5 by multiplying the entries in rows 3 and 4; this is only approximately the increase in height, based on the assumption of constant speed over the whole of the first time-step. It is clearly an underestimate, because the speed of the rocket is increasing.

When column 1 is complete, start column 2 by adding the increases in time and height from column 1 to the previous entries for time and height. Then repeat the procedure.

Some spaces in columns 4 and 5 have been left blank for you to fill in for yourself. You should arrive at a value of 85.1 km for the estimated height after 50 seconds.

You can use this step-by-step method to approximate to the solution of a differential equation. The only difference is that the third row is not determined by numerical data, but is calculated from the differential equation.

Starting from a given initial point (x_0, y_0) on the solution curve, you find a sequence of points (x_1, y_1), (x_2, y_2), ... whose x-coordinates form an arithmetic sequence with a suitable common difference δx. The y-coordinates are then calculated so that the points lie as close as possible to the solution curve.

Example 14.1.2

Use the step-by-step method to find an approximation to the solution of $\dfrac{dy}{dx} = \sqrt{x + y}$, with an initial value $y = 0.2$ when $x = 0$. Use 5 x-steps, each of size 0.2, to estimate values of y from $x = 0$ to $x = 1$.

The calculations are set out in Table 14.3, and illustrated by Fig. 14.4.

x_r	0	0.2	0.4	0.6	0.8	1.0
y_r		0.2	0.289 44	0.429 36	0.611 50		1.087 11
Gradient at (x_r, y_r)	0.447 21	0.699 60	0.910 69			
x-step	0.2	0.2	0.2			
Estimated y-step	0.089 44	0.139 92	0.182 14			

Table 14.3

In Table 14.3 x_r and y_r are the entries in rows 1 and 2 of any column. You then calculate the gradient g as $\sqrt{x_r + y_r}$ and enter it in row 3. Row 4 shows the chosen x-step, h (0.2 in this example), and you then calculate the y-step, $k = gh$. This completes the column. You then start the next column by calculating $x_{r+1} = x_r + h$, $y_{r+1} = y_r + k$.

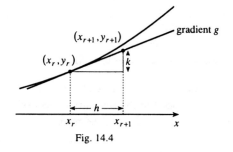

Fig. 14.4

Some spaces have been left in columns 4 and 5 for you to fill in yourself. You should arrive at 1.087 11 as the estimated value of y when $x = 1$.

Fig. 14.4 shows what is happening. When you go from x_r to x_{r+1}, what you would like to find is the y-coordinate at x_{r+1} on the solution curve through (x_r, y_r). But you can't do this, because you don't know the equation of the curve. All you do know, from the differential equation, is the gradient of the tangent at (x_r, y_r). So the best guess you can make is to take the point on this tangent corresponding to $x = x_{r+1}$ as an approximation to the point on the solution curve.

The approximate step-by-step method illustrated in Example 11.4.2 is attributed to Euler, although the basic idea can be traced back to earlier mathematicians, including Fermat and Newton.

Euler's step-by-step algorithm

To find an approximate numerical solution of a first order differential equation:

Step 1 Choose an x-step.

Step 2 In column 1, enter the given initial values of x and y in rows 1 and 2. Denote these by x_0, y_0.

Step 3 In row 3 enter the gradient g, calculated from the differential equation for the values of x_r and y_r in rows 1 and 2.

Step 4 Enter the chosen x-step in row 4. Denote it by h.

Step 5 Calculate the y-step $k = gh$, and enter it in row 5.

Step 6 Calculate $x_{r+1} = x_r + h$, $y_{r+1} = y_r + k$ and enter these in rows 1 and 2 of the next column.

Step 7 If you want to go further, return to Step 3.

Exercise 14A

1 A racing car accelerates from 0 to $80\ \mathrm{m\,s}^{-1}$ (about 180 m.p.h.) in 12 seconds. Its speed after successive intervals of 2 seconds is given in the table. Estimate how far the car travels while accelerating.

Time (seconds)	0	2	4	6	8	10	12
Speed ($\mathrm{m\,s}^{-1}$)	0	8	20	40	58	74	80

Is your answer too large or too small?

2 The driver of a train travelling at $100\ \mathrm{m\,s}^{-1}$ applies the brakes and brings the train to rest in 25 seconds. The speed of the train after successive intervals of 5 seconds is given in the table. Approximately how far does the train travel in coming to rest?

Time (seconds)	0	5	10	15	20	25
Speed ($\mathrm{m\,s}^{-1}$)	100	88	60	30	12	0

Is your answer too large or too small?

3   For the differential equation and initial value in Example 14.1.2, carry out similar step-by-step calculations with

    (a) 10 x-steps, each of 0.1,   (b) 20 x-steps, each of 0.05.

    Keep your answers to Question 4 for use in Exercise 14B Questions 1 and 2.

4   Use Euler's step-by-step method to find points on the solution curves of the following differential equations.

    (a) $\dfrac{dy}{dx} = \cos\tfrac{1}{2}(x+y)$; solution curve through $(0,0)$ over the interval $0 \le x \le 1$, taking

        x-steps of   (i) $h = 0.5$,   (ii) $h = 0.25$;

    (b) $\dfrac{dy}{dx} = \dfrac{1}{x+2y}$; solution curve through $(1,2)$ over the interval $1 \le x \le 5$, taking

        x-steps of   (i) $h = 1$,   (ii) $h = 0.5$;

    (c) $\dfrac{dy}{dx} = \sqrt{y} + e^{-x}$; solution curve through $(0,1)$ over the interval $0 \le x \le 2$, taking

        x-steps of   (i) $h = 1$,   (ii) $h = 0.5$,   (iii) $h = 0.25$;

    (d) $\dfrac{dy}{dx} = \dfrac{\sqrt{x}+\sqrt{y}}{2}$; solution curve through $(1,2)$ over the interval $0 \le x \le 2$, taking

        x-steps of   (i) $h = \pm 0.5$,   (ii) $h = \pm 0.25$.

5   The speed v of an object falling from a height satisfies the equation $\dfrac{dv}{dt} = 10 - 0.01v^{\frac{3}{2}}$, and $v = 0$ when $t = 0$. Use a step-by-step method with t-steps of 4 and 2 to estimate v when $t = 20$.

6   The level, h metres, of water in a reservoir satisfies the differential equation $\dfrac{dh}{dt} = 0.5t - 0.1h$, where t is the time in weeks. When $t = 0$, the level is 10 metres.

    Find the level when $t = 10$,

    (a) by using Euler's step-by-step method with step lengths of 2 weeks and 1 week,
    (b) by solving the differential equation exactly.

    Calculate the errors in using the step-by-step method.

14.2 Slope fields

Another approach is to use numerical values of $\dfrac{dy}{dx}$ given by the differential equation to sketch approximate solution curves. You have already used this idea with homogeneous differential equations in Section 12.3. This method is especially effective if you want to know the nature of the general solution of the differential equation.

It is useful first to introduce some new notation. An expression like $\sqrt{x+y}$ is an example of a **function of two variables** x and y. Such a function is defined for a **domain** which is a set of number pairs (x,y). For $\sqrt{x+y}$ the natural domain is the set such that $x + y \ge 0$, represented in a coordinate plane by the points to the 'north-east' of the line $x + y = 0$, shown by the shaded part of Fig. 14.5.

For each point of the domain the function defines a
unique value, denoted in general by $f(x,y)$. The set of
values taken by the function is its **range**; for $\sqrt{x+y}$ the
range is the set of non-negative real numbers.

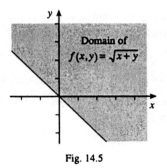

Fig. 14.5

A general first order differential equation can be written
as

$$\frac{dy}{dx} = f(x,y)$$

for some function f. This defines, at each point of the
domain of f, the gradient of the solution curve through
that point. These gradients constitute the **slope field**, or
tangent field, for the differential equation. It is
illustrated in Fig. 14.6, for the differential equation
$\frac{dy}{dx} = \sqrt{x+y}$, by the 'needles' drawn at the corners of
the grid. (You can't, of course, show it at more than a
few typical points. In Fig. 14.6 these are restricted to the
square $0 \le x \le 1$, $0 \le y \le 1$, but the slope field extends
throughout the domain of f.)

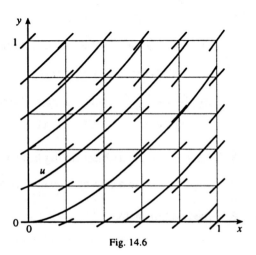

Fig. 14.6

There is a solution curve of the differential equation
through each point of the domain of f. Fig. 14.6 shows
a few such solution curves, and the needles help you to
imagine how others could be drawn starting at any point
of the domain. The curve labelled u is the one in
Example 14.1.2 with initial condition $y = 0.2$ when
$x = 0$.

14.3 Errors in Euler's method

The reason why Euler's method is only approximate is that it is based on the assumption that the value of
$\frac{dy}{dx}$ remains constant over an interval of values of x. This is obviously not true, but it suggests that the
method will be most accurate where $\frac{dy}{dx}$ is not changing very rapidly, that is where $\left|\frac{d^2y}{dx^2}\right|$ is small.

The simplest way of improving the accuracy is to reduce the length of the x-steps. In this way you can
allow for the change in $\frac{dy}{dx}$ more frequently. The downside is that you have to use more intervals to reach
your destination. Halving the length of the x-steps doubles the number of intervals you need, and so
doubles the amount of arithmetic. But this may not matter if you are using a computer or calculator
program.

The purpose of this section is to investigate the effect on the accuracy of reducing the step length. This
will be done by comparing the results obtained for the differential equation in Example 14.1.2 with
different values for the x-step.

The differential equation in Example 14.1.2 can in fact be solved algebraically, but the solution

$$\sqrt{y+x} - \ln\left(1+\sqrt{y+x}\right) - \tfrac{1}{2}x = \sqrt{0.2} - \ln\left(1+\sqrt{0.2}\right)$$

is too complicated to be of much use. You cannot find from it an equation for y in terms of x, or for x in terms of y. The values described as 'exact' (correct to 5 decimal places) in row 2 of Table 14.7 have not been calculated from this equation, but by using a more advanced modification of Euler's method. However, if you like you can check for yourself that these values do satisfy the above equation.

When you use Euler's method you begin by choosing an x-step. Rows 3 to 5 of Table 14.7 show the results you get if you use x-steps of 0.2, 0.1 and 0.05 respectively. Of course, the shorter the x-step, the more steps you must take to get to a particular value of x. The entries in row 3 are the same as those found in Example 14.1.2, with 5 steps of 0.2.

The numbers of steps in rows 4 and 5 are 10 and 20, but only the values of y for $x = 0.2, 0.4, \ldots, 1$ are shown in the table. You calculated these in Exercise 14A Question 3.

Rows 6 to 8 of Table 14.7 are the errors in the values calculated in rows 3 to 5, found by subtraction from the exact entries in row 2.

	x	0	0.2	0.4	0.6	0.8	1.0
	y (exact)	0.2	0.318 05	0.484 61	0.692 67	0.938 41	1.219 38
	0.2	0.2	0.289 44	0.429 36	0.611 50	0.831 64	1.087 11
y (approx.) with $h =$	0.1	0.2	0.303 43	0.456 51	0.651 48	0.884 32	1.152 45
	0.05	0.2	0.310 68	0.470 46	0.671 95	0.911 22	1.185 75
	0.2	0	0.028 61	0.055 25	0.081 17	0.106 77	0.132 27
error with $h =$	0.1	0	0.014 62	0.028 10	0.041 19	0.054 09	0.066 93
	0.05	0	0.007 37	0.014 15	0.020 72	0.027 19	0.033 63

Table 14.7

Look first along rows 6 to 8 of the table. You can see that the error gets larger with each step taken, but according to a regular pattern. For example, the bottom row shows that after 4 steps of 0.05 the error is about 0.007; after 8 and 12 steps it is about 0.014 and 0.021, roughly twice and three times as much. You will find a similar pattern in rows 6 and 7.

Look down the columns in rows 6 to 8. Each time the x-step is halved, the error is roughly halved. So you can achieve greater accuracy by using a larger number of smaller steps.

Table 14.7 is typical of the results obtained when you use Euler's method. They can be summarised as the following error rules:

Error rules in Euler's method

For a given x-step, the error is approximately proportional to the number of steps taken.

For a given value of x, the error is approximately proportional to the size of the x-steps used.

Another way of improving the accuracy of numerical solutions is to modify the algorithm. For example, in Example 14.1.1 you might get a more accurate estimate of the height of the rocket by taking the time interval boundaries at 5, 15, 25, 35 and 45 seconds, so that the tabulated speeds are at the middle rather than the start of each interval. A number of ways of modifying Euler's method have been devised, some of which can produce very accurate numerical solutions. These are described in specialist books on numerical analysis.

14.4* A graphical explanation of the error rules

Fig. 14.8 illustrates the step-by-step process in Example 14.1.2. You begin at the point A (0, 0.2). The basis of the Euler method is to suppose that, for the first x-step, the solution can be approximated by a line with gradient equal to the gradient at A. This takes you from A to P, which has coordinates (0.2, 0.289 44).

Now you would like P to be on the solution curve u, but in fact it is on a different solution curve, labelled v. The next step therefore takes you from P to Q, where the gradient of [PQ] is equal to that of the tangent to v at P. The coordinates of Q were calculated in Table 14.3 as (0.4, 0.429 36), and this lies on the curve labelled w. A further step takes you from Q to R, where R has coordinates (0.6, 0.611 50) and the gradient of [QR] is equal to that of the tangent to w at Q.

The exact values of y in row 2 of Table 14.7 correspond in the figure to the points A, B, C, D,... on u, and the step-by-step approximations correspond to A, P, Q, R,..., so the errors are represented by the lengths PB, QC, RD, ... You can see that the error increases by about the same amount at each step, so the total error is roughly proportional to the number of steps.

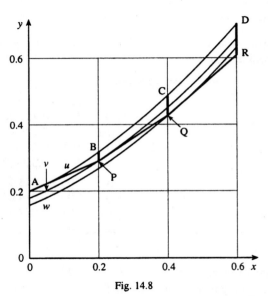

Fig. 14.8

The effect of halving the x-step is shown on a larger scale in Fig. 14.9. The points A, P, B and the curves u, v are the same as in Fig. 14.8, so that with $h = 0.2$ Euler's method takes you from A to P. But with an x-step of $h = 0.1$, the first step will go only as far as the mid-point S of [AP], and the next step will take you to T, where [ST] is the tangent to the solution curve through S. The error at $x = 0.2$ is therefore reduced from PB to TB. You can see that the effect of halving the step length is roughly to halve the error.

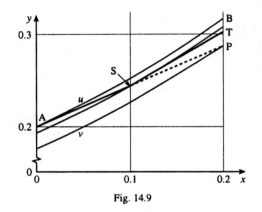

Fig. 14.9

Exercise 14B

1 For the differential equations in Exercise 14A Question 4, draw the slope fields and use these to make freehand sketches of the solution curves through the given points. On the same diagrams plot the points which you found from the step-by-step method, and compare these with the curves you have sketched.

2 The actual solution curves for the differential equations in Exercise 14A Question 4 pass through the points given in the table below. For each curve, find the errors in using the step-by-step method, and see whether these conform with the results summarised in the shaded box in Section 14.3.

(a)	(0.5, 0.479 91)	(1, 0.854 59)		
(b)	(2, 2.176 78)	(3, 2.320 01)	(4, 2.441 24)	(5, 2.546 76)
(c)	(0.5, 2.003 07)	(1, 3.033 18)	(1.5, 4.121 94)	(2, 5.292 99)
(d)	(0, 1.060 83)	(0.5, 1.457 16)	(1.5, 2.659 55)	(2, 3.425 15)

3* This question is designed to establish the error properties stated at the end of Section 14.3 for simple differential equations of the form $\dfrac{dy}{dx} = f(x)$. The notation for points and curves corresponds to that used in Fig. 14.8.

Let the solution curve have equation $y = F(x)$ passing through the point A with coordinates $(a, f(a))$. This satisfies the differential equation $F'(x) = f(x)$.

(a) Referring to Fig. 14.8. let the x-coordinate of B be $a + h$. Express the y-coordinates of B and P in terms of a, h and F. Use a Taylor polynomial (see Section 11.2) to show that the error in using Euler's method when $x = a + h$ is approximately $\frac{1}{2}h^2 f'(a)$.

(b) If the solution curve v through P has equation $y = F_1(x)$, explain why $F_1(x) = F(x) + k$, and show that $k = hf(a) + F(a) - F(a + h)$. Hence find the y-coordinate of Q, and deduce that the error when $x = a + 2h$ is approximately double that when $x = a + h$.

(c) Suppose that Euler's method is used with a single step of $2h$. State what the error would be when $x = a + 2h$, and show that doubling the step has the effect of approximately doubling the error.

Review exercise

1 If S_n denotes $\sum_{i=1}^{n} \frac{1}{i}$, prove that $S_{2n} - S_n > \frac{1}{2}$. Show that, if S_n tends to a limit S as $n \to \infty$, then

$\lim_{n \to \infty} (S_{2n} - S_n)$ would equal 0.

What can you deduce about the infinite series $\sum \frac{1}{i}$?

2 (a) If $\lim_{n \to \infty} u_n = 0$, what is $\lim_{n \to \infty} \frac{1}{1 + u_n}$?

   (b) Use the limit comparison test to show that, if $u_i > 0$ for all i and $\sum u_i$ is convergent, then so is

   $\sum \frac{u_i}{1 + u_i}$.

3 (a) Use a calculator to find $\sum_{i=1}^{999} \frac{1}{i^3}$.

   (b) Prove that $\sum_{i=1000}^{9999} \frac{1}{i^3} < \frac{9}{1000^2}$, and find a similar inequality for $\sum_{i=10\,000}^{99\,999} \frac{1}{i^3}$.

   (c) Prove that $\sum_{i=1000}^{\infty} \frac{1}{i^3} < \frac{1}{110\,000}$. Hence give the value of $\sum_{i=1}^{\infty} \frac{1}{i^3}$ correct to as many decimal places as these calculations allow.

4 A sequence u_n of positive numbers has $\lim_{n \to \infty} u_n = L$.

   (a) If $L > 0$, use the identity $\left(\sqrt{u_n} - \sqrt{L}\right)\left(\sqrt{u_n} + \sqrt{L}\right) = u_n - L$ to prove that $\sqrt{u_n} - \sqrt{L} < \frac{u_n - L}{\sqrt{L}}$.

   Hence prove that $\lim_{n \to \infty} \sqrt{u_n} = \sqrt{L}$.

   (b) If $L = 0$, use the definition of limit to prove that $\lim_{n \to \infty} \sqrt{u_n} = 0$.

5 The Maclaurin polynomial of degree 6 is used to approximate to the value of e^x. Over what range of values of x can you be sure that the error is less than 0.001 in absolute value?

6 (a) Find an expression for $\sum_{i=1}^{n} \frac{1}{i(i+2)}$ in terms of n.

   (b) For what values of x is the power series $\sum \frac{x^i}{i(i+2)}$ convergent?

7 State the limits, as $n \to \infty$, of

   (a) $\frac{n^2}{2^n}$,

   (b) $n \tan \frac{1}{n}$,

   (c) $\frac{n(2n-1)}{(3n-2)(4n-3)}$.

8 Use the integral test to prove that the value of $\sum_{i=1}^{\infty} \frac{1}{1+i^2}$ is between $\frac{1}{4}\pi$ and $\frac{1}{4}\pi + \frac{1}{2}$.

9 By grouping the terms of the series in two different ways, prove that $1 + \dfrac{1}{2^p}G < \displaystyle\sum_{i=1}^{2^k}\dfrac{1}{i^p} < G + \dfrac{1}{2^{kp}}$,

where G is the sum of the geometric series $\displaystyle\sum_{j=1}^{k}\left(\dfrac{1}{2^{p-1}}\right)^{j-1}$.

Hence find lower and upper bounds for the value of $\displaystyle\sum_{i=1}^{\infty}\dfrac{1}{i^p}$ if $p > 1$.

10 (a) If the Maclaurin series for $\tan x$ begins $a + bx + cx^2 + dx^3 + \dots$, use the identity
$\tan x \times \cos x = \sin x$ to find a, b, c and d.

(b) Use a similar method to find the Maclaurin series for $\sec x$ as far as the term in x^4.

(c) Why is there no Maclaurin series for $\csc x$? Show that, when x is small, $\csc x \approx \dfrac{1}{x} + \dfrac{1}{6}x + \dfrac{7}{360}x^3$.

11 Prove that, if $f(x) = \cos^n x$, then $f''(x) = n(n-1)\cos^{n-2}x - n^2\cos^n x$. Hence expand $\sqrt{\cos x}$ as a Maclaurin series as far as the term in x^4.

Check by squaring your answer and showing that the resulting series agrees with the series for $\cos x$ as far as the term in x^4.

12 Find (a) $\displaystyle\lim_{x \to 1}\dfrac{\cos\frac{1}{2}\pi x}{1 - x^2}$, (b) $\displaystyle\lim_{x \to 0}\dfrac{\left(e^x - 1\right)^2}{1 - \cos x}$.

13 A curve C passes through the origin and satisfies the differential equation $\dfrac{dy}{dx} + 2xy = x^3$.

(a) Use Euler's method to approximate to the value of y when $x = 1$ using x-steps of length
    (i) 0.2,   (ii) 0.1.

(b) Solve the equation to find the value of y when $x = 1$ correct to 4 decimal places.

(c) If you make the assumption that the error in Euler's method is exactly halved when the length of the x-steps is halved, what value would your answers to part (a) suggest for the value of y when $x = 1$?

14 Find the implicit equation of the curve which passes through $(1,0)$ and satisfies the homogeneous differential equation $\dfrac{dy}{dx} = \dfrac{2x}{x+y}$. Check your answer by differentiation.

15 (a) Use Euler's method starting from $x = 0$ to find an approximation to the solution of the differential equation $\dfrac{dy}{dx} = y$ which passes through the point $(0,1)$. Take steps of length
(i) 0.1 and (ii) 0.05 to find approximations to the value of y when $x = 1$.
Compare your approximations with the exact value of y when $x = 1$.

(b) For the same equation, take a step length of $\dfrac{1}{n}$, giving n steps between $x = 0$ and $x = 1$. Denoting the value of y after the rth step by y_r, show that $y_{r+1} = \left(1 + \dfrac{1}{n}\right)y_r$, and deduce that the value of y when $x = 1$ is given by $\left(1 + \dfrac{1}{n}\right)^n$.

(c) Try calculating $\left(1 + \dfrac{1}{n}\right)^n$ for large values of n. (See Exercise 7 Question 3.)

Examination questions

1 For positive integers k and n let $u_k = \dfrac{1 + 2(-1)^k}{k+1}$ and $S_{2n} = \displaystyle\sum_{k=1}^{2n} u_k$.

   (a) Show that $S_{2n} = \displaystyle\sum_{k=1}^{n} \dfrac{4k-1}{2k(2k+1)}$.

   (b) Hence or otherwise, determine whether the series $\displaystyle\sum_{k=1}^{\infty} u_k$ is convergent or not, justifying your

   answer.   (© IBO 2003)

2 (a) Describe how the integral test is used to show that a series is convergent. State all the necessary
        conditions.

   (b) Test the series $\displaystyle\sum_{n=1}^{\infty} \dfrac{n}{e^{n^2}}$ for convergence.   (© IBO 2003)

3 (a) Find the first four non-zero terms of the Maclaurin series for

        (i) $\sin x$,   (ii) e^{x^2}.

   (b) Hence find the Maclaurin series for $e^{x^2} \sin x$, up to the term containing x^5.

   (c) Use the result of part (b) to find $\displaystyle\lim_{x \to 0}\left(\dfrac{e^{x^2}\sin x - x}{x^3} \right)$ (© IBO 2003)

4 Find the Maclaurin series of the function $f(x) = \ln(1 + \sin x)$ up to and including the term in x^4.

                                                                                                (© IBO 2004)

5 Determine whether the following series is convergent or divergent.

   $$\sum_{k=1}^{\infty} \cos\left(\frac{(k-1)\pi}{2k} \right)$$ (© IBO 2004)

6 Let $S_k = \displaystyle\sum_{k=1}^{n} \dfrac{\sin\left(\dfrac{k\pi}{2}\right)}{k + \sin\left(\dfrac{k\pi}{2}\right)}$.

   (a) Show that, for $m \in \mathbb{Z}^+$, $S_{4m} = 0$.

   (b) Show that $S_n \to 0$ as $n \to \infty$.

   (c) Hence, or otherwise, show that the series converges as $n \to \infty$, and find its limit.

                                                                                                (© IBO 2004)

7 Find the range of values of x for which the following series is convergent.

   $$\sum_{n=0}^{\infty} \frac{x^n}{n+1}$$ (© IBO 2004)

8 (a) Show that the series $\displaystyle\sum_{n=1}^{\infty} \sin\frac{2\pi}{n^2}$ is convergent.

Let $\displaystyle S = \sum_{n=1}^{\infty} \sin\frac{2\pi}{n^2}$.

(b) Show that for positive integers $n \geq 2$, $\dfrac{1}{n^2} < \dfrac{1}{n-1} - \dfrac{1}{n}$.

(c) Hence or otherwise show that $1 \leq S < 2\pi$.   (© IBO 2004)

9 (a) Show that the series $\displaystyle\sum_{k=1}^{\infty} \frac{k-1}{k!}$ is convergent.

(b) Find the sum of the series.   (© IBO 2005)

10 The function f is defined by $f(x) \equiv e^{-x}\cos 2x$.

(a) (i) Show that $f''(x) + 2f'(x) + 5f(x) = 0$.

   (ii) Show that $f^{(n+2)}(0) + 2f^{(n+1)}(0) + 5f^{(n)}(0) = 0$, for $n \in \mathbb{Z}^+$.

(b) Find the Maclaurin series for $f(x)$ up to and including the term in x^4.   (© IBO 2005)

11 Given that $e^x \equiv 1 + x + \dfrac{x^2}{2!} + \dfrac{x^3}{3!} + \ldots$, and $\ln(1+x) = x - \dfrac{x^2}{2} + \dfrac{x^3}{3} - \dfrac{x^4}{4} + \ldots$, find the first four

non-zero terms of the Maclaurin series for $e^{-x}\ln(1+x)$.   (© IBO 2005)

12 Find the radius of convergence of the series $\displaystyle\sum_{k=1}^{\infty} \frac{(2k-2)!}{k!(k-1)!}x^k$.   (© IBO 2005)

Answers

1 Summing finite series

Exercise 1A (page 4)

2 (a) $\frac{1}{4}i(i+1)(i+2)(i+3)$;

$\frac{1}{4}n(n+1)(n+2)(n+3)$

(b) $-\frac{1}{2(i+1)(i+2)}$; $\frac{1}{4}\left(1-\frac{2}{(n+1)(n+2)}\right)$

3 $6i^5+2i^3$; $\frac{1}{12}n^2(n+1)^2(2n^2+2n-1)$

4 (a) $\ln(n+1)$ (b) $1-\frac{1}{n!}$

5 $(n+1)!-1$

6 $\frac{100}{201}$

7 $160i^4+80i^2+2$; $722\,666$

8 $\dfrac{1-(n+1)r^n+nr^{n+1}}{(1-r)^2}$

9 $\dfrac{\sin\left(n+\frac{1}{2}\right)\theta}{2\sin\frac{1}{2}\theta}-\frac{1}{2}$

Exercise 1B (page 8)

1 (a) $\dfrac{1}{x+5}+\dfrac{1}{x+3}$ (b) $\dfrac{3}{x-1}+\dfrac{7}{x+5}$

(c) $\dfrac{-4}{x-4}+\dfrac{5}{x-5}$ (d) $\dfrac{8}{2x-1}-\dfrac{4}{x+3}$

2 (a) $\dfrac{5}{x+2}+\dfrac{3}{x-1}$ (b) $\dfrac{5}{x-4}-\dfrac{5}{x+1}$

(c) $\dfrac{4}{x-3}+\dfrac{6}{x+3}$ (d) $\dfrac{3}{x}-\dfrac{6}{2x+1}$

3 (a) $\dfrac{3}{x+2}-\dfrac{5}{x-1}+\dfrac{2}{x-3}$

(b) $\dfrac{9}{x+3}-\dfrac{2}{x+1}+\dfrac{1}{x-1}$

(c) $\dfrac{3}{x}+\dfrac{5}{x-6}+\dfrac{7}{x+4}$

Exercise 1C (page 11)

1 (a) $\frac{1}{2}\left(1-\dfrac{1}{2n+1}\right)$ (b) $\frac{1}{3}\left(\dfrac{1}{2}-\dfrac{1}{3n+2}\right)$

(c) $\frac{1}{4}\left(\dfrac{1}{3}-\dfrac{1}{(2n+1)(2n+3)}\right)$

(d) $\frac{1}{15}-\dfrac{n+1}{(2n+3)(2n+5)}$

2 (a) $\dfrac{2^{n+1}}{n+2}-1$ (b) $\frac{1}{2}-\dfrac{\left(\frac{1}{2}\right)^n}{n+2}$

(c) $\frac{1}{4}\left(1-\dfrac{\left(\frac{1}{3}\right)^n}{2n+1}\right)$

2 Infinite series

Exercise 2A (page 14)

1 (a) 1   (b) $\frac{1}{4}$ (c) $\frac{1}{2}$

(d) $\frac{1}{6}$ (e) $\frac{1}{4}$ (f) $\frac{1}{12}$

2 (a) $\frac{1}{6}$ (b) $\frac{1}{4}$ (c) 2

3 (b) 1

Exercise 2B (page 18)

1 (a) $\lim_{i\to\infty}\dfrac{i}{2i-1}=\frac{1}{2}\neq 0$

(b) $\dfrac{1}{\sqrt[3]{i}}\geq\dfrac{1}{\sqrt{i}}$, and $\sum\dfrac{1}{\sqrt{i}}$ is divergent.

2 (a) $\dfrac{1}{i^{2.5}}\leq\dfrac{1}{i^2}$, and $\sum\dfrac{1}{i^2}$ is convergent.

(b) $\dfrac{1}{i^2+1}<\dfrac{1}{i^2}$, and $\sum\dfrac{1}{i^2}$ is convergent.

(c) $\dfrac{1}{2^i+1}<\dfrac{1}{2^i}$, and $\sum\left(\frac{1}{2}\right)^i$ is convergent.

3 (b) $\frac{1}{3}\pi^2-1\approx 2.29$

(c) For example $S_{56}\approx 1.879\,853\,862$

4 (a) $\dfrac{1}{i^4}\leq\dfrac{1}{i^2}$, and $\sum\dfrac{1}{i^2}$ is convergent.

(b) E.g. $S_{999}\approx 1.082\,323\,233$.   (c) 90

5 (a) $\dfrac{1}{i^3}\leq\dfrac{1}{i^2}$, and $\sum\dfrac{1}{i^2}$ is convergent.

(b) For example $S_{999}\approx 1.202\,056\,403$.

(d) $\sum\dfrac{1}{(i-1)i(i+1)}$ is not defined for $i=1$.

(e) $\displaystyle\sum_{i=2}^{\infty}\dfrac{1}{i^3}\leq\sum_{i=2}^{\infty}\dfrac{1}{(i-1)i(i+1)}=\frac{1}{4}$, so $\displaystyle\sum_{i=1}^{\infty}\dfrac{1}{i^3}\leq 1\frac{1}{4}$.

6 (a) $\sum\dfrac{1}{i}$ is divergent

(b) $S_{1000}>5\frac{1}{2}$ (c) $7.485\,471$

7 (a) $i = 1, 2$; $S_\infty \leq 2$

(b)   For $i > 2$, $i! \geq 2 \times 3^{i-2}$ $(=$ when $i = 2, 3)$;
$M = 8$
(Exact values of S_∞ are (a) $e - 1$, (b) $e^2 - 1$.)

8 (c)   For example $S_{168} \approx 0.736\,399\,859$.

Exercise 2C (page 22)

2 (a) $\frac{3}{4}$

3 6

3 Tests for convergence

Exercise 3A (page 28)

1 (a)   For example, $S_\infty \leq \frac{5}{16} = 0.3125$,
$S_{100} = 0.3017\ldots$

(b)   For example, $S_\infty \leq \frac{4}{7} = 0.5714\ldots$,
$S_{15} = 0.5644\ldots$

(c)   For example, $S_\infty \leq 7\frac{11}{56}$, $S_{100} = 6.000\ldots$

2 (a) $\lim\limits_{i \to \infty} \dfrac{u_i}{u_{i-1}} = \frac{1}{2}$ (b) $\lim\limits_{i \to \infty} \dfrac{u_i}{u_{i-1}} = \frac{1}{3}$

3 No; in fact it diverges.

4 (b) $\lim\limits_{i \to \infty} \dfrac{u_i}{u_{i-1}} = 1$

5 (a) $q < 1$ (b)   all q (c) $q < 1$

Exercise 3B (page 31)

1 (a)   1   (b) $\frac{1}{2}$

3 (a),(b),(d),(f) convergent; (c),(e) divergent

4 Series and integrals

Exercise 4A (page 37)

1 (a)   3.5, 4.5; 3.9, 4.1; 3.99, 4.01; exact value 4
(b)   4.875, 9.375; 6.555, 7.455;
6.95505, 7.04505; exact value 7
(c) $4.146\ldots, 5.146\ldots; 4.616\ldots, 4.716\ldots;$
$4.661\ldots, 4.671\ldots$; exact value $4\frac{2}{3}$
(d)   20, 43; 27.4375, 38.9375; exact value 33.75

2 (a) $50\left(1 - \dfrac{1}{n}\right)$, $50\left(1 + \dfrac{1}{n}\right)$; 50

(b) $\frac{1}{6}a^3\left(1 - \dfrac{1}{n}\right)\left(2 - \dfrac{1}{n}\right)$, $\frac{1}{6}a^3\left(1 + \dfrac{1}{n}\right)\left(2 + \dfrac{1}{n}\right)$;
$\frac{1}{3}a^3$

(c) $\dfrac{e-1}{n\left(e^{\frac{1}{n}} - 1\right)}$, $\dfrac{e^{\frac{1}{n}}(e-1)}{n\left(e^{\frac{1}{n}} - 1\right)}$; $e - 1$

3 (a)   0.2   (b)   0.01   (c) $\dfrac{1}{n}$

4 (a)   0.3   (b)   0.015   (c) $\dfrac{3}{2n}$

5 $S - s = \dfrac{\big(f(a) - f(b)\big)(b - a)}{n}$,
otherwise unchanged

Exercise 4B (page 43)

2 (a)   4246, 4243
(b)   30.69, 30.18
(c)   57.29, 56.29
(d)   0.007 854, 0.007 803

3 (a) $\dfrac{(n+m-1)(n-m+1)}{2(m-1)^2 n^2}$, $\dfrac{(n+m+1)(n-m+1)}{2m^2(n+1)^2}$

(b) $\frac{1}{2}\ln\dfrac{1+n^2}{1+(m-1)^2}$, $\frac{1}{2}\ln\dfrac{1+(n+1)^2}{1+m^2}$

(c) $\dfrac{(n+1)^{n+1}}{(m+1)^{m+1}}e^{-(n-m)}$, $\dfrac{n^n}{m^m}e^{-(n-m)}$

5 (b) $\frac{3}{4}\left(9^{\frac{4}{3}} - 1\right)$

(c) $\frac{3}{4}\left(201^{\frac{4}{3}} - 101^{\frac{4}{3}}\right)$; $\frac{3}{4}\left(200^{\frac{4}{3}} - 100^{\frac{4}{3}}\right)$

5 Infinite integrals and infinite series

Exercise 5A (page 46)

1 (a)   1   (c)   3   (d)   1   (f)   1
(b), (e) do not converge.

2 (a) $p < 0$ (b) $p < -1$

3 (a) $\frac{1}{2}$ (b)   1   (c) $\frac{1}{2}\pi$
(d) $\frac{1}{2}$ (e) $\frac{1}{4}$ (f) $2e^{-1}$

4 No, $f(x) = \dfrac{1}{x}$ is a counterexample.

Exercise 5B (page 52)

2 (a) $\ln 2$, $1 + \ln 2$; $S_{999} = 1.3857\ldots$
(b) $\frac{1}{6}\pi - \frac{1}{3}\arctan\frac{1}{3}$, $\frac{1}{10} + \frac{1}{6}\pi - \frac{1}{3}\arctan\frac{1}{3}$;
$S_{999} = 0.4670\ldots$
(c) $\ln\frac{3}{2}$, $1 + \ln\frac{3}{2}$; $S_{999} = 1.1683\ldots$
(d) $\sin 1$, $\cos 1 + \sin 1$; $S_{999} = 1.1437\ldots$
(e)   0.2, 0.208; $S_{999} = 0.2024\ldots$

4 $\dfrac{1}{\left(1+x^2\right)^{\frac{1}{2}}}, \dfrac{1}{\left(1+x^2\right)^{\frac{3}{2}}};\ 1-\dfrac{1}{\sqrt{2}},\ 1-\dfrac{1}{2\sqrt{2}}$

Exercise 5C (page 54)

1 (a) 1.644 933 567, 1.644 934 567
   (b) 0.392 699 050, 0.392 699 112

2 (a) 1.386 29   (b) 0.468 043
   (c) 1.168 524   (d) 1.144 79
   (e) 0.203 41

6 Series with positive and negative terms

Exercise 6 (page 64)

1 (a) 21; 0.901 498, 0.901 593
   (b) 5; 0.783 429, 0.783 451
   (c) 7; 0.632 118, 0.632 143
   (d) 10; 0.864 620, 0.864 673

2 (a) absolutely convergent
   (b) conditionally convergent
   (c) oscillates finitely
   (d) conditionally convergent
   (e) oscillates infinitely
   (f) oscillates infinitely
   (g) oscillates infinitely
   (h) conditionally convergent
   (i) absolutely convergent
   (j) diverges to $+\infty$
   (k) oscillates finitely
   (l) oscillates infinitely

3 (a) $-\dfrac{1}{1440}\pi^4$ (b) $\dfrac{1}{96}\pi^4$ (c) $\dfrac{7}{720}\pi^4$

4 (a) $1-\dfrac{1}{2}-\dfrac{1}{4}+\dfrac{1}{3}-\dfrac{1}{6}-\dfrac{1}{8}+\dfrac{1}{5}-\dfrac{1}{10}+\dfrac{1}{7}-\dfrac{1}{12}$
   (b) $1+\dfrac{1}{3}-\dfrac{1}{2}+\dfrac{1}{5}+\dfrac{1}{7}-\dfrac{1}{4}+\dfrac{1}{9}+\dfrac{1}{11}-\dfrac{1}{6}+\dfrac{1}{13}$
   (c) $-\dfrac{1}{2}+1-\dfrac{1}{4}-\dfrac{1}{6}-\dfrac{1}{8}-\dfrac{1}{10}-\dfrac{1}{12}+\dfrac{1}{3}-\dfrac{1}{14}-\dfrac{1}{16}$
   The series of positive terms diverges to $+\infty$ and the series of negative terms diverges to $-\infty$.

6 (a) $\sum\left(-\dfrac{1}{2}\right)^{i-1}i$ (b) 4
   (c) $-\dfrac{16}{9}$ (d) $\dfrac{4}{9}$

7 The theory of limits

Exercise 7A (page 68)

1 (a) If $p<2$, $\dfrac{2n+3}{n+2}>p$ if $n>\dfrac{2p-3}{2-p}$.

   (b) If $q>\dfrac{1}{2}$, $\dfrac{n}{2n-1}<q$ if $n>\dfrac{q}{2q-1}$.

2 (a) 300   (b) 3000   (c) $\dfrac{3}{q}$

3 (a) 30   (b) $\max\left(-\dfrac{1}{p},\dfrac{3}{q}\right)$

4 (a) $\dfrac{3}{2}$ (b) 1

6 1
8 1

Exercise 7B (page 72)

1 (a) 1   (b) $-\dfrac{1}{5}$ (c) $\dfrac{1}{3}$

2 (a) 0   (b) $\dfrac{1}{2}$ (c) $\dfrac{1}{2}$ (d) 1

3 For example,   (a) $u_n=\dfrac{1}{n}$

      (b) $u_n=-\dfrac{1}{n}$ (c) $u_n=\dfrac{(-1)^n}{n}$

Exercise 7C (page 78)

1 (a) $\dfrac{3}{5}$ (b) 4
2 (a) $\dfrac{1}{3}$ (b) 1   (c) 0   (d) 1
3 a, e^a; that if $\lim_{n\to\infty} u_n=L$, then $\lim_{n\to\infty} e^{u_n}=e^L$.
4 (a) $\dfrac{2}{3}$ (b) $\dfrac{4}{9}$ (c) $\ln 3$
5 (a) 0 (b) 0

8 Power series

Exercise 8 (page 84)

1 (a) $[-1,1]$ (b) $[-1,1[$ (c) $\mathbb{R}$
   (d) $\left[-\dfrac{1}{2},\dfrac{1}{2}\right[$ (e) $x=0$ (f) $]-1,1[$
   (g) $]-1,1[$ (h) $]-1,1[$ (i) $\left]-\dfrac{1}{4},\dfrac{1}{4}\right[$

2 (a) 1   (b) 1   (c) 2   (d) $\sqrt{2}$

9 Maclaurin series

Exercise 9A (page 90)

1 (a) $1+\dfrac{3}{2}x+\dfrac{3}{8}x^2-\dfrac{1}{16}x^3$
   (b) $1+\dfrac{3}{2}x+\dfrac{15}{8}x^2+\dfrac{35}{16}x^3$

2 (a) $x-\dfrac{1}{6}x^3+\dfrac{1}{120}x^5$
   (b) $2x-\dfrac{4}{3}x^3+\dfrac{4}{15}x^5$
   (c) $1+x+\dfrac{1}{2}x^2+\dfrac{1}{6}x^3+\dfrac{1}{24}x^4$
   (d) $1-3x+\dfrac{9}{2}x^2-\dfrac{9}{2}x^3+\dfrac{27}{8}x^4$
   (e) x^2
   (f) $1-x^2$
   (g) $-x-\dfrac{1}{2}x^2-\dfrac{1}{3}x^3-\dfrac{1}{4}x^4$

(h) $1+x+\frac{3}{2}x^2+\frac{5}{2}x^3$

(i) $1-\frac{1}{2}x^2+\frac{1}{8}x^4$

(j) $x^2-\frac{1}{2}x^4$

4 $1,\frac{1}{2}$

5 $1+px+\frac{p(p-1)}{2}x^2+\frac{p(p-1)(p-2)}{6}x^3$
$+\frac{p(p-1)(p-2)(p-3)}{24}x^4$

Exercise 9B (page 93)

1 (a) 1.6487   (b) 0.8415
  (c) 0.9655   (d) 0.9397
  (e) −0.0513   (f) 0.8109
  (g) −0.9900

2 $2x+\frac{2}{3}x^3+\frac{2}{5}x^5+...+\frac{2}{2i+1}x^{2i+1}+...$,
$-1<x<1$; $x=\frac{1}{2}$, 1.099;
$x=2$ is outside interval of validity.

3 (a) $1+\frac{1}{2}x^2+\frac{5}{24}x^4$, $8.5\times10^{-6}\%$

  (b) $x-\frac{1}{3}x^3$, $2.0\times10^{-3}\%$

4 0.0433, 0.0063 too large; the second, which uses a value of x closer to 0

Exercise 9C (page 100)

1 (a) $1+3x+\frac{3}{2}x^2-\frac{1}{2}x^3+\frac{3}{8}x^4$

  (b) $1-2x+2x^2-\frac{4}{3}x^3+\frac{2}{3}x^4$

  (c) x^3 (d) x^3

2 (a) $1+3x+\frac{9}{2}x^2+...+\frac{3^i}{i!}x^i+...$, $\mathbb{R}$

  (b) $1-\frac{1}{8}x^2+\frac{1}{384}x^4-...+\frac{(-1)^i}{2^{2i}(2i)!}x^{2i}+...$, $\mathbb{R}$

  (c) $x-\frac{1}{6}x^2+\frac{1}{120}x^3-...+\frac{(-1)^{i-1}}{(2i-1)!}x^i+...$,
    positive $\mathbb{R}$

  (d) $-x-\frac{1}{2}x^2-\frac{1}{3}x^3-...-\frac{1}{i}x^i-...$,
    $-1\le x<1$

  (e) $2x-2x^2+\frac{8}{3}x^3-...+\frac{(-1)^{i-1}2^i}{i}x^i+...$,
    $-\frac{1}{2}<x\le\frac{1}{2}$

  (f) $e+ex+\frac{1}{2}ex^2+...+\frac{e}{i!}x^i+...$, $\mathbb{R}$

  (g) $1-x^2+\frac{1}{3}x^4+...+\frac{(-1)^i2^{2i-1}}{(2i)!}x^{2i}+...$, $\mathbb{R}$

(h) $1+\frac{1}{e}x-\frac{1}{2e^2}x^2+...+\frac{(-1)^{i-1}x^i}{ie^i}+...$,
  $-e<x\le e$

(i) $\cos1-(\sin1)x-(\frac{1}{2}\cos1)x^2+...$
$+\frac{(-1)^i\cos1}{(2i)!}x^{2i}$
$+\frac{(-1)^{i+1}\sin1}{(2i+1)!}x^{2i+1}+...$, $\mathbb{R}$

3 (a) $x-x^2+\frac{1}{3}x^3$

  (b) $1-\frac{1}{2}x-\frac{5}{8}x^2+\frac{3}{16}x^3+\frac{25}{384}x^4$

  (c) $1+\frac{1}{2}x^2-\frac{1}{3}x^3+\frac{3}{8}x^4$

  (d) $x+\frac{3}{2}x^2+\frac{1}{3}x^3-\frac{1}{12}x^4$

  (e) $3x-\frac{21}{2}x^2+24x^3-\frac{205}{4}x^4$

  (f) $-6x^2-6x^3+x^4$

4 (a) $1-\frac{1}{2}x^2+\frac{5}{24}x^4$

  (b) $\ln2+\frac{1}{2}x+\frac{1}{8}x^2-\frac{1}{192}x^4$

5 $x+\frac{1}{6}x^3+\frac{3}{40}x^5+...$
$+\frac{3\times5\times7\times...\times(2i-1)}{(2i+1)i!2^i}x^{2i+1}+...$,
$\frac{1}{2}\pi-x-\frac{1}{6}x^3-\frac{3}{40}x^5-...$; 3.1416

6 $x-\frac{1}{18}x^3+\frac{1}{600}x^5-...$
$+\frac{(-1)^i}{(2i+1)(2i+1)!}x^{2i+1}+...$

7 $x+\frac{1}{4}x^2+\frac{1}{18}x^3+...+\frac{1}{i(i)!}x^i+...$; 0.570

9 $-\frac{1}{3}x^3+\frac{1}{30}x^5$; $-\frac{1}{3}$

10 (a) 2   (b) $\frac{1}{2}$
   (c) 1   (d) $-\frac{1}{2}$

11 $\frac{1}{3}\theta+\frac{2}{81}\theta^3$; 0.82 radians

10 The error term

Exercise 10 (page 113)

1 (a) 0.818 733 333
  (b) −0.000 002 580
  (c) $-\frac{e^c}{5!}(0.2)^5$ where $-0.2<c<0$,
    0.000 002 667
  (d) 0.000 002 667

2 (a) 0.479 427 083   (b) −0.000 001 545

(c) $R_5(0.5) = -\frac{\sin c}{6!}(0.5)^6$ where $0 < c < 0.5$,

0.000 021 701

(d) 0.000 001 550

(e) For the $\sin x$ series $p_5(x)$ and $p_6(x)$ are the same, so the error in part (c) could be found as $R_6(0.5)$ rather than $R_5(0.5)$; this is $-\frac{\cos c}{7!}(0.5)^7$ where $0 < c < 0.5$, with $\frac{(0.5)^7}{7!}$ as an upper bound for the magnitude of the error. This is the same as part (d).

3 (a) $\frac{(0.2)^6}{6} = 0.000\,010\,667$

(b) $(0.2)^5 = 0.000\,32$

(c) $\frac{(0.2)^6}{6} = 0.000\,010\,667$,

$\frac{(0.2)^6}{6 \times 0.8} = 0.000\,013\,333$

4 (a) $-2.62 < x < 2.62$

(b) $-0.517 < x < 0.664$

5 (a) 14   (b) 13

6 (a) $-\frac{1 \times 3 \times 5 \times \ldots \times (2i-3)}{2^i \times i!}$

(b) $-\frac{1 \times 3 \times 5 \times \ldots \times (2n-1)}{2^{n+1} \times (n+1)!} \times \frac{x^{n+1}}{(1-c)^{n+\frac{1}{2}}}$

(d) 5   (e) 1.56×10^{-6}

7 (a) $R_n(x) = (-1)^{n+1} \frac{(n+2)(n+3)x^{n+1}}{2(1+c)^{n+4}}$ where

$0 < c < x$, $|R_n(x)| < \frac{(n+2)(n+3)}{2} x^{n+1}$

(b)

$\int_0^x \frac{(n+1)(n+2)(n+3)}{2}(1-t)^{-(n+4)}(x-t)^n dt$

$\leq \frac{(n+1)(n+2)(n+3)}{6} x^n \left(\frac{1}{(1-x)^3} - 1\right)$

8 $\left(1 + 3x + 6x^2 + \ldots + \frac{(n+1)(n+2)}{2}x^n\right)$

$\frac{(n+2)(n+3)x^{n+1} - 2(n+1)(n+3)x^{n+2}}{}$

$+ \frac{+(n+1)(n+2)x^{n+3}}{2(1-x)^3}$

10 Expressions for successive derivatives soon become very complicated. 6 terms

11 Taylor series and l'Hôpital's rule

Exercise 11 (page 120)

1 $e^a\left(1 + (x-a) + \frac{(x-a)^2}{2!} + \ldots\right) = e^a \times e^{x-a}$;

$\int_a^x \frac{e^t}{n!}(x-t)^n dt$,

$\frac{e^c(x-a)^{n+1}}{(n+1)!}$ where c is between a and x.

2 $\frac{1}{\sqrt{2}}\left(1 + (x - \frac{1}{4}\pi) - \frac{(x-\frac{1}{4}\pi)^2}{2!} - \frac{(x-\frac{1}{4}\pi)^3}{3!}\right.$

$\left.+ \frac{(x-\frac{1}{4}\pi)^4}{4!} + \frac{(x-\frac{1}{4}\pi)^5}{5!} - \frac{(x-\frac{1}{4}\pi)^6}{6!}\right)$;

$\int_{\frac{1}{4}\pi}^x \frac{-\cos t}{6!}(x-t)^6 dt$;

$p_6(x) - \frac{1}{\sqrt{2}} \times \frac{(x-\frac{1}{4}\pi)^7}{7!}$, $\int_{\frac{1}{4}\pi}^x \frac{\sin t}{7!}(x-t)^7 dt$

3 $1 + \frac{1}{3}h - \frac{1}{9}h^2 + \frac{5}{81}h^3$,

$-\frac{10}{243}h^4(1+\theta h)^{-\frac{11}{3}}$, where $0 < \theta < 1$;

1.047 708, too large, 0.000 021

4 $(x-2)(x^2+2x-1)$, $(x-2)(x^2+x+2)$; $\frac{7}{8}$

5 $(x-2)^2(x+1)$, $(x-2)^2(x+4)$; $\frac{1}{2}$

6 (a) 4   (b) −2   (c) $-\frac{2}{\sqrt{e}}$ (d) 2

7 (a) $\frac{8}{9\pi^2}$ (b) $\frac{25}{4}$ (c) −2   (d) $-\frac{1}{4}$

12 Homogeneous differential equations

Exercise 12A (page 128)

1 $y = \sqrt{x^2 + k}$

2 (a) $y = (\sqrt{x}+2)^2$, $y = (\sqrt{x}+1)^2$, $y = x$,

$y = (\sqrt{x}-1)^2$ for $x > 1$,

$y = (\sqrt{x}-2)^2$ for $x > 4$

(b) $y=\left(x\sqrt{x}+26\right)^{\frac{2}{3}}$, $y=\left(x\sqrt{x}+7\right)^{\frac{2}{3}}$, $y=x$,

$y=\left(x\sqrt{x}-7\right)^{\frac{2}{3}}$ for $x>7^{\frac{2}{3}}$,

$y=\left(x\sqrt{x}-26\right)^{\frac{2}{3}}$ for $x>26^{\frac{2}{3}}$

3 $y=x\sqrt{2\ln x+k}$

4 (a) $y=\sqrt{x^2+3x}$, $y=\sqrt{x^2+6x}$,

$y=\sqrt{x^2+5x}$; all for $x>0$

(b) $y=\sqrt{5x-x^2}$, $y=\sqrt{10x-x^2}$,

$y=\sqrt{13x-x^2}$

5 $x=y\sqrt{1+2\ln y}$

6 $y=\dfrac{x}{\ln x+k}$

7 $\frac{1}{2}\ln\left(x^2+y^2\right)+\arctan\left(\dfrac{y}{x}\right)=k$

Exercise 12B (page 131)

1 $\sqrt{3}$

2 $y=(\sqrt{x}+2)^2$ is an enlargment of $y=(\sqrt{x}+1)^2$, and $y=\left(\sqrt{x}-2\right)^2$ is an enlargement of $y=\left(\sqrt{x}-1\right)^2$, both with a factor of 4.

3 (a) 2, $1\frac{2}{3}$ (b) 2, 2.6

4 Yes; $y=\dfrac{x}{\ln x}$ is transformed by an enlargement of factor c to $y=\dfrac{x}{\ln x-\ln c}$, and $\ln c$ can take all real values.

6 $y=0, y=-x$. But in fact the solution is $y=\dfrac{x}{k-\ln|x|}$ with stationary points at $\left(\pm e^{k+1},\mp e^{k+1}\right)$, so all stationary points are on $y=-x$; there are no points on solution curves at which $y=0$, since the differential equation is meaningless at $(0,0)$.

13 Linear differential equations

Exercise 13 (page 140)

1 (a) $y=\frac{1}{3}x^2+\dfrac{k}{x}$ (b) $x=(t+k)\csc t$

(c) $y=-\dfrac{1}{2x}+kx$ (d) $u=(2x+k)e^{-x^2}$

2 (a) $y=\dfrac{x-1}{x^2}$ (b) $y=\csc x$

(c) $y=\dfrac{x^2+3}{4\sqrt{x}}$

3 (a) $u=\frac{1}{3}x+\dfrac{k}{x^2}$ (b) $y=k\sec x-\cos x$

(c) $x=ke^{4t}-\frac{1}{2}e^{2t}$ (d) $y=kx^3-x^2$

(e) $y=(t+k)\cos t$ (f) $y=\cos x+k\cot x$

4 (a) $y=3x-1+ke^{-3x}$ with $k=-1,0,1,2,3$

(b) $y=\frac{1}{4}x^2+\dfrac{k}{x^2}$ with $k=-\frac{1}{4},\frac{3}{4},\frac{7}{4},-4,0,4$

(c) $y=\sec x+k\cos x$ with $k=-3,-2,-1,0,1$

(d) $y=kx^3-x$ with $k=2,1,0,0,1,2$

5 $y=x(1-\ln x)$

6 $\dfrac{dx}{dt}=-0.1x$, $\dfrac{dy}{dt}=0.1x-0.2y$; $x=50e^{-0.1t}$, $y=50\left(e^{-0.1t}-e^{-0.2t}\right)$; 12.5 litres, after 6.93 hours

7 $\dfrac{dx}{dt}=c(a+b\sin ct-x)$

9 $y=2x+kx^2$; gradient positive within the acute angles between $y=x$ and the y-axis, negative within the obtuse angles

10 $y=\dfrac{k}{x}-\dfrac{1}{x^2}$; solution curves are concave up above $y=\dfrac{2}{x^2}$, are concave down below.

14 Approximate methods

In this chapter your answers may differ from those given by 1 or 2 in the last decimal place. This will usually depend on whether or not you have rounded intermediate values in the calculations. Don't spend time trying to get an exact match between your answers and those given if they are close enough to indicate that you have used a correct procedure.

Exercise 14A (page 144)

1 400 m; too small

2 1450 m; too large

3 Values at selected points are given in (a) line 4, (b) line 5 of Table 14.7 in Section 14.3.

4 (a) (i) (0.5, 0.5), (1, 0.938 79)
       (ii) (0.5, 0.492 23), (1, 0.898 21)
   (b) (i) (2, 2.2), (3, 2.356 25), (4, 2.485 91), (5, 2.597 37)
       (ii) (2, 2.187 72), (3, 2.337 25), (4, 2.462 60), (5, 2.571 05)

(c) (i) (1,3),   (2,5.099 93)
    (ii) (0.5,2),   (1,3.010 37),
        (1.5,4.061 83),   (2,5.181 10)
    (iii) (0.5,2.000 89),   (1,3.020 01),
        (1.5,4.088 86),   (2,5.232 72)
(d) (i) (0,0.924 24),   (0.5,1.396 45),
        (1.5,2.603 55),   (2,3.313 13)
    (ii) (0,0.990 54),   (0.5,1.427 08),
        (1.5,2.631 18),   (2,3.368 43)

5 With t-step 4, 97.68; with t-step 2, 95.46

6 (a) 19.7 m, 20.9 m   (b) 22.07 m
   Errors 2.4 m, 1.2 m

Exercise 14B (page 149)

2 (a)

x	0.5	1.0
$h = 0.5$	−0.020 09	−0.084 20
$h = 0.25$	−0.012 32	−0.043 62

(b)

x	2	3
$h = 1$	−0.023 22	−0.036 24
$h = 0.5$	−0.010 94	−0.017 24

	4	5
	−0.044 67	−0.050 61
	−0.021 36	−0.024 29

(c)

x	0.5	1
$h = 1$	−	0.033 18
$h = 0.5$	0.003 07	0.022.81
$h = 0.25$	0.002 18	0.013 17

	1.5	2.0
	−	0.193 06
	0.060 11	0.111 89
	0.033 08	0.060 27

(d)

x	0	0.5
$h = -0.5$	0.136 59	0.060 71
$h = -0.25$	0.070 29	0.030 08

	1.5	2.0
$h = +0.5$	0.056 00	0.112 02
$h = +0.25$	0.028 37	0.056 72

3 (a) $y_B = F(a+h)$, $y_P = F(a)+hf(a)$
   (b) $y_Q = F_1(a+h)+hf(a+h)$
   (c) $2h^2 f'(a)$

Review exercise

(page 150)

1 The series is divergent.

2 (a) 1

3 (a) 1.202 056 403   (b) $\sum_{i=10\,000}^{99\,999} \frac{1}{i^3} < \frac{9}{10\,000^2}$
   (c) 1.2021 correct to 4 d.p.

5 $-1.26 < x < 1.08$

6 (a) $\frac{3}{4}-\frac{1}{2}\left(\frac{1}{n+1}+\frac{1}{n+2}\right)$ (b) $-1 \le x \le 1$

7 (a) 0   (b) 1   (c) $\frac{1}{6}$

9 $\frac{2^{p-1}-\frac{1}{2}}{2^{p-1}-1}$, $\frac{2^{p-1}}{2^{p-1}-1}$

10 (a) 0, 1, 0, $\frac{1}{3}$ (b) $1+\frac{1}{2}x^2+\frac{5}{24}x^4$
   (c) If $f(x)=\csc x$, $f(0)$ doesn't exist.

11 $1-\frac{1}{4}x^2-\frac{1}{96}x^4$

12 (a) $\frac{1}{4}\pi$ (b) 2

13 (a) (i) 0.1391   (ii) 0.1624
    (b) 0.1839   (c) 0.1857

14 $(2x+y)(x-y)^2=2$

15 (a) 2.593 74, 2.653 30; e ≈ 2.718 28

Examination questions

1 (b) Not convergent

2 (b) Convergent

3 (a) (i) $x-\frac{1}{6}x^3+\frac{1}{120}x^5-\frac{1}{5040}x^7$
       (ii) $1+x^2+\frac{1}{2}x^4+\frac{1}{6}x^6$
   (b) $x+\frac{5}{6}x^3+\frac{41}{120}x^5$ (c) $\frac{5}{6}$

4 $x-\frac{1}{2}x^2+\frac{1}{6}x^3-\frac{1}{12}x^4$

5 Divergent

6 (c) 0

7 $-1 \le x < 1$

9 (b) 1

10 (b) $1-x-\frac{3}{2}x^2+\frac{11}{6}x^3-\frac{7}{24}x^4$

11 $x-\frac{3}{2}x^2+\frac{4}{3}x^3-x^4$

12 $\frac{1}{4}$

Index

The page numbers refer to the first mention of each term, or the shaded box if there is one.

Lightning Source UK Ltd.
Milton Keynes UK
08 July 2010

156696UK00001B/60/P